PRAISE FOR
THE UNFIT HEIRESS

NAMED A BEST BOOK OF 2021 BY THE *NEW YORK POST*
AND *BOOK RIOT*

NAMED A BEST TRUE CRIME BOOK OF 2021
BY CRIMEREADS

"In the early 1930s, socialite Maryon Cooper Hewitt got doctors to declare her 'promiscuous' daughter Ann mentally unfit—and sterilize the young woman without her knowledge. Her goal was to prevent Ann from claiming millions of dollars from her father's will, which contained a child-bearing clause. A riveting court case ensued, as detailed in this equally fascinating book."

—*New York Post*

"In Audrey Clare Farley's book, the fascinating and unsettling case—and the worldwide media sensation it caused—is carefully revisited to expose what it meant to be considered an unfit parent and how easily family can become foes." —*Town and Country*

"A disturbing yet thought-provoking tale of family strife and ethically unsound medical practice." —*Kirkus Reviews*

"This book is as timely as ever. A gripping tale about the atrocity of systematic reproductive control." —*Booklist*, starred review

"Farley sets a brisk pace and persuasively reimagines the dynamic between Ann and Maryon. This is an eye-opening portrait of an obscure yet fascinating case."   —*Publishers Weekly*

"Expertly blending biography and history, and using the life of Ann Cooper Hewitt as a backdrop, Farley has created an absorbing biography effectively explaining how the legacy of eugenics still persists today. Hewitt's story will engage anyone interested in women's history."   —*Library Journal*

"This book, and the case it covers, are in many ways still a current issue. Farley takes a look at the court case and story of Maryon Cooper Hewitt, who had her daughter, Ann Cooper Hewitt, sterilized without her consent or knowledge for an inheritance. It also takes a look at the history of eugenics and how it created the laws that allowed this, and how this is not a long-ago history."   —*Book Riot*

"THE UNFIT HEIRESS is a sensational story told with nuance and humanity with clear reverberations to the present. Historian Audrey Clare Farley's writing jumps off the page, as Ann Cooper Hewitt, once a one-dimensional tabloid fixation, is brought into full relief as a complicated victim of her time, standing in the crosshairs of the growing eugenics movement and the emergence of an 'oversexed' and 'dangerous' New Woman. But most importantly, this book is a necessary call to remember the high stakes and terrible history of the longstanding fight for control over women's bodies."   —Susannah Cahalan, #1 *New York Times* bestselling author of *Brain on Fire*

"THE UNFIT HEIRESS is the propulsive tale of a high-society scandal that triggered a high-stakes courtroom battle. It is also an illuminating exploration of America's long, dark history of eugenics and forced sterilization. By braiding together these narrative threads, Audrey Clare Farley has accomplished the rare feat of writing a book that is as thought-provoking as it is page-turning."

—Luke Dittrich, *New York Times* bestselling author of *Patient H.M.*

"THE UNFIT HEIRESS is not only a fascinating look at a wildly dysfunctional high-society family, it's also a compulsively readable account of the reproductive myths and bigotry-driven pseudo-science that still shape our world today."

—Rachel Monroe, author of *Savage Appetites*

"THE UNFIT HEIRESS is a triumph of compassion, historical inquiry, and intellectual rigor. In her elegant telling of Ann Cooper Hewitt's story, Farley shines her bright, empathetic light on profoundly imperfect humans and the myriad, often tragic ways we grapple for fulfillment. At the same time, she renders with crystalline precision the history of American eugenics, insisting—gently, yet steadfastly—that we look where we'd rather avert our gaze. This book startled me, seized my attention, and summoned my empathy when I least expected it."

—Rachel Vorona Cote, author of *Too Much*

"Shocking." —*Daily Mail*

"Well-researched and endlessly readable... Part biography and part history of eugenics, this one is intriguing and terrifying."

—*Ms. Magazine*

"[Farley] keenly investigates the culture of eugenics that surrounded and pervaded both Ann's life and court case... The most indicting feature of Farley's book is not America's eugenic past but America's eugenic present."
                                                                    —*Lady Science*

"In [THE UNFIT HEIRESS], Audrey Clare Farley untangles this dark and complex chapter of American history and shines a light on official and medical complicity in a horrifying system. Her book is exceedingly well-researched yet reads with the momentum of a thriller."
                                                                    —CrimeReads

"Gripping, unsettling reading."   —*The Progressive*

"Farley has presented an excellent case here. The book is fascinating on a variety of levels... not just a titillating story about greed, but one that delves further into the human mind and poor judgement, to say the least."
                                                        —*New York Journal of Books*

THE UNFIT
HEIRESS

THE UNFIT HEIRESS

THE TRAGIC LIFE AND SCANDALOUS
STERILIZATION OF ANN COOPER HEWITT

AUDREY CLARE FARLEY

GRAND
CENTRAL

New York Boston

Grand Central Publishing
Hachette Book Group
1290 Avenue of the Americas, New York, NY 10104
grandcentralpublishing.com
twitter.com/grandcentralpub

Originally published in hardcover and ebook by Grand Central Publishing in April 2021.
First Trade Edition: April 2023

Grand Central Publishing is a division of Hachette Book Group, Inc. The Grand Central Publishing name and logo is a trademark of Hachette Book Group, Inc.

The publisher is not responsible for websites (or their content) that are not owned by the publisher.

Library of Congress Cataloging-in-Publication Data
Names: Farley, Audrey Clare, author.
Title: The unfit heiress : the tragic life and scandalous sterilization of Ann Cooper Hewitt / Audrey Clare Farley.
Description: First edition. | New York : Grand Central Publishing, [2021] |
    Includes bibliographical references. | Summary: "At the turn of the
    twentieth century, American women began to reject Victorian propriety in
    favor of passion and livelihood outside the home. This alarmed
    authorities, who feared certain "over-sexed" women could destroy
    civilization if allowed to reproduce and pass on their defects. Set
    against this backdrop, THE UNFIT HEIRESS chronicles the fight for
    inheritance, both genetic and monetary, between Ann Cooper Hewitt and
    her mother Maryon. In 1934, aided by a California eugenics law, the
    socialite Maryon Cooper Hewitt had her "promiscuous" daughter declared
    feebleminded and sterilized without her knowledge. She did this to
    deprive Ann of millions of dollars from her father's estate, which
    contained a child-bearing stipulation. When a sensational court case
    ensued, the American public was captivated. So were eugenicists, who saw
    an opportunity to restrict reproductive rights in America for decades to
    come. This riveting story unfolds through the brilliant research of
    Audrey Clare Farley, who captures the interior lives of these women on
    the pages and poses questions that remain relevant today: What does it
    mean to be "unfit" for motherhood? In the battle for reproductive
    rights, can we forgive the women who side against us? And can we forgive
    our mothers if they are the ones who inflict the deepest wounds?"--
    Provided by publisher.
Identifiers: LCCN 2020053583 | ISBN 9781538753354 (hardcover) | ISBN 9781538753347 (ebook)
Subjects: LCSH: Hewitt, Ann Cooper, 1914-1956. | Hewitt, Ann Cooper,
    1914-1956--Trials, litigation, etc. | Heiresses--United
    States--Biography. | Socialites--United States--Biography. | Involuntary
    sterilization--United States--History--20th century. | Reproductive
    rights--United States--History--20th century.
Classification: LCC CT275.H5888 F37 2021 | DDC 362.198/1780092 [B]--dc23
LC record available at https://lccn.loc.gov/2020053583
ISBNs: 978-1-5387-5336-1 (trade pbk.), 978-1-5387-5334-7 (ebook)

Printed in the United States of America
LSC-C
Printing 1, 2023

For my family

CONTENTS

PART III: THE AFTERMATH

THE UNFIT
HEIRESS

PART I:

THE NEW WOMAN AND THE RISE OF EUGENICS

1

THE STERILIZED HEIRESS

B ulbs flashed as the socialite, sporting rouge and fur, took her seat alongside her attorney, who had called a press conference in his San Francisco office. The image of the solemn-faced, perfectly coiffed twenty-one-year-old would appear in newspapers across the country. Some, like the *New York Times*, would print nearly fifty stories detailing the woman's private life—her childhood, romantic relationships, spending habits, even the lingerie she was wearing. (It was imported from France.) It was January 1936, and heiress Ann Cooper Hewitt was suing her mother, Maryon Cooper Hewitt, in court for half a million dollars. The plaintiff claimed that her mother paid two doctors to "unsex" her during a scheduled appendectomy in order to deprive her of an inheritance from her millionaire father's estate.

Ann's father was Peter Cooper Hewitt, whose invention of the mercury-vapor lamp in 1901 earned him more than $1 million. The money from this creation supplemented an already sizable bank account, as Ann's father was also the grandson of an even more famous engineer—Peter Cooper. Cooper was behind a slew of inventions in the nineteenth century, including gelatin dessert and a steam locomotive. His ingenuity, coupled with investments in real estate, railroads, and the insurance industry, made him one of the richest men in New York City before his death in 1883. Cooper's children and grandchildren dutifully expanded the family wealth with their own business enterprises. When Ann's father died in 1921, his estate was worth over $4 million (the equivalent of $59 million today).

Peter Cooper Hewitt's will stipulated that two-thirds of his estate was to go to Ann and one-third to his wife, Ann's mother, after his death. The will also stipulated that Ann's share reverted back to her mother if she died childless. Knowing this, Ann asserted in her civil complaint, her mother had secretly paid two California doctors to remove her fallopian tubes. Mrs. Cooper Hewitt had done this with money obtained from Ann's trust fund eleven months before her twenty-first birthday—the point at which the woman would have no further say in her daughter's medical care.

The plot was set in motion in August 1934, when Ann and her mother were at the Coronado beachside resort outside San Diego. Over lunch, Ann talked of becoming an adult and finding a man to marry when she was suddenly struck with stomach pains. Their driver rushed them back to San Francisco, where Ann's private physician, Dr. Tilton Tillman, was waiting for her at Dante Sanatorium on Broadway. "Well, Ann, I understand you have appendicitis," said Tillman, upon her arrival at the hospital.

According to the plaintiff, Tillman never examined her abdomen. Instead, he led her to another room, where an alienist (an early-twentieth-century term for a psychologist) named Mary Scally began to ask her civics questions: Why did the Pilgrims come to America? What is the duration of a presidential term? What is the longest river in the United States? When was the Battle of Hastings fought?

"I didn't pay much attention or know what it was about," Ann recalled at the press conference. "Four days later, I returned to the hospital for my appendectomy, which was performed by Dr. Samuel Boyd. No one told me anything else."

The heiress reported that she stayed at the hospital for several weeks to recover from the procedure. During this time, she overheard a few staff members asking her nurse how the "idiot patient" was doing. Ann also heard her nurse make several phone calls to Dr. Tillman assuring him that his patient "didn't suspect a thing."

"I learned then that my mother and Dr. Tillman had told everyone that I was a mental case," Ann testified. "I discovered that I had undergone a salpingectomy, having my tubes removed along with my appendix."

After her discharge, she went home and was kept a prisoner in her room. "My mother made me act as my own maid," Ann claimed. "Not one housekeeper entered my room during my convalescence. I was forced to live with little more than the bare necessities or comforts of a poorhouse waif."

When a reporter asked what she meant by the second statement, Ann explained that the telephone and reading lamp had been removed from her room. She couldn't communicate with anyone or even read the newspaper after dusk—not that one had been delivered to her. At mealtime, she'd hear a knock at the door and open it to find a maid holding some paltry, unappealing dish. Perhaps a biscuit without butter or jam, or a cold leg of chicken with a few lifeless spears of asparagus. The maid would wait for her to take the plate and then re-lock the door behind her.

The reporter hurried to record these details. Only in fiction did people encounter little rich girls imprisoned and made to live a miserly existence.

The *Little Princess* treatment was not new, the young heiress told reporters. "I was locked up all the time," she said. "In fact, as a baby, I was put in a crib with very tall sides. That was so I couldn't climb out of it. We were living in Paris then." The heiress recalled how her father, who was not yet married to her mother at the time, would visit the apartment and pick her up. "He was the only one who ever let me out of that cage. My mother never came near me. The maid would come and dress me in the morning, then leave me there for the day. I would often go to sleep in my clothes."

"So you remember your father?" one journalist inquired. "What was he like?"

"I remember my father very well," said Ann. "He was one of the few precious gifts of my life. He was a tall man, very kind and gentle. I think of him walking beside me, suiting his long gait to mine. It seems to me I spent all my happy times with him. He died when I was seven."

After her father's death, Ann related, she hardly ever left their apartment. She was forbidden from making friends or having boy-friends when she grew older. "Mother didn't have one spark of affection for me, and she refused to permit others who did. She always called me an 'imbecile' and an 'ugly duckling.' She hated my buck teeth and my humped shoulders. And the way my eyes cross when I am tired. She sometimes struck me when she noticed my eyes were going."

The reporters looked around in disbelief. They knew wealthy women weren't keen on parenting, but Ann's claims were truly extraordinary. What would Maryon have to say for herself?

Ann revealed a small scar on her forehead, where she claimed to have been cut with a wineglass. She said her mother had smashed a glass of Cabernet over her head one evening, when a gentleman did not appear for a dinner date with the two of them. "She blamed me whenever things didn't work out with a man."

The slight, ninety-pound heiress also revealed a burn on her forearm, where she claimed her mother had extinguished a cigarette. "That was for telling her I didn't like one of her suitors."

Even had it not been for Ann's claims of abuse, some present might have turned against her mother, believing that female smoking was a sign of modern women's depravity. Men could withstand the habit; but in women's bodies, cigarette smoke compromised judgment, inflamed the imagination, and unleashed all sorts of profane desires. Women knew this and still puffed away.

Ann contended that, for many years of her life, she didn't realize that her situation was extraordinary. "I thought all mothers treated their daughters the way mine treated me. Until I went to school, I thought that was the usual way people behaved."

"You mean you've never had anyone else to love you? Besides your father?" a reporter asked.

"Well, most of the men my mother married were kind to me. I suppose that's one of the few things she has done for me—seen that I had nice stepfathers," said Ann. "I've also had a few people paid to take care of me who were kind. I did have this one maid, Nini, who was especially affectionate. My father hired her. She was there the night he died and comforted me when Mother sent me away from his bed."

"Did any of the help mistreat you?" this same reporter pressed. "Perhaps because your mother told them to?"

"No one ever struck me like Mother did. Though there was one maid in Paris, Eugenie, who used to follow along when my father would take me around the city. Every time I'd turn around, she'd make faces and obscene gestures at me."

"Why would she do such a thing?"

"I don't know," said Ann. "Probably because she was devoted to Mother. She used to clean my mother's shoes with her fur coats. Ordinary rags weren't good enough, she said."

"Do you believe your mother hatched a plot to kill you?" another reporter asked. "Your suit claims your mother would benefit if you died without any children. But one would expect your mother to die before you. How do you explain this?"

Ann froze for a moment, then bowed her head to wipe a tear from her cheek. Her attorney, Russell P. Tyler, put his hand on her shoulder and answered the question for her. "Mrs. Cooper Hewitt has always said that her daughter is sickly," he explained. "She has also refused to acknowledge her own aging. The woman probably presumed her life expectancy exceeded her daughter's."

The reporter looked to Ann to corroborate this, but the heiress refused to look up. Tyler added, "My client hasn't seen her mother since the day she turned twenty-one. As soon as she came of age, she demanded to live independently. She contacted me to set her up financially, and that's when I learned of this whole tragedy."

"Before you discovered you were sterilized, had you planned to marry?" someone else asked.

"No," Ann replied, finally raising her head.

"What you mean to say, Ann," said Tyler, "is that you had no specific man in mind. But you did hope to marry someone someday, didn't you?"

"Yes, that's right," said the heiress. "But I don't know if anyone will have me now."

Wanting to lighten the mood—and also to get a sense of the young woman's intellect—another correspondent asked what book Ann was currently reading. The heiress told him that she was enjoying a title by a contemporary of William Thackeray. "It's called *Ten Thousand a-Year*," she said. "I like it so well because of the sarcasm in it. It just reveals to you what the world really is."

"Have you read Voltaire?" the man asked.

"I peeked into Voltaire and found him insipid," Ann replied. "One author I love is Arthur Conan Doyle. He is so real."

"Have you read his ghost stories?"

"Yes," said Ann.

"Do you believe them?" The other journalists looked up with raised eyebrows.

"Of course not," Ann disappointed. "I don't read them to believe in them. I just read them."

"What will you do with the money if you're awarded it?" the same reporter pressed. "Take a holiday? Buy a new wardrobe?" The fur on Ann's coat was matted. Shortly after leaving her mother's home with a single trunk, the heiress had purchased the coat for $1 from a laundress, along with a few other items patrons had neglected to retrieve. Ann had since re-acquired many of her belongings, but Tyler had instructed her to dress modestly. He didn't want people to be distracted by her fancy clothes.

Before Ann could answer, Tyler interrupted to say that such a question was irrelevant and inappropriate. Ann was pursuing this lawsuit to protect others, not because the money was needed or wanted. The attorney explained that, in addition to sterilizing her daughter, Maryon had squandered hundreds of thousands of dollars from Ann's trust fund at gambling resorts across the world, including the Villa d'Este in Italy, the Deauville in France, and the Monte Carlo in Mexico. This showed clear disregard for her daughter's well-being, and Mrs. Cooper Hewitt now needed to compensate her daughter for the losses.

Ann elaborated that her mother had been gambling for as long as she could remember. "Mother always left me in the hotel suite with a maid when she went downstairs to roll the dice," she recalled. "I once told her, 'No, I'm not staying here another night. I want to come with you.' She promised me a nice moleskin coat if I stayed. I said, 'I don't want that,' and she called me a brat and slammed the door in my face."

According to Ann, her mother promised many gifts that she never received—a rocking horse, a dollhouse, a baby pram. This was despite the fact that Maryon often made money from gambling with her daughter's inheritance. "I always woke up when she came back to the suite, usually around two or three in the morning. If she'd done well, she'd turn on all the lights and begin to count her money, saying how clever she was."

"And if she lost?" Ann's attorney asked for the benefit of reporters. "What then?"

"Then she would be very angry. She'd turn over the furniture and break things. She once called her broker in the middle of the night and threatened to kill him if he didn't make better trades. Mother always assumed he made bad deals to spite her. She suspected many people in her life of conspiring against her."

In connection with her civil suit, Ann had demanded a full accounting of her mother's spending for the last ten years. Though this accounting had not yet been produced, her attorney indicated that the court would be appalled by the handling of the money bequeathed to her from the Cooper family trust.

Tyler explained to the reporters present that a lawsuit was his client's only recourse—and that lawsuit needed to be filed hastily. The statute of limitations for filing a complaint related to malpractice was one year.

The reporters peppered the attorney with questions. When these ended, Ann powdered her nose and readied herself for the cameramen again. She endured over one hundred flashes of light, prompting one photographer to observe that she couldn't be feebleminded—she didn't have a fit. A few approached to say how awfully sorry they were about what happened. One told her she had really lovely blue eyes. Another gave her his card, in case she wanted to talk off the record.

Ann went home feeling satisfied. After months of fretting, she'd finally told her story, and people were horrified to learn what she'd endured. It was plain to them that Maryon, not she, was the one unfit to be a mother. Ann figured it wouldn't be long before Maryon agreed to settle the lawsuit, allowing her to move on with her life.

The heiress had no idea that her mother would respond by telling the court—and the world—about Ann's own private life, saying Ann had given her no choice. Nor did she have a clue how dramatically her lawsuit would change her life and those of untold numbers of women for decades to come. What seemed to her a personal matter to be settled by the courts would spark a nationwide debate on the changing nature of womanhood, the purpose of sexuality, and the merits of allowing doctors to decide who did and didn't reproduce.

2

"OVER-SEXED"

You were born on an evil day," Ann's mother often told her, when she behaved in a way that displeased her parent. "A very evil day."

Maryon was referring to the fact that World War I had begun on the day of Ann's birth in Paris. No sooner had the three-and-a-half-pound, dark-haired baby come into the world than Austria-Hungary declared war against Serbia, prompting other nations to take sides before troops rolled into their cities. The new mother had not been about to let this unfortunate event interfere with her postpartum convalescence. After all, Maryon used to say, the pain of giving birth to Ann had nearly killed her. However, fearing that Germans might bombard Paris from the skies, Ann's father had pleaded with her to take the newborn out of the country. So she'd put the little girl in a reed basket and taken her to England and then to the United States until it was deemed safe for them to return.

As a child, Ann had long believed that the ill-fated day of her birth had doomed her to be a bad, sickly girl. She often thought how much she would have liked to have been born on Christmas or the Fourth of July. A little girl who shared a birthday with Jesus or the greatest nation on earth surely wouldn't require regular trips to a sanatorium to be cured of bronchial trouble, nor a truss to straighten an unsightly double hernia.

"It's a good thing your father left you money," Ann's mother began to remark after Peter's death. "Or else I'd go bankrupt paying for your care."

Maryon made a point of telling young Ann exactly how much she spent on private nurses, governesses, and extended trips to institutions, where physicians often looked at Ann with disgust after being told that she'd been caught with her hand in her undergarments at three years of age. Some of these professionals promised to cure Ann, only to later explain that she was beyond hope. "She has retarded growth, arrested mental development, and a disturbance of the endocrine system that has resulted in impulsive tendencies," one doctor had told Ann's mother. "There's little we can do to correct these problems here. Have you tried a home for feebleminded children?"

Mrs. Cooper Hewitt had little patience for doctors like this one, often accusing them of taking her money knowing they could do nothing for Ann. But in this case, soon after her husband's passing, she'd taken the doctor's word and sent Ann to a place in Switzerland. It was at this facility, tucked in the Alps, that eight-year-old Ann committed a deed for which her mother would never forgive her.

After a few days at the institution, the girl found a peer her age—an English boy who made her laugh by twisting his arm and drooling the way some of the other patients did. "Look, I'm an imbecile!" he'd said. Then, turning serious, he'd asked Ann what she'd done to warrant being sent to such a place.

Not wanting to repeat what her mother had told the staff—that she had "erotic tendencies"—Ann had responded, "My mother is vacationing in the Riviera."

"What's that got to do with anything?" the boy had asked.

"Mother says I don't deserve to go. My French is terrible, and I don't know my sums. It's all because I am ornery."

"Mm," said the boy.

"What about you?" Ann had asked before he could press for more.

"I have fits."

The two youngsters began to take walks and, when staff members weren't looking, exchange notes and sketches of places they'd encountered in their reading, such as the Wild West and the Galapagos Islands. Then the boy began to weave stories about the places he'd drawn. He was a cowboy riding across the desert with a crew of bandits at his heels. A sea serpent reigning over a marine kingdom. Sometimes he dramatized these scenes for a wide-eyed Ann.

One evening, when his tale-telling was cut short by their curfew, the boy told the young heiress to find his room after the night nurse made her rounds. And that's exactly what she did, tiptoeing down the hall to the boys' wing in her nightgown. Her friend had already made room for her under the blankets; and after a moment's hesitation, she slid into the bed and pulled the quilt to her chin. They lay there for a moment, imagining the rage of authorities coming across them. Then the boy resumed his story.

Not wanting to be caught, Ann stayed only an hour. But when she returned the next evening, she lingered a little longer. The evening after that, she lingered longer still. The trend continued until one night, she drifted off to sleep to the image of a lost orphan exploring an enchanted forest in search of treasure.

A nurse discovered them when she made her rounds at dawn. "You wicked, wicked girl," she shrieked, grabbing Ann by the elbow and pulling her out of the bed. "Imagine what your mother will say. After all she has done for you!"

Ann could only hope that her mother would send a maid to fetch her, as she often did. But it was Mrs. Cooper Hewitt herself who arrived at the asylum a few days after receiving a telegram about the incident. Ann sat, flush-faced, while the director related the details of her crime, then as Maryon pulled a handkerchief from her pocket to dab her eyes. "I don't know what to do," Ann's mother said. "God knows I've tried to set her on the right path, but there's something terribly wrong with her."

The director stood and approached Maryon, placing his hand on her shoulder. "See what you've done, Ann? See what grief you've caused?"

Ann bowed her head.

Mrs. Cooper Hewitt waited until they were alone in the room to reach over and slap her daughter. Though Ann's lip began to quiver, she managed not to shed a tear.

In the early twentieth century, a "New Woman" was emerging in Europe and the United States, who inspired widespread societal panic. Though adolescent Ann hardly resembled this adult, middle-class cultural figure, she was haunted by her specter from a very young age.

The New Woman was a defiant white woman who refused to dwell at home and avoid strenuous activity, as her Victorian counterpart of the nineteenth century had. Instead she rode her bicycle around town, attended college, and worked in offices typing reports. She even began to engage in political conversations with co-workers and friends—that is, if her companions indulged her. Many worried that intense conversations endangered a woman's health; they had long been told that the gentler sex required rest and seclusion to avoid overtaxing the nervous system.

Traditionalists narrowed their eyes at the New Woman, who had no regard for the "separate spheres" Victorians had delineated between private and public life in the previous century. A woman's place, according to convention, was in the home. Only there could she be a guardian of virtue, raising her children to be moral, righteous, and productive members of society. A woman who spent her days in an office was apt to raise wanton, individualistic offspring, her critics believed. After all, the younger generation was prone to imitate the behaviors of their mothers. If a mother forsook her family to pursue her whims, was there any reason to believe that her children would not do the same, eventually becoming criminals, alcoholics, or other unprincipled creatures?

There was something even more disturbing about the New Woman, which physicians claimed to observe about Ann: She was over-sexed. Whereas the Victorian woman of yesteryear was prudent and passionless, blushing if a crass friend or neighbor raised the topic, the New Woman talked about sex as casually as she talked about what she was preparing for dinner on her new steel cookstove. The Victorian woman had understood that men needed to limit their marital relations, so as not to sap their virility. (If any organ overexerted itself, illness or insanity might ensue.) She'd further understood that sex was purely for procreative purposes, as too much of it endangered society. As one of her popular magazines explained, "Every man has a quantity of dynamite in him, and the frequent explosion of that dynamite is a tragic part of the world's history." But the New Woman didn't see it as her job to contain the male sex's natural barbarism. Nor did she respect the natural function of sex. Using new methods of contraception, she sought to separate sex from motherhood. As a result, the New Woman's critics feared, she was going to unleash the male species's baser instincts.

As far as Ann's European physicians were concerned, a little girl caught masturbating was sure to become such a danger to men and society—that was, if she didn't obviate the need for men altogether. "Ann is 'man-like' in her urges," one physician told her mother, after hearing about her alleged fondness for self-gratification. "And if she keeps at her nasty habit, she won't perceive any need to marry one day."

Across the Atlantic, anxiety about nonprocreative female sexuality was growing even more intense, as Americans feared for the future of the white race. In the early decades of the century, African Americans were migrating from southern to northern cities, and Asians and Eastern Europeans were emigrating in record numbers. Cities like New York, Boston, Chicago, and San Francisco didn't look like they had during the Civil War. In this context, white middle-class women's seeming rejection of motherhood caused great alarm. Authorities noted with indignation, "In 1840, the average American woman produced six children. Now she births a pitiful three. 'Liberated' women are going to cause the downfall of civilization!"

Former president Teddy Roosevelt went so far as to call women of "good stock" (white, able-bodied, middle- to upper-class women) who refused to have children "race criminals." Like other Progressives of the era, who were determined to resolve the perceived abuses of industrial capitalism without actually undermining that system, he resented that working-class and minority women seemed to be reproducing at alarming rates, while "fit" women were having fewer children or even none at all.

Believing social reforms could save the race, Progressives took action. With funding from John D. Rockefeller Jr., the son of the famous oil tycoon, they established "vice commissions" to regulate the sexual activity of shop girls, factory workers, and other low-class women. Undercover investigators trailed women from their tenements to their jobs, taking notes on everything from their boots to their professional tasks. "There is no question that this woman is on terms of sexual intimacy with her male companions," one concluded, having observed a manicurist massaging the hands of businessmen all day. "The salesgirl is especially promiscuous," another investigator wrote after spying on a girl at Macy's. "All day, she is surrounded by expensive clothing, jewels, and other finery, and so she will sacrifice anything—including her virtue—to obtain these items."

But while city authorities could prosecute brothel owners and known prostitutes, they had little recourse against women who worked or went out after their shifts, even if their companions were married men. If Progressives were going to save society from the sexually active women on the streets, they required more aggressive measures—ones informed by burgeoning scientific fields like evolutionary biology.

Eugenic sterilization appeared to provide such a solution. By surgically preventing poor, disabled, and "wayward" individuals from reproducing, Progressives could reduce the number of unsound people in the population. In 1907, Indiana passed the first law authorizing the sterilization of such individuals within state homes; and other states quickly followed suit. California was one of them. There the sterilization program became so robust that officials in other nations began to take note. But in 1936, when Ann's case came into the spotlight, the fate of this social program hung in the balance; and the outcome of the mother-daughter drama promised to reverberate far and wide.

3

REMAKING THE WORLD

In 1883, English intellectual Francis Galton coined the term
eugenics (meaning "wellborn") to advocate a selective breeding
program among humans. Galton had long been bothered that his
country was becoming overrun by wretched people who de-
pended upon the charity of affluent families like his. After
reading his cousin Charles Darwin's book *On the Origin of the
Species*, Galton determined to influence the evolution of human
beings. The Englishman argued that it was imperative for members of the upper class to pass down the characteristics associated
with it, such as superior intelligence. If wellborn women had
more children, then many social evils, such as poverty, could be
eliminated.

Though he revered science and had little time for religion,
Galton imagined that eugenics would be taken like a religious
creed—on faith and without scientific proof. He often compared
eugenical marriage (the marriage of two high-class individuals) to
other religious duties and cited instances of selective breeding in
Jewish and Christian texts. "It is easy to let the imagination run
wild on the supposition of a whole-hearted acceptance of eugenics
as a national religion," Galton wrote in 1905. His British followers

agreed that eugenics could only thrive as a religion—and that "nothing but a eugenic religion [could save] civilization," in the words of playwright George Bernard Shaw.

While Galton made an impression on fellow countrymen like Shaw, he most enthralled an American biologist named Charles Davenport. A colleague recalled that Davenport entered a trance-like state whenever he spoke of eugenic concepts, such as protoplasm (the genetic material needed to create a more perfect race): "He used to lift his eyes reverently, and, with his hands up-raised as though in supplication, quiver emotionally as he breathed, 'Protoplasm. We want more protoplasm.'"

In 1910, Davenport founded the Eugenics Record Office at Cold Spring Harbor Laboratory on Long Island. He intended to identify—and then eliminate—traits associated with poverty, intellectual disability, criminality, promiscuity, and other perceived genetic conditions. Like Galton, he believed that social conditions like poverty were biologically inherited, just like blue eyes or brown hair. But whereas Galton had emphasized increased breeding among elites (what would become known as positive eugenics), Davenport desired to give equal attention to the other side of the eugenic coin: negative eugenics. He wanted to take measures to prevent those deemed "unfit" from becoming parents. He claimed that Austrian monk Gregor Mendel's recently rediscovered work on the reproductive patterns of peas provided the know-how to implement such a program.

With funding from philanthropic families in leading industries, such as the Rockefellers (oil), Carnegies (steel), Kelloggs (cereal), and Harrimans (railroad), Davenport appointed Harry Laughlin as the Eugenics Record Office's first director; and together, the two hired field-workers to collect family pedigrees from the public. With this data, much of it based on field-workers' biased observations, Davenport and Laughlin came to many unscientific conclusions about epileptics, alcoholics, prostitutes, "shiftless" persons, immigrants, and other classes of people. For instance, the two determined that epileptics were morally degenerate, as they were stuck in a primitive stage of development that didn't allow for the higher reasoning needed to live according to social norms. Davenport and Laughlin regularly presented their findings to lawmakers and government agencies, helping to pass stringent immigration restrictions, expand anti-miscegenation laws (prohibiting marriage between races), and implement involuntary sterilization programs across the country.

Inspired by Davenport and Laughlin's crusade, two California men came together in 1913 to expand sterilization in their home state. They were Paul Popenoe and Ezra Gosney.

The Kansas-born Popenoe had recently left the university, where he studied heredity, to care for his father, when his former academic adviser asked him to edit the Journal of Heredity, a scholarly publication focused on the subject of inheritance. One of his first editorial assignments was to cover the progress of California's five-year-old forced-sterilization law, which authorized directors of state institutions to sterilize inmates against their will and even without their knowledge. For this assignment, Popenoe visited asylums across the state to inspect the inmates subjected to the new legislation. He found that people from Scandinavia, Britain, Italy, Russia, Poland, and Germany constituted the majority of sterilizations, though African Americans and those of Mexican descent were operated upon at double their rate within the general population. He didn't question these numbers, believing that immigrants and persons of color were the original sources of degeneracy and that African Americans and Mexicans were "hyperbreeders," whose children could seldom support themselves.

Based on his observations, Popenoe then argued in his journal that approximately ten million Americans—then, a tenth of the population—should be sterilized.

Gosney financed the study, in addition to commissioning it. The lemon grove owner had amassed a considerable fortune from selling citrus crops in Southern California. A Kentucky native who shared Popenoe's background in agriculture, Gosney wanted to apply horticultural practices to human beings. Why, he wondered, were measures being taken to grow the plumpest, most appealing fruit and the sturdiest cattle, but nothing was being done to ensure the quality of the human species?

In 1928, after more than a decade of advocating for sterilization in academic circles, the two men established the Human Betterment Foundation in Pasadena, whose stated purpose was "to foster and aid constructive and educational forces for the protection and betterment of the human family in body, mind, character, and citizenship." More plainly, their mission was to increase public knowledge about the good of sterilization and educate policy makers in other parts of the country (and even the world) on ways to implement their own sterilization programs. Once again, Gosney provided the funding for the venture. He served as its president, while Popenoe served as secretary. Both men recognized that the Golden State was far outpacing others in terms of its eugenic measures, and therefore that they were in a position to lead the nation.

Although other states had similar sterilization statutes, many officials in those states were reluctant to exercise their laws. The two Californians corresponded with these authorities to assuage their worries about the safety, morality, and legality of involuntary surgery. They promised these skeptics that vasectomy (for males) and salpingectomy (for females) were "no more serious than pulling a tooth" and that most individuals were grateful after undergoing either procedure. Gosney and Popenoe even struck up a dialogue with some German officials who were very intrigued by the idea of using surgery as a means of population control. The Germans had first encountered the idea in a translation of Popenoe's 1916 college textbook, *Applied Eugenics*, co-authored by Roswell Johnson. In addition to advocating for selective breeding, this text encouraged the segregation of "waste humanity" in manual labor camps.

Popenoe and Gosney, too, collaborated to write a number of influential texts, such as *Sterilization for Human Betterment: A Summary of Results of 6,000 Operations in California, 1909–1929*. This text was based on data gathered from the California inmates whom Popenoe studied, and it quickly found its way into the hands of officials in Nazi Germany. In 1930, Eugen Fischer, the director of the Kaiser Wilhelm Institute for Anthropology, Human Heredity, and Eugenics in Berlin, wrote a letter of gratitude to Gosney for his and Popenoe's insights, saying that "these issues will be of great importance for legislation here in Europe." Five years later, Fischer drew upon the text to help craft the Nuremberg Laws, which forbade intercourse and marriage between Jews and Germans and declared only those of German or related blood to be eligible for Reich citizenship. He went on to use Popenoe and Gosney's work as a rubric for selecting children to sterilize under the Nazi regime.

Hermann Simon, the director of another eugenic institute in Germany, praised the book as well. Shortly after its publication, he wrote to the authors, "I do hope the time will come that also in Germany this knowledge will be generalized." Simon got his wish in 1933, when his country enacted a eugenic statute based on California's program. Shortly thereafter, a Human Betterment Foundation board member wrote to Gosney, "I want you, my dear friend, to carry this thought with you for the rest of your life, that you have really jolted into action a great government of 60 million people."

There was momentum for eugenics in the United States, as well. The year prior to the opening of the Human Betterment Foundation, the US Supreme Court had reaffirmed the legality of involuntary sterilization by upholding the state of Virginia's decision to operate on a woman deemed feebleminded after becoming an unwed mother. The targeted individual, Carrie Buck, was a poor woman from rural Virginia, whose pregnancy resulted from her rape at sixteen years of age. Buck's foster parents' nephew had violated her while his aunt and uncle were out of town. Shortly after Buck gave birth to a daughter in 1924, her foster parents committed her to the Lynchburg Colony, where authorities decided to remove her fallopian tubes under the state's brand-new involuntary sterilization law.

Before operating, however, these authorities arranged to use Buck to test said law, which, like the one in California, authorized officials of state-run institutions to order surgeries. They wanted to cement the legislation against future court challenges. Toward this end, the superintendent of the colony, Albert Priddy, appointed a colleague, Irving Whitehead, to serve as Buck's attorney. These two men corresponded throughout the legal proceedings to guarantee that Priddy prevailed on behalf of the colony.

The defense's case against Buck was simple: Carrie was cognitively impaired. She had a chronological age of eighteen but a mental one of nine. To prove Carrie's hereditary deficiencies, the defense counsel cited her poor performance on an intelligence test; her "life of immorality, prostitution, and untruthfulness"; and the fact that both her mother and daughter were defective. The defense attorney claimed that Carrie's mother was also unwed at the time of her birth and that Carrie's six-month-old had inherited both mother and grandmother's defects. (According to a nurse who interacted with her, the baby had a queer look in her eyes.) The defense attorney did not acknowledge that Buck had no more than a sixth-grade education, due to her foster parents' decision to have her work on their farm instead of attending school. And his claim about Buck's illegitimacy was false; Emma Buck was married to, but separated from, Carrie's father at the time of her birth.

Whitehead didn't challenge any of the statements against his client; nor did he call any witnesses to testify about the circumstances of Buck's pregnancy or about her commitment to the colony. Many believed that Buck's foster parents had her locked up to conceal their nephew's crime.

When the Circuit Court of Amherst County ruled in favor of the colony, Whitehead appealed to the Supreme Court of Appeals of Virginia. He was again simply executing his and Priddy's plan. When that court upheld the first court's ruling, following Priddy's death and replacement as the named defendant, Whitehead took the case to the US Supreme Court. Again, Whitehead poorly argued his client's case, leading to a verdict for the defense and for sterilization advocates across the country. In his majority opinion for *Buck v. Bell*, Justice Oliver Wendell Holmes wrote, "It is better for all the world, if instead of waiting to execute degenerate offspring for crime, or to let them starve for their imbecility, society can prevent those who are manifestly unfit from continuing their kind...Three generations of imbeciles are enough."

The decision reaffirmed that unwed motherhood was pathological, legitimating the psychologists at state institutions who incorporated social codes into diagnostic criteria. It further allowed state officials to forcibly cut into individuals' bodies in the name of enforcing those codes. Eugenicists everywhere were delighted.

The same year that the Supreme Court handed down the Buck decision, Americans had encountered eugenic ideals on the big screen with the popular film *Are You Fit to Marry?* In it, viewers found messages about there being "no love without sacrifice" and the need to use medical science to improve human society. It was not the first film to urge young moviegoers to select mates with the gene pool in mind. Eugenic propaganda also saturated other forms of entertainment, such as state fairs, where the public participated in "Better Babies" and "Fitter Families" contests. These competitions, begun in the 1910s, subjected humans to the same physical inspections that livestock underwent, awarding medals to those with white pigment, straight teeth, and flawless family trees. "Yours is a goodly heritage," medals read, assuring recipients that they should get married and have children—plenty of children.

Many liberal Protestant Americans also encountered eugenic principles in Sunday services. While Catholic and orthodox Protestant church officials vehemently opposed involuntary sterilization, some progressive Methodist, Presbyterian, and Episcopal ministers encouraged selective breeding, participated in Eugenics Sermon contests, and contributed to popular publications like *Eugenics* magazine. These more worldly leaders instructed that Christians and eugenicists were fighting a common battle, as both were occupied with removing the causes of weakness. The sooner the causes of weakness were removed, the sooner weakness would be removed; and the sooner weakness was removed, the closer to the Lord's kingdom human civilization would be. Liberal Protestants often drew upon scripture to promote eugenics, such as the following from the Gospel of Matthew: "A good tree cannot bear bad fruit, and a bad tree cannot bear good fruit. Every tree that does not bear good fruit is cut down and thrown into the fire" (7:18–19). By suggesting philosophical overlap between Christian teachings and notions of racial integrity, these religious officials quelled fears that eugenicists were trying to "play God."

But despite these noteworthy legal and cultural gains, the race crusade was on unstable ground when the Human Betterment Foundation opened its doors in 1928, and both Popenoe and Gosney knew it. By the end of the third decade of the century, geneticists and biologists had begun to claim that the science behind eugenics was quite shoddy. According to these experts, the transmission of positive and negative traits was far more complicated than eugenicists assumed. To start, the inheritance of traits extended well beyond one generation, meaning that even if all the feebleminded persons in the country were sterilized, it could take sixty-eight generations to substantially decrease the proportion of feebleminded persons in the population. Critics also claimed that it was impossible to identify potential carriers of bad genes since "normal" people could carry negative traits. In addition, eugenicists completely disregarded the role of the environment in the development of traits. Environmental conditions hadn't been on many scientists' radar at the beginning of the century, but burgeoning fields like behavioral and social science were beginning to change this.

Some of eugenics' most vocal critics were figures who had previously espoused the movement's ideals. Respected individuals like Herbert Spencer Jennings and Alexander Graham Bell were quietly retiring from eugenics boards and committees, and the Nobel Prize–winning Thomas Hunt Morgan was lambasting the idea that Mendelian inheritance patterns could be easily applied to humans. Henry Goddard, who had developed intelligence tests to identify feebleminded persons like Buck, was also among the defectors. "I think I have gone over to the enemy," the psychologist would confess in the early 1930s. Goddard would claim to have realized that the difference between human beings was "intellectual, not racial" and that there actually wasn't much evidence that moron parents were likely to have moron children after all.

Margaret Sanger, the birth control advocate and early eugenics supporter, appeared to Gosney and Popenoe to be jumping ship as well. When eugenics was first gaining currency, she had promised Davenport that the birth control she promoted would weed out idiots, delinquents, alcoholics, and prisoners. In 1918, she wrote, "All of our problems are the result of overbreeding among the working class... [Birth control] must lead to a higher individuality and ultimately to a cleaner race." But in reality, she was using birth control to do the opposite. She was promoting birth control to all women, regardless of their skin color or social station. As a result, the lower classes were breeding more prolifically than ever, while middle-class white women were taking birth control and going to college or the workforce.

In 1933, under the new leadership of Adolf Hitler, the Nazis had implemented a eugenic-sterilization program that impacted more than 350,000 individuals. At first, Gosney and Popenoe had been thrilled to see what the Germans had accomplished using their own programs as blueprints. But they soon realized that Hitler's persecution of the Jews could seriously undermine support for sterilization in the United States, as the dictator was extremely unpopular among Americans. The public now bristled at terms like *racial integrity*, which the eugenicists had long used to describe their work.

Having poured decades of their lives and, in Gosney's case, private wealth into the expansion of eugenic programs in California and beyond, both Gosney and Popenoe feared the combination of scientific turns and events abroad could be the death knell for their movement. They desperately needed to find a new idiom to promote eugenics. One that would resolutely convince people of the great danger of allowing just anyone to reproduce.

4

MAYHEM

Shortly after Ann's press conference in San Francisco, the district attorney got wind of her case. At first, Matthew Brady's eyes widened as he read the girl's accusations in the *San Francisco Examiner*. Then his mind began to turn. Here was an opportunity to charge four individuals (Mrs. Cooper Hewitt, the doctor who ordered the operation, the doctor who performed it, and the alienist) with a felony not often encountered outside of legal textbooks: mayhem. This criminal charge was reserved for cases involving the act of disabling or disfiguring an individual, and it was punishable by up to fourteen years in prison.

Brady immediately conferred with his assistant, August Fourtner, and Police Inspector George Engler about the matter. The group's cursory research revealed that over ten thousand individuals in the state had been sterilized in public institutions since California had passed a law authorizing sterilization in 1909. There existed no record of the number of sterilizations performed in private practice, though some legal experts predicted the number was large. The law didn't authorize these procedures, meaning that there could be hundreds—or even thousands—of individuals like Ann, whose rights had been violated.

The most frequent techniques for sterilization were vasectomy and salpingectomy, which Ann had undergone. Castration and spaying were generally avoided, as these procedures didn't merely render individuals incapable of producing children—they desexualized them. This last fact might present a conundrum for the San Francisco prosecutors, Brady realized. Mayhem cases hinged on proving that one's body had been maimed, rendered useless, or substantially changed in physical character. What if defendants argued that the primary purpose of sex was pleasure, rather than procreation, and therefore that the operation did not amount to an act of mayhem?

Brady imagined his opponent declaring in court, "The woman has not been 'unsexed,' as she claims. She has only had her tubes removed. She can still gratify her desires—no one has taken that from her." If the court accepted this logic, the case could be dismissed, and he would be harangued for drawing the public's attention to such an impolite fact.

But on another legal point, Brady and the other two men were emboldened. Criminal liability for mayhem required proof of gross negligence, criminal intent, or the fact of being engaged in the commission of another felony. There was no question that Ann's mother had acted with malice and insidious intent. As far as they were concerned, she had debilitated her daughter simply to tighten her grip on the family money. The doctors, too, had acted wickedly. Each had accepted $9,000 for a procedure for which they ought to have been paid a few hundred.

"Of course, the court will see that they were bribed," Fourtner said. "The monstrous woman paid them to execute her plot and then keep quiet about it."

"What about the psychologist?" Engler asked. "What did she get out of this?"

The mayhem charge against her might prove more difficult, Brady agreed. But perhaps forthcoming facts would implicate Mary Scally, too.

A meeting with Ann's attorney assured the three city officials that a parallel criminal case was imperative. There was no question that the salpingectomy had been completed without the girl's knowledge. And it would be easy to prove that this procedure—and not the appendectomy—was the primary reason for cutting the girl open. Boyd had foolishly revised the medical records after the fact, inserting "organs infantile" to explain why an incision had been made in the girl's abdomen at the site of the fallopian tubes, rather than the appendix. The operating physician also recorded on a later date that the fallopian tubes had only been tied, when, in fact, they were removed, making it impossible to reverse the procedure. It was as if the severity of the crime had struck Boyd later and he went back to cover his tracks. Brady had already arranged for the paper to be chemically tested to substantiate in court that the doctor had, indeed, revised the medical notes well after the operation took place.

The testimony of the nurses attending to Ann before and after the procedure also strengthened the prosecutors' case. Ann was completely normal, these persons maintained. One of them, Grace Wilkins, had just received a sealed letter from Mrs. Cooper Hewitt's attorney warning her "not to talk." Another said that she had received a telephone call threatening death if she testified.

This case was a winner, the prosecutors thought.

To avoid being accused of collaborating with the heiress, Brady and Fourtner planned to tell the press that Ann had neither requested nor attended the meeting and that they had no intentions of involving her in the investigation. "It would be most unfair that she assume the duties and obligations of the police department," they'd say. "The poor woman is dealing with enough as it is."

Of course, both district attorneys had confirmed with Tyler that Ann would cooperate by signing the criminal complaint and, if necessary, taking the stand against her mother. "The case is dead if the girl gets cold feet," they cautioned.

"You don't need to worry about that," Tyler had assured them. "She is determined to prevail against her mother. And also to prevent such a terrible crime from happening to anyone else."

With this assurance, Brady and Fourtner held their own press conference. Brady did the talking. "I am not prepared to make a definite statement on the law in this case," the man told the scribbling reporters outside his office. "There are many angles to be investigated. I can say, however, that the charges will probably be presented to a grand jury very soon. And justice will be served."

"Tell us what angles you are considering," a man from the *San Francisco Examiner* urged.

"The legality of the sterilization, to start," Brady responded. "There's only one state law pertaining to sterilization, and it allows superintendents of state mental hospitals to authorize operations of feebleminded persons. There's no record of such persons being involved in this case. Dr. Tillman is not a superintendent, and the plaintiff is not feebleminded."

"Are you saying that Mrs. Scally's investigation didn't count?"

"That's for the courts to decide," said Brady. "However, the psychologist's supervisor has since demanded that all requests for psychological examination of minors be made in writing and approved by his office."

Earlier that day, the district attorney had received a telephone call from California State Health Officer J. C. Geiger with this policy update, as well as a request for all pertinent information related to the investigation to be shared. Tongues were wagging, and authorities needed to assure everyone that the laws were strictly enforced. "It's not as though anyone can be plucked off the street and snipped," Geiger had insisted. "We must communicate this fact, or else there will be riots."

But as Brady had recently learned, Californians *were* being plucked off the streets and forcibly operated upon. In fact, those on the streets—impoverished, unemployed, and wayward individuals—were the most likely to find themselves strapped to a table. For many decades, such individuals had been sent to homes, where they could be rehabilitated following a pregnancy or cured from deviant habits like masturbation or inversion (homosexuality). But sexual deviance—especially among women—had grown too rampant to be contained this way, sterilization advocates said. There simply weren't enough homes to house all the wayward women to be found on the streets.

Apparently, most physicians agreed with these practices. For decades, they had been arguing that sexually deviant behaviors were medical, not moral, matters. They said the same about poverty and other social circumstances. The "conditions once considered criminal are really pathological, and come within the province of the physician," the editor of *The Medical Record* had opined in 1884. To justify their oversight of sexual abnormality, doctors observed that morally loose individuals tended to have congenital defects, such as enlarged reproductive organs.

Brady had also received a telephone call from a representative of a physicians association, who was worried that a criminal case posed a threat to the profession's authority, though not exactly in matters related to sterilization. "Doctors in the state are concerned about the implications of a criminal mayhem case," the representative had claimed. "Many of them routinely perform"—she'd lowered her voice to say the next word—"*abortions* upon minors, at the parents' request. In these cases, it is rightfully assumed that the parents know best. How can a thirteen-year-old girl who has gotten into trouble possibly be trusted to make responsible decisions?"

Brady had told this caller that he had never considered the repercussions of a particular case when deciding upon a course of action, and he wasn't prepared to start now. As a district attorney, it was his job to seek justice for crimes committed in his city and to let the chips fall where they may. If the state of California determined that a minor could seek recourse against her parents for an unwanted operation—abortion or otherwise—then so be it.

The prosecutor was not surprised to observe one physician with his black bag in attendance at the press conference he gave outside his office. The medical man stood quietly, arms crossed, as he listened to Brady relate the facts of the case and the relevant points of law.

Before the small crowd dispersed, Brady reiterated that, while he did not intend to involve the heiress in the criminal suit, he had her full blessing. "Miss Hewitt has quite courageously decided to share her story so that no one else experiences the same pain and anguish," he said.

Unfortunately for the prosecutor, Ann's attorney was wrong about his client's willingness to sign the criminal complaint. This meant that the prosecutors could not take the case to municipal court without a judge's permission.

"I don't see why I have to be involved in that case," Ann told Tyler when he put the papers in front of her.

"Without you, the case is flimsy," Tyler explained. "The court will wonder if the prosecution has all the facts straight."

"But I've told all the facts to you, and you've related them."

Tyler sighed and returned the papers to the district attorney, who slammed his fist on his desk upon hearing the news.

"What is wrong with her? Is she as dimwitted as they say?" Brady stood from his chair to close the door behind Ann's attorney. Already he knew that the details in this case needed to be tightly protected. He couldn't afford to have the newspapers report his next move, citing some anonymous clerk or secretary in his office.

"Tell me," the prosecutor continued. "Is she going to make a fool of us on the stand?"

"I don't believe so," said Tyler. "She's very sympathetic when she gets talking about the matter."

That morning, Ann had met with a reporter from the *Los Angeles Times* who had hopped on an early-bird train to come and see the sterilized heiress for himself. "I never intended to be an old maid," Ann had told the man with a wistful look in her eyes. "I still want to marry and have a house of my own. There just won't be any children." She'd posed for several photographs for his story.

"But is she going to talk in court? That's the question." Brady couldn't count the number of times over the course of his career that a witness had hung him out to dry.

"I'll talk to her again," Tyler assured him. "You proceed with the case."

Without Ann's signature, Brady and Fourtner had no choice but to request a municipal hearing to determine if they had the authority to file criminal charges on their own. Much to their relief, the twenty-one-year-old appeared to testify at this proceeding. She even seemed to impress Judge Sylvain J. Lazarus with her poise and intellect.

When describing the mental exam administered by Scally, Ann recalled asking the psychologist in disgust, "Why are you asking me these asinine questions?"

At this, the judge turned to her and asked, "Did you really say 'asinine'?"

"Oh, yes," said Ann. "I also corrected her French pronunciation during another part of the exam."

"Never dispute a psychiatrist," said Judge Lazarus. "She probably marked you down a couple of points just for that."

At the end of Ann's testimony, the man in robes assured the girl, "You have been a wonderful witness. I know very few who think as clearly as you do."

Anne B. Lindsay, the nurse who had assisted Dr. Boyd with the operation, also performed splendidly. "The doc asked me to take the case two days before the operation," this woman stated on the stand. "He said Miss Hewitt had the mentality of a child of eleven and a sex complex. But later, he admitted that he didn't think she was a moron after all. He said he'd simply taken all of Dr. Tillman's findings."

Judge Lazarus listened to every word, leaning toward the witness box so as not to miss a single detail. When the testimony ended, he declared that he would consider the case and decide whether to order the arrest of Ann's mother and the two physicians. He didn't see any reason why the alienist ought to be charged with the same crime. "She could have been more discerning—there's no question about that," said the judge. "But I don't believe it is reasonable to think she, too, engaged in mayhem."

The newspapers remarked on Ann's charm. "When comfortable, talk makes her forget that she's supposed to be homely," wrote one reporter. "And she has a broad, smooth brow, and well-modeled nose, which counteract the effect of the hated buck teeth."

Less than one week later, Lazarus ruled to issue warrants for the arrest of the three defendants. He made clear that he had not considered possible motives for Ann's sterilization—only whether or not her personal rights had been violated. "The question is whether mothers, fathers, or guardians can set themselves up to say whether minors should be sterilized," he explained. "There are dangers in such a thing."

Officers arrested Tillman and Boyd and then released both men on bail to await trial. The doctors didn't delay in making a statement. "The girl was feebleminded," Dr. Tillman read from a paper in his hand. "Mrs. Cooper Hewitt came to me and said she wanted her daughter examined. I had her under my observation for six or eight months. Mrs. Scally, a state psychiatrist, gave the tests and confirmed my observations as to the girl's condition. The actual operation was performed by Dr. Boyd. Mrs. Cooper Hewitt was perfectly within her legal rights in deciding on an operation."

Tillman added that money had nothing to do with Maryon's choice to have her daughter sterilized. In fact, he explained, if money had *anything* to do with the matter at all, it was only that it delayed Ann's sterilization. "A girl of ordinary means with her intellect would've been committed years ago to Sonoma, where authorities would have demanded that she be operated upon," he said.

Founded in 1884, the Sonoma State Home was a clearinghouse for young women like Ann, who were perceived to be intellectually (morally) deficient. In contrast with other state institutions, which detained patients indefinitely, Sonoma sterilized patients and then released them back into the population. This business model alleviated the cost of maintaining inmates, the home's director, F. O. Butler, claimed. It also allowed for more people to be sterilized. By 1936, physicians at Sonoma had sterilized more "defective" individuals than any other asylum in the world. Many of these persons' own parents had referred them by alerting social workers they feared, in the case of "delinquent" daughters, that their child would become pregnant out of wedlock. An illegitimate pregnancy threatened the family's economic stability by ruining the family's reputation. (People didn't want to patronize a business owned by someone who couldn't keep his own children out of trouble.) Maryon was by no means the only parent complicit in her daughter's sterilization, even if her motivations seemed unusual.

Tillman had nothing to say about the suggestion that his relationship with Maryon was unprofessional. In the criminal complaint, Brady and Fourtner had squeezed in a detail about Maryon affectionately calling the doctor "Uncle Tilt" and instructing her daughter to do the same. This nugget had come from Tyler, who reported that the physician had regularly visited the Cooper Hewitt residence for at least a year before the procedure. According to his client, Maryon and the doctor had spent many evenings on the sofa, whispering in each other's ears while a servant refilled their champagne flutes.

In trying to shift the spotlight from Ann to Maryon's romantic life, Tyler and the two prosecutors implicitly reinforced the doctors' views that amorous women made bad mothers. It remained to be seen whether this counterattack would serve their respective cases.

When it was his turn to speak, Dr. Boyd stated that he had been consulted about Ann's case and had found no reason to dispute his colleague's findings. Thus, he'd agreed to perform the procedure. "There was nothing out of the ordinary about what happened," he, too, maintained. "Cases like this, in which a parent orders a moron child's sterilization, occur every day."

By the time the two doctors had issued their statements, newspapers across the country had picked up the story. The premise—an heiress alleging that her mother had plotted to sterilize her to secure the family money—was enough to rivet readers on its own. But with the unfolding testimony related to Ann's and Maryon's private lives, the case was growing even more intriguing. Many middle-aged and elderly readers remembered Mrs. Cooper Hewitt from the society pages years before. The beautiful, much-betrothed woman had gained a reputation for "keeping the record complicated" and "securing the jobs of genealogists." The newspapers had portrayed Ann's mother as a social climber who married for money instead of love. The prospect of this society pet falling from the upper echelons all these years later was too absorbing for these readers to ignore.

The legal dimensions of the case also stirred readers' interests. In 1936, many Americans didn't know that tens of thousands of individuals had been sterilized in state institutions nationwide. Or if they did, they didn't think or talk much about this fact; what happened behind the closed doors of an asylum was not considered polite conversation. Ann's case provoked readers' curiosity about sterilization practices in their home states and around the nation.

Some experts predicted that the case's greatest impact would not be upon sterilization practices, but rather upon the practice of performing other surgeries without written consent. These experts reasoned that the number of patients receiving such surgeries (often within their own homes) far exceeded the number of those being sterilized beyond the walls of a state institution. Citing the frequency with which doctors performed undocumented abortions, *New York Medical Week* warned its readers on January 18, 1936, "not to substitute personal judgment for the law." If a physician were to be found incompliant with statutory requirements, it would matter little whether that physician acted according to his conscience, the author of that piece maintained. Ignorance of statutory requirements was no excuse. "There are readable, authoritative books on the subject, and every physician should have at least one—and be thoroughly familiar with its contents," the writer posited.

No more than a few weeks after it had been filed, the criminal case was already being applied to conversations ranging from population control to medical ethics. Given the case's vast scope—and, of course, the salacious nature of Ann's charges—Americans from many walks of life carefully followed the proceedings. In mid-January, people were frantically opening their morning papers to see if Maryon had been brought in on charges, and if so, how she had pleaded.

To readers' great dismay, Maryon Cooper Hewitt never found herself in handcuffs. By the time a police officer knocked on the door of her penthouse apartment at the Ritz-Carlton in downtown San Francisco, Ann's mother had boarded a train for the East Coast.

5

THE NEWCOMER

When nineteen-year-old Maryon Andrews first arrived in New York in 1903, she knew at once that the metropolis would suit her. Like her, the city moved in one direction: up.

Skyscrapers loomed where four- and five-story buildings once stood, and hotels and apartments pushed farther and farther into the sky. She couldn't ride through the cobblestone streets without hearing the sound of workers hammering iron beams or slapping bricks one on top of the other. The owner of the tallest building never enjoyed the distinction for long. "Still higher" was the motto of every architect.

The expansion was partly due to an increasing population. Between 1866 and 1900, the city boomed from 800,000 residents to 3.4 million. Gotham's financial capital also had something to do with its changing skyline. National banks in the city had financed the $2 billion Civil War, along with railroads, telegraph networks, and mining projects. Thanks to these ventures, real estate and the value of goods had doubled; and New York now had the infrastructure to produce and bankroll even more.

Maryon wasted no time finding the shopping district on

Broadway between 14th and 23rd Streets. There she opened accounts at Arnold Constable and Lord & Taylor, and outfitted herself with silk stockings, imported lingerie, ostrich-plumed hats, and other finery.

The future mother of Ann Cooper Hewitt had recently wed California physician Pedar Bruguiere, a Spanish don whose family had come to the United States in the early days to open one of its first banks. Dr. Bruguiere had divorced his first wife for Maryon, and the haste of his remarriage raised some eyebrows out west. But no one could say with certainty whether he and Maryon had fled to Reno to skirt the Golden State's mandatory one-year waiting period, as the records of his divorce had been lost in a fire.

Beginning with this first marriage, Maryon became known as a temptress who used her good looks to lure men, often away from their more respectable wives. Over the years, she did little to discourage this characterization, seeming to accept the fact that flaunting herself provided unparalleled advantages. Like other attractive, socially mobile women of the era, she faced intense scrutiny. Women weren't to embrace their sexuality, much less leverage it for personal gain.

Because of her beauty, Maryon expected her husbands to be fully devoted, at least for a time. Pedar was no exception. The newlyweds had first settled in San Francisco, but there, Maryon had grown very jealous of Pedar's relationships with his patients. In fact, she'd accused him of seeing patients only to take advantage of indisposed women. She wanted him out of that office, and it wasn't an impossible request. When Pedar's father had died, the forty-niner had left between $8 million and $10 million for his wife and three sons; Pedar's share provided more than enough for him to retire comfortably.

Maryon often approached ladies outside Pedar's office, demanding to know if they had intimate knowledge of her husband. "Did he undress you to examine your throat?" she once asked a young woman having a coughing fit on the way to her carriage. "Don't lie to me." This lady hurried to climb into her seat and snap the reins.

"You're just his type. He likes his blondes," Maryon told another. "Tell me—did my husband say those locks look like they were dipped in gold?"

Maryon had pressed a note into the hands of a patient who pushed a pram with one hand and guided a toddler with the other. "He's married to *me* now. Find another doctor or else there will be consequences," it read.

Most of these women had been agape at Maryon's suggestions and assured her that she was paranoid. But half a mile down the road, they'd beamed at the prospect of stirring such a gorgeous woman's envy.

Pedar had been less amused. His new wife's suspicions made his medical practice difficult, especially when some of his patients began to ask for an escort outside. Those who hadn't been personally accosted had heard about Maryon's antics or watched through the window as she shook her finger in some poor housewife's face. The doctor's secretary had obliged them, but Pedar knew that she was annoyed to have to leave her desk every hour simply to keep his wife at bay. He could hear his assistant complaining under her breath at the sight of each patient coming down the hall. "The missus needs to find a charity or hobby, if you ask me," she'd told a delivery boy. "She has too much time on her hands and so looks over his shoulder every minute. She calls at least a dozen times a day just to check on him."

One day, after receiving a letter from Pedar's sister-in-law, Maryon had suggested that they move to New York City where Pedar's brother Louis lived. "I'm tired of San Francisco," she'd complained. "The city is so drab, and now it's becoming unclean, too."

Maryon referred to the epidemic that was spreading across the city. The previous year, a ship had docked that carried rats infected with the bubonic plague. The creatures had scurried down the gangplank and onto the streets of Chinatown, leading to dozens of deaths before anyone had thought to quarantine. Even after the animal source of the outbreak had been discovered, officials blamed the "Orientals" whose numbers were growing in the city.

"And you suppose New York is better?" Pedar had asked his wife. "The streets are dank with the smell of manure. Even in the good parts of town, you'll see rotting horse carcasses."

"I know I'll find it more tolerable than here," Maryon had retorted. "Besides, your mother is getting on in her years. She'd be happy to have another son on the East Coast."

Dr. Bruguiere agreed with her on that point. He'd also wondered if a change of scene might assuage his wife's marital anxieties. So he'd given his patients notice—in some cases, behind closed doors. More than one had to wipe away tears, and one had sobbed so loudly that his secretary came to see what was going on. Pedar had been relieved to leave it all behind.

Maryon made arrangements for them to stay with Louis Bruguiere and his wife while they looked for an apartment. This wasn't merely for the sake of convenience. The Bruguieres were known in the social circles that Maryon eagerly wished to join. Years ago, Louis had been in her shoes, coming from the West in need of social backing. He had been accepted when Mrs. Hermann Oelrichs, the wife of a prominent businessman and millionaire, had vouched for him. For a time, Maryon's brother-in-law had been so popular among young crowds that he developed the nick-name Louis le Grand. After a few years in the scene, he'd gained the privilege of ordaining others.

But when the time came, the spunky Maryon refused to grovel for favor from her new relatives, even though it would have proved socially advantageous. Doing so would have required her to admit her lowly origins. For years, Maryon had told people, including her husband, that she had been born into an aristocratic family in Baltimore. In truth, she'd been born in the back woods of Alabama. Before moving the family to California, her father had been a horse car driver, not a landowner. Unsurprisingly, she and her family were now estranged.

After her and Pedar's arrival on the East Coast, Louis's wife expressed skepticism about Maryon's lineage, claiming that the genealogies of genteel families in Maryland were well known and that Maryon didn't appear in any of them. Nor did Maryon speak or write like an Englishwoman, a mark of good breeding. She always used a *z* where an *s* belonged, and she was neither fluent in foreign languages nor cultivated in the arts. As Mrs. Bruguiere further told her friends, Maryon never opened a book, only ever reading receipts to identify charges to dispute. Despite now having large sums at her disposal, Maryon often refused to pay bills for items ranging from furniture to lingerie. Less fortunate women in the city were jailed for shoplifting items worth much smaller sums.

Angry about Mrs. Bruguiere's attempts to expose her, Maryon refused to kowtow to her new in-laws. Once she and Pedar moved into their own place, she no longer asked for permission to use the family's resort in Newport, the breezy Rhode Island town where New Yorkers went for respite from the summer heat. Nor did she show the slightest interest in attending Louis's wife's parties. "What a shame we already have plans," she would say when an invitation was delivered.

"What plans?" her husband would inquire. "I haven't seen my brother for nearly three months, and he only lives on the other side of the park."

"We're going to the theater," Maryon would reply, leaving the room before he could contradict her.

Outraged that she had rejected them before they could reject her, Louis and his wife redoubled their efforts to sully her name. There was nothing unusual about their exclusion. New York society demanded that those seeking entry first prove their allegiance to the existing elite. Those who refused to comply with this unspoken mandate faced exile. Caroline Astor, wife of William Backhouse Astor Jr., had initiated this trend in the closing decades of the nineteenth century when she'd acted as the establishment's first gatekeeper. She'd distinguished between the "old rich" who lived on the proceeds from land purchased by their Dutch ancestors and the "new rich" (*nouveau riche*) who made their fortunes through entrepreneurship. Fancying herself one of the former, Mrs. Astor had scoffed at the vulgar "shoddyites" trying to elbow their way into her circles without going through her. With the help of a social arbiter, Ward McAllister, she'd refused to admit certain families into the aristocracy by denying them coveted invitations to her costume balls and charity events. She and her sidekick had a particular disliking for the Vanderbilts, who had earned their money from "filthy railroads."

But as Mrs. Astor and the Bruguieres eventually learned, it was risky to shun those certain individuals favored by the press. The Gilded Age woman had never forgotten the time she'd refused to call upon the Vanderbilts when they built their palatial mansion down the street, since it had resulted in her own debuting daughter not receiving an invitation to the Vanderbilts' elaborate house-warming ball. After the slight, Caroline Astor had no choice but to call upon her rivals in their French Renaissance–style chateau, while newsmen snapped photographs of her stepping out of her carriage. A decade later, the Bruguieres learned that they, too, had something to lose by distancing themselves from the social up-and-comer: relevance. Maryon attracted photographers and society writers wherever she went, prompting all of the Bruguieres' friends to inquire about her.

Maryon spent much of her time at Delmonico's, the restaurant in Lower Manhattan where menus were offered in French and dinners cost $3 a plate ($90, in today's money). At this haunt, the beautiful and witty woman lured many bachelors and divorced men to her table. If she cast a look in an admirer's direction, his ego swelled.

The *San Francisco Examiner* reported that at the opening of the Horse Show in Newport, two Vanderbilt brothers "pranced eagerly to the box occupied by Mrs. Bruguiere." Other men followed, gathering in such numbers that people came to see what was being given away. They found Maryon "giving away smiles and a clever word or two." Women beckoned their husbands to return to their seats and then demanded that they explain what they saw in such a person. The clever ones claimed to enjoy the spectacle of a silly woman pretending to have airs. The husbands who stuttered faced a cold shoulder for the rest of the afternoon.

Dr. Bruguiere did not enjoy scenes like the one at the Horse Show, and he might have stayed home on this and other occasions, if respectable establishments had admitted women without an escort. Pedar was beginning to realize that such was his position in New York—an escort and nothing more. He grew increasingly tired of simply holding his wife's fur wherever they went. His brother and sister-in-law only aggravated his discontentment, telling him he was known in their circles as "Mrs. Bruguiere's husband."

Pedar also began to worry about his wife's extravagance and her interest in gambling to augment their fortune. At the Saratoga tracks upstate, Mrs. Bruguiere's eyes twinkled at the prospect of doubling or even tripling their money. More than once, Pedar had to stop his wife from betting sums that might have turned them into paupers. Perhaps he hoped that motherhood would clip her wings.

If so, he was wrong. After Maryon gave birth to a boy named Pedar Jr., she left the infant in the care of her mother-in-law—a neutral party to the family feud—to go about her business. There was no way she was going to stay home with a screaming babe when she could sip cocktails with the elite. Especially now that her name was gaining recognition.

If Maryon had entered the scene during Mrs. Astor's reign, the latter would have had no choice but to admit her to "The Four Hundred"—a term coined by McAllister to denote the number of individuals who could count themselves among the fashionable of New York. (The Astor ballroom had a maximum occupancy of four hundred.) The Bruguieres didn't have bank accounts or property comparable to the Vanderbilts, Morgans, Rockefellers, or other families newly integrated into the city's elite, which was ordinarily sufficient cause for Mrs. Astor's rejection. But Maryon's fashionable clothing, combined with her popularity and the frequency with which her name appeared in the society pages, would have made her a force that Mrs. Astor couldn't easily ignore.

Maryon and Pedar resided in an apartment hotel, rather than a single-family home on Millionaire Row. Lavish, art-filled, and well-situated places like the Fifth Avenue Hotel and the Waldorf Astoria hosted distinguished guests, including presidents and heads of state, and were becoming increasingly popular as residences among the affluent classes. Their first-floor restaurants and saloons attracted New York's most famous patrons, making it easy for residents to mingle with beloved and influential people. Plus, there was room service. In a single-family residence, one couldn't demand a baked potato at three in the morning—the kitchen staff was bound to be sleeping. At a hotel, one could.

This amenity especially pleased Maryon, a night owl whose tabs sometimes exceeded $100. Mrs. Bruguiere would call the concierge and ask for the finest bottles of champagne to be sent to her suite, along with enough cigarettes to last her until the morning, when she could send someone for the gold-tipped ones she preferred.

Apartment life suited Maryon even more when Pedar faded out of the scene. Tired of being sidelined, the doctor began to make frequent trips to California, where he considered resuming his practice. If Maryon had once demanded her husband's attentions, she now cared little about his absence. In fact, she used their time apart to hunt for someone with even deeper pockets to pay her bills. Having attracted so much notice from men in high circles, she did not worry one bit about her chances of landing one.

In 1904, the doctor officially moved back west. Maryon made a trip to California to visit friends in October that year. While staying at the Hotel St. Francis in San Francisco, she wrote a letter to her husband, begging him to obtain a divorce as soon as legally possible:

Dear Doctor Bruguiere:

I arrived last night with my baby and maid from New York. Doctor Flint advised me not to remain east during the severe weather with baby just cutting his stomach teeth. I trust our return will not interfere with your plans in the least. I do not wish to see you at any time. An interview is quite unnecessary. Should you wish to say anything at all it must be done entirely by letter, as I shall refuse to receive at all times any person sent by you to me. So please do not do it.

There really can only be one topic worth while discussing, and that is divorce, and you must get one from me as soon as the year of my desertion is over. It is quite useless for me to remain your wife longer. It would only mean this sooner or later, but I have decided never to live again with you. I could never think of continuing so sad an existence. Of course, before, I wanted to try for baby's sake and a little bit for my own. If then it was affection, my love for you is so different now.

But to continue about divorce: I shall have the child always, and I think that you would be a fool as to try to take baby. How-ever, it is just as well to have these things understood beforehand. I shall be glad to send him to see you with his nurse whenever you shall wish it. He has grown to be a lovely, large boy and really looks much like you. Kate Murray thought he even played with his little toys as you did when you were his age. He really is a beautiful child. He has grown so you would hardly know him, and talks all the time.

There is no use continuing this, with love from baby to you,

MARYON ANDREWS BRUGUIERE

Maryon's contention that it was "useless" to stay in an unhappy marriage, even for the sake of her child, was certainly unconven-tional. Most women at the turn of the century didn't think of leaving their spouses simply because they lived "a sad existence." Social stigma and financial dependence prevented them from seeking a divorce. Although courts awarded maintenance (what is now called alimony or child support), women weren't guaranteed to receive this, especially if the judge disagreed with a woman's choice to dissolve the marriage. (Courts also retained the right to deny women a divorce.) Moreover, the maintenance allotted to a divorced woman didn't normally match the household income to which she had access as a married person, significantly curtailing her lifestyle. Once divorced, a woman couldn't obtain a loan or credit application unless a man agreed to co-sign. It didn't matter how much money she had to her name.

From the disparaging tone of this letter, the prospect of assuming a humbler existence after divorce seems never to have occurred to Maryon. Nor did the socialite have any inkling that the letter would be introduced as evidence against her in court.

Not long after her and Pedar's union was dissolved, Maryon married Stewart Deming, a wealthy Wall Street man. That union was annulled within a mere three months, when Deming told a New York court that something wasn't right with her divorce from Bruguiere. Since Maryon's second marriage hadn't taken her up the notch she'd expected, she was desperate to reverse her steps. She needed a steady income—at least, until she could find her third spouse. Maryon resumed her previous surname and went to Nevada, where Pedar had filed for divorce, to allege that her ex didn't have residency in that state when he'd submitted the pleading. This, Maryon argued, meant that she was still married to Pedar and, therefore, entitled to financial support. Claiming to be dependent on the charity of friends and relatives for her basic needs, she asked for $400 a month ($250 for herself and $150 for Pedar Jr.).

Pedar accused Maryon and her second husband of conspiring to get money out of him. He had learned from the gossip mill that Stewart Deming had left Maryon with the same complaint he'd had: He was tired of being a coat hanger. Pedar's New York sources told him that Deming had once stormed out of a crowded restaurant when his wife spoke to him with the same tone she used with the wait staff. As far as the physician was concerned, the Wall Street man's sudden change of attitude could only mean one thing: that Maryon had convinced him to participate in a scheme that would benefit both of them at his expense.

When the matter finally went before a judge, the physician explained that he'd gone to Nevada with the intent of establishing a medical practice among the rapidly growing mining camps in that state. "I wanted to get back to writing prescriptions and not checks!" he declared. Once in that state, he'd filed the paperwork necessary to divorce his spendthrift wife. But then the 1906 earthquake damaged some family property in San Francisco, requiring his presence. There he'd met Nannie King, with whom he was immediately taken. They'd married, and Nannie had given him a daughter. "*They* are my family now," he urged. "I can't abandon them."

If his ex-wife dared to smear his current one, Dr. Bruguiere was prepared to produce some very "unsavory details" about her, the *San Francisco Call* reported.

Maryon knew a judge wouldn't look kindly upon a woman accused of infidelity, even if the charges couldn't be proven. Pedar had suspected, but couldn't establish, that she'd cheated on him as early as their second year of marriage. So rather than discrediting the new Mrs. Bruguiere, she simply pretended that she had neither wanted the divorce from Pedar nor received a summons for the action. "I was on holiday in Paris with his mother, when she received a letter from her son declaring that he was a free man," Maryon told the court. "I had no idea what he was talking about."

Pedar's attorney swiftly produced the letter written in the Hotel St. Francis, in which Maryon had begged for Pedar to file for divorce from her. This forced her to change her strategy on the stand. "He abused me," she testified. "Mostly with his words. His language shocked my ears. No one ever spoke to me that way before."

Her attorney took pains to characterize her as innocent and confused, as if lost in the labyrinth of American divorce courts and begging someone to clarify her marital status. On the stand, Maryon played the part, saying, "I am told by Nevada that I am divorced. I am told by the New York courts that I am still Mrs. Bruguiere. What am I to do?"

Her theatrics proved futile. The judge sided with Pedar, citing concern for the physician's current wife and child. "What will become of them, legally speaking, if they are declared illegitimate?" he asked.

It wouldn't be the last time Maryon found her fate in the hands of the court, a reality she'd come to resent. Many judges didn't look kindly upon women (even honest ones) who pursued divorce for reasons other than severe physical abuse. Women had to preserve their families, even if it meant sacrificing their own happiness.

After the Nevada ruling, the divorcée returned to the East Coast to resume life with her son. Fortunately, Maryon's mother-in-law continued to serve as Pedar Jr.'s primary caregiver, even letting him live with her. Some newspapers reported that the elder Mrs. Bruguiere was disgusted to be in the same small town (Newport) with Maryon during the summer months. In this insular community, Pedar's mother couldn't avoid gossip about where and with whom Maryon was spotted. If it hadn't been for the little boy, members of the press speculated, she would have severed all ties with her former daughter-in-law. But others claimed that the relationship between the two women was unaffected by Maryon and Pedar's nasty spat. One columnist even reported that the elder Mrs. Bruguiere paid Maryon the $400 a month that the Nevada courts had denied her.

It hadn't taken much for Maryon to persuade her ex-relative to fund her lifestyle, as Mrs. Bruguiere believed Maryon was truly distressed over Pedar's leaving her. When the vacationing women had received the telegraph from Pedar announcing the split, Maryon had immediately burst into tears, insisting she couldn't live without her husband. The elder Mrs. Bruguiere had thrown her arms around her and assured her everything would be all right. She hadn't known about the letter sent from the Hotel St. Francis.

Back in New York and Newport, Maryon set her sights on the next phase of her career. Her three-month marriage to a Wall Street man had lasted just long enough to expand her social circle. Mr. Deming had many connections and famous clients, including the Gould family. Jay Gould had made his money underhandedly, buying and then manipulating stock in small railways. He'd also become involved with the corrupt Tammany Hall, a political ring that passed legislation in exchange for payments. (The cartoonist Thomas Nast famously satirized Gould and his colleagues in the pages of *Harper's Weekly*.) Negative public sentiment surrounding a client of her husband's like Gould might have disturbed a more scrupulous wife, but not Maryon. She was greatly intrigued by Wall Street and the frenetic activity said to take place inside the stock exchange building. The woman later called "the greatest woman gambler in the world" imagined what she could do if among the throngs on the trading floor.

"It's no place for a lady," her husband had told her before they'd split. "You would be trampled to death."

"I could at least watch from the balcony." Maryon had seen photographs of men reaching over guardrails waving their hats and canes to attract the attention of a dealer below. From this position, she might be able to make a purchase.

Her husband, however, had assured her that no one of importance ever appeared in the exchange. They conducted all of their business by telegraph.

Once divorced from Deming, Maryon enticed some of society's most eligible single, widowed, and even married men. One of them was Williams Proudfoot Burden, whose family gained its fortune by establishing Troy Iron Works in Schenectady, New York, home to the first waterwheel in the United States. Burden was so enamored with Maryon that he consulted a divorce attorney within a month of meeting her. But the married man got cold feet when the woman who had introduced him to Maryon wrote a story about the two in *Town Topics*. The editor of this society journal, Colonel William d'Alton Mann, often bribed or blackmailed household staff to divulge gossip about the upper classes. He also got his news from individuals harboring grudges, as was the case with his information on Maryon. An anonymous source, identified in print as "The Widow," penned a lurid tale about the nature of beautiful, social-climbing women and the foolish men who fall for them.

The story did not identify Maryon or Burden by name. To avoid libel charges, Mann omitted names within an exposé, but printed a news item about the lady or gentleman elsewhere in the issue so readers knew exactly who was being discussed. An excerpt from The Widow's story reads:

She caught him by her attractiveness of person, and the belief that everybody was in the running for her, and she keeps her hold by telling all sorts of little details about the attentions through which she is being annoyed...She tells him of invitations to this and to that that she never had; she tells him of the importuning of strangers who want to meet her; she sends flowers to herself—without cards—and then wonders, in his presence, "who could have sent them?" or else refuses flatly to tell who did; she writes messages and telegrams to herself, and bribes the messenger "not to tell"; she buys paste jewelry and passes it off as a valuable present she has received, and she resorts to every known device to convince him she is popular—popular—and that he has won a prize. She does these tricks to get him, and she keeps them up to make him feel fortunate in having title to her.

According to The Widow, a woman would only go to such lengths to impress a man if she was looking to secure someone who would shower her with gold and jewels and pay the bills. Such a woman prefers "to capture a husband," The Widow wrote, "but gold as a bank account is the sacred tie, and not gold in the wedding ring."

The first account of Maryon written by someone close to her, the profile validated the Bruguieres' views. But ordinary Americans may not have unquestioningly adopted this position. Middle-class readers probably had mixed feelings about Maryon, as they often did when it came to unruly women.

The popular stage actress Sarah Bernhardt, who had first risen to fame in the 1860s and '70s, provoked a range of reactions with her deviant behaviors. Bernhardt wore a pantsuit, dated men well beneath her station, conceived a child out of wedlock, drank from a skull, and slept in a satin-lined coffin, in which she allowed herself to be photographed. The actress also flaunted a body that didn't conform to Victorian ideals. Critics complained that she was too skinny and therefore shouldn't wear clothing that accentuated her small waist. Cartoonists mocked her corseted figure, titling sketches "Too thin, or Skeleton Sarah."

But many news readers adored Bernhardt, admiring her stubborn resistance to the social codes that were smothering them. They made scrapbooks of the actress, compiling newspaper clippings and other paraphernalia to celebrate the starlet's achievements on stage and in public life. Other news readers resented her economic privilege, which allowed her to thwart the conventions to which they were bound. In their quest to take the actress down a notch, journalists often pandered to their readers' envy, detailing Bernhardt's extravagant lifestyle, such as her habit of riding bicycles with a jewel-encrusted nameplate.

Though she was by no means as famous as Bernhardt, Maryon's exploits were already being reported in newspapers across the country. At a time when many women were struggling to redefine womanhood, some may have viewed her as an inspiring figure. After all, she bore little resemblance to the Victorian matriarch with whom many wanted to do away. Of course, as was the case with Bernhardt, certain women readers probably also resented her for enjoying more social mobility than they did.

The Widow's scathing profile of Maryon resonated with at least one reader: her suitor. After its publication, Burden distanced himself from the divorcée. He was disgusted with himself for being duped and sought to restore his reputation for the sake of his family business. Unfortunately, tongues wagged about Burden again in 1908, when his wife committed suicide, a grave crime punishable with jail time if unsuccessful. Mrs. Burden's maid found her dead in bed with the tubing of her gas reading lamp misfitted and her Pomeranian wheezing on the floor. A coroner told the *New York Times* that the death was undoubtedly accidental, but close friends insisted that Mrs. Burden was depressed. Not only had she been suffering from "the grip" (influenza), she was married to a man with roving eyes.

Maryon was sore when Burden withdrew his affection, if only because she had invested so much time in the romance. At least she still had the attention of James J. Van Alen, a sportsman and politician; Reginald C. Vanderbilt, a millionaire equestrian within the distinguished clan; and many other wealthy men. Society columnists weren't the least surprised that men of this stature took pleasure in a social butterfly like her. But they were really knocked off their feet when Peter Cooper Hewitt's head was turned a few years later.

6

THE CHRYSALIS

Not only was the fifty-four-year-old married and many years Maryon's senior, Peter Cooper Hewitt was a much-respected scientific man from a much-respected clan. His maternal grandfather had established the family name with his numerous inventions, then used his fortune to open a tuition-free school, the Cooper Union for the Advancement of Science and Art, and fund other educational and public programs in the city. New Yorkers revered their benefactor, as well as his son-in-law (Peter's father), Abram Hewitt, who had become the city's mayor and overseen the family's many business and charitable interests. Peter, too, had earned the public's esteem. In the 1890s, the man had developed his famous lamp to improve the efficiency of the popularly used incandescent ones, which converted only 5 percent of energy into light and turned the remainder into heat. This invention swiftly transformed factories across the nation.

Cooper Hewitt had further delighted society when he claimed that he was going to use the same technology he had used for his lamps to enable wireless, transatlantic conversations. His grandfather had contributed to the laying of the first transatlantic cable, so no one doubted Peter's ability to follow in his footsteps. Ann's father never succeeded in this particular task, but he had gone on to invent a telephone relay and electric wave amplifier, among other telephone and telegraph apparatuses, and to assist Thomas Edison with the perfection of an electric storage battery. Peter also helped to develop the hydro-aeroplane (an airplane made to operate on water) and the high-speed motorboat.

Peter's passion for his trade was long believed to have turned him off romance. For years, he had been too buried in research to pay much attention to his wife. Finding him uninterested, Lucy Cooper Hewitt had moved to Europe some years ago to pursue charity work. The couple was estranged, but still married, when Maryon flitted before him. Something about this new woman "was more fascinating than anything the test tubes in his scientific laboratories had ever revealed," the *San Francisco Chronicle* reported a few year later, when the affair came to light.

Maryon and Peter met at the Horse Show in Newport. Peter didn't usually attend the event, but his friend Reginald Vanderbilt was competing in this one. After watching his chum win a few ribbons, Peter went with the man to the crowded box of the former Mrs. Bruguiere. Reginald wanted to show him the object of his affection. The Vanderbilt brother had no idea that the man dubbed a "woman-hater" would steal his prize from right under his nose and initiate a union that would rock high society's foundations. Nor that this union would perturb members of the press, as Maryon's critics scrambled to better understand—and ultimately contain—the power that brazen women like her were increasingly wielding over men.

"From the moment he entered Mrs. Bruguiere's box, Peter Cooper Hewitt was hopelessly lost," the *San Francisco Chronicle* later reported. He hung on her every word and begged to see her again.

Soon after the Horse Show, Maryon and Peter reunited at the mansion where she'd been staying for the summer. Peter came armed with jewelry.

Maryon opened the box, smiled, and then lifted the golden locks from her neck so that he could clasp it for her. From then on, she rebuffed all her other suitors and began to accompany the married man around the island. The two took afternoon drives and dined at fashionable restaurants, where Peter insisted that they occupy corner booths and bow their heads to avoid being seen.

A few months later, when the leaves turned crimson and the ocean breeze brought shivers, Maryon accompanied her new lover to Palm Beach, where she attracted photographers in a highly ornamental bathing suit unlike any other they'd seen. "Are you the 'beautiful unknown'?" one asked. This man had seen a news profile about a mysterious lady who had come to Newport and reigned over the crowds there.

"I am," Maryon said with a smile.

Peter pulled her away before she could remind the man of her name. He didn't need Lucy opening the newspaper to see an image of him canoodling with another woman in the Florida sun.

When they returned to Newport, a few friends discovered their romance, and Peter worried his family would get word of it. Not willing to lose her greatest catch yet, Maryon proposed that they spend the winter in Paris. The scientist agreed on one provision: that they establish separate residences. He had business interests in the city that could be compromised if one of his associates learned of their affair.

Maryon had no choice but to bring Pedar Jr. with them, as the boy's grandmother was getting too old to care for him. But she soon found a French governess to mind her son while she accompanied Peter to dinner, the theater, and other high-end establishments in the city. It wasn't long before Maryon learned she had conceived a child.

When she rang the bell of Peter's Champs-Élysées townhome and blurted out the news, the inventor's eyes darted between the figures passing by his stoop. He breathed a sigh of relief that none resembled a colleague or member of the press and then pulled Maryon inside to explain everything.

"It's quite simple," she said, looking around for the maid to take her fur. "I'm to have a baby around Thanksgiving."

"But how?"

Maryon tilted her head at Peter. "Does the scientist need a lesson in anatomy?"

"I—of course not. I just mean, at my age…" Peter and his wife had never managed to conceive a child; and at sixty years old, he'd presumed parenthood wasn't in the cards for him. Now he was being told otherwise.

For the next six months, he withdrew, often telling Maryon he was too busy to meet for lunch or dinner. She began to wonder if the pregnancy was a grave mistake. Instead of nudging Peter to break things off with Lucy, as she'd hoped, it was pushing him away. But perhaps things would be different when he saw his first-born and held him in his arms, she thought.

Peter was in the United States, tending to business, when Maryon went into labor unexpectedly early. When the first pains struck, she sent for Dr. I. L. Hill, who had traveled all the way from the United States for the occasion. The doctor found her thrashing in bed and cursing the man who had brought the situation upon her.

Maryon labored for another ten hours before Ann finally arrived. She took one look at the child and startled. It was half the size of her firstborn and had jet-black hair slicked to the scalp.

"What is it?" she asked.

"It's a girl," said Dr. Hill.

"Hmph," said Maryon, sinking back into her pillows.

"She's a tiny thing," said Hill. "Best to get her warm right away." He handed the babe to a nurse, who had prepared a warm basin in the next room.

"You did swell," said the physician, patting Maryon on the hand. "Shall I telegraph Mr. Hewitt?" But the new mother of two didn't hear the question, for she was fretting about Ann's sex. She'd presumed she was carrying Peter's son.

"Tell the nurse to keep her," Maryon told Dr. Hill. "I need my rest."

"I'm afraid that's not possible. A small thing like that—she'll need to nurse very soon."

"Fine," said Maryon. Perhaps if the girl gained weight and shed some of that ghastly hair, Peter would take to her.

The very next day, she received a telegram from her lover, who'd gotten word of the birth. The message bore no congratulations—only an order to immediately take Ann and Pedar Jr. to England, where they were to board a vessel for the States. It wasn't safe for them to stay in Paris, Peter said. Maryon reluctantly obeyed, evacuating just in time for German aircraft and artillery to assault the city. In Britain, she found a nurse to attend to her children in an adjacent suite on the ship. Maryon sometimes went days without once seeing her newborn. One day, when the nurse had gone to the deck, she was lured to Ann by the sound of the infant screaming like the dickens. Maryon looked down at the flailing little creature in the crib and wished she had never been born.

Pedar Jr. appeared at her side.

"She's not right," Maryon explained, putting her arm around the boy. "I'm afraid she'll never be right." She then led her son out the door and closed it behind them.

Maryon had written to Dr. Hill about Ann's frequent crying, calling it "insufferable." He assured her colic was common and suggested syrup. Had Maryon been a middle-class mother, she might have been chastised for her impatience. Physicians were growing concerned about modern women's seeming lack of devotion to their offspring, penning manuals about proper care and reminding their readers that children were a blessing.

When Ann was a little more than a month old, they arrived in the New York harbor, where Peter was waiting. The moment he saw his child, the scientist took her in his arms and kissed her, forgetting Maryon. He then took the trio to an apartment in Upper Manhattan, a few blocks from his laboratory but out of the way of peering eyes. For the next few months, he visited whenever he could, holding Ann up to the window and whispering about passersby.

Maryon wondered what it was that he saw in the plain-looking little girl, whose miserable hair continued to grow in thick. Not wanting to be pushed to the side, she insisted that Peter take her to Delmonico's. "You know I can't do that," he said. In December, she told him that she was returning to Paris. With the front lines moved north, the city had been declared secure again. The government had resumed business, and pedestrians were walking freely.

"But it's safer here," said Peter.

"Well, I don't want to live under a rock," Maryon replied. "I refuse."

After failing to persuade her, Peter made arrangements for Maryon and the children to sail in the New Year. He promised to meet them as soon as he resolved some matters in New York. But it was nearly six months before Maryon saw him again, as the scientist was tapped to serve on a government scientific advisory committee. President Woodrow Wilson had declared the United

States neutral at the outbreak of the war, but he still needed to prepare for the possibility of entering the conflict.

Ann could move on all fours by the time Peter arrived in France. Seeing this, the aging man got down on her level and chased her around the velvet carpet, delighting her. When Maryon chided him, he explained that his own father and grandfather had shunned decorum to give him such a thrill. A few months later, when Ann's legs could support her, he began to move her across the room to the sound of the Victrola. Then, when he grew tired, he'd take her in his lap, where she'd stay until Maryon ordered a nurse to take her to bed.

For a time, life went on like this, and Maryon imagined it wouldn't be long before Peter left Lucy and they were a family. She knew that Pedar Jr.'s grandmother might not like the idea of Peter adopting the boy, but she could live with her relative's disdain. It turned out that Maryon never had to break the news, for her former mother-in-law drowned unexpectedly. Mrs. Bruguiere was on the White Star liner *Arabic* with her son Louis when a German submarine sank the vessel, forcing all passengers to go overboard. The newspapers reported that Louis had fastened a life belt onto his mother and jumped in the sea with her, swimming at her side for half an hour before hitting his head on a piece of wreckage. Stunned, he'd lost his grip and then never seen his mother again. Rescuers had saved him some time later.

Maryon wished that *he* had died and Mrs. Bruguiere lived. She hadn't forgiven her brother-in-law for slandering her name in Newport. She had no idea that her mother-in-law had also taken to gossiping about her, as Louis had finally coaxed her to take his side. Before her tragic death, Mrs. Bruguiere had told the press that Newporters had ostracized her family because Maryon was so attractive and flirty. In a 1914 *San Francisco Examiner* story titled "Too Beautiful for 'The 400': How the Ambitious Bruguieres Spent Millions Getting into Newport and Lost Millions Getting Out When Perfectly Gorgeous Sister-in-Law Appeared," Maryon's mother-in-law was quoted as saying, "We as a family have been cursed by too great a beauty. It was not ours by birth; it married into the family, and alas, our sorrows have been many." It wouldn't be the last time Maryon was condemned for her looks.

With Peter and Maryon out of the country, the American press didn't get wind of their affair until December 1918, when the inventor's first wife filed for divorce. Lucy had long known of the affair, but assumed that her husband would eventually grow bored of his new plaything and come back to her. With Ann's birth, it had become clear that this was not going to happen.

At last, Peter proposed to Maryon, who promptly took his check-book to a dressmaker to be fitted for wedding attire. The couple then sailed to New York to respond to Lucy's court proceeding. Before the ink recording the dissolution of the marriage was dry, the lovers rushed to the Third Presbyterian Church in Paterson, New Jersey, to wed.

Peter and Maryon could have moved to Ringwood Manor, which Peter and his siblings had inherited from his paternal ancestors. The renovated estate was grand and opulent enough to satisfy Maryon. The legendary architect Stanford White had added a new wing with a gabled roof, installed Ionic columns on the veranda, and transformed the interior to resemble the Italianate mansions of Gramercy Park. With Peter's ex-wife planning to return abroad to assist with war efforts, there was no need to worry about her scrutinizing eye. But there were Peter's siblings to worry about. Immediately upon learning of Ann's existence, they'd pressed their brother to consider the possibility that Maryon had falsified his paternity. Maryon knew that her new relatives would never forgive her for putting Peter's name in the papers for something other than his inventions. So instead of staying at the complex, the couple returned to Paris, where they finally combined their residences. This delighted little Ann and even Pedar Jr., whom the scientist soon adopted.

Peter and Maryon's marriage intrigued the press more than any of her previous nuptials. Columnists burned to know how Maryon had possibly managed to land a man of Peter's stature. Her previous husbands had been wealthy and professionally successful, but they were not in the same league as the inventor of the mercury-vapor lamp, the son of a mayor, and the grandson of "Old New York's First Citizen." What in the world was Peter Cooper Hewitt doing with a little enchantress?

The *Richmond Times-Dispatch* tackled this question in a full-page story titled "Why Brainy Men Often Marry Frivolous Wives." The author of that piece opined that "the charm of a frivolous woman for a serious man has been observed since the dawn of human history," citing Hercules, Samson, Lord Byron, and other men of talent ensnared by ladies who sang, danced, or laughed prettily. Then he turned to physics and psychology to explain the phenomenon. Perhaps the attraction between brainy men and frivolous women was due to the law of opposites. Or perhaps it was that men had nervous energy to expel. They could be drawn to coquettes because those types brought out their boyishness and allowed them to escape the mundaneness of professional life. Then again, maybe "men of genius...marry a pretty doll in the hope of being able to educate her into an attractive companion." If so, their judgment was flawed, according to this writer. It "rarely happens that the minds of those beauties are 'wax to receive and marble to retain.' Pretty girls are commonly lazy—spoiled by the thought that their beauty atones for everything and regardless for the future when this apology for indolence will have lost its persuasiveness."

This writer wasn't alone in thinking that a woman was either pretty or smart—seldom both. Such an opinion surely underestimated Maryon. Though uninterested in the few intellectual pursuits available to women, such as the crusade for the vote, Ann's mother was far from stupid. Her successful efforts to exploit the legal system certainly demonstrated this. Her skills at the card table also suggested that she was by no means empty-headed. In Europe, she made casino owners sweat, walking away with record earnings.

Maryon, however, attributed her winnings to her lucky mascot, the yapping lapdog she took with her every night. Once, at the Casino Barrière Deauville in Normandy, this little creature bit the ankle of a gentleman at the roulette table where Maryon had had a four-night winning streak. The patron winced before grabbing the dog and tossing him out the first-floor window. After this, the manager had refused to allow the pet back in. Fearing her streak was over, Maryon never returned.

Soon after she and Peter nestled into their Parisian love nest—a penthouse in the Ritz Hotel—Peter's health began to decline. The scientist's woes began with stomach pains, which made digestion difficult. He consulted a physician, who suggested a possible gastrointestinal condition and advised a change of diet. For a while, this helped, and Peter was able to maintain his workload, travel between the continents, and dote on Ann. He took the girl around the city, climbing the towers of Notre Dame and chasing pigeons in the gardens below. He carried her home on his shoulders, pointing to landmarks along the way. Sometimes, Maryon went along, only to catch sight of some shiny object in a storefront and go her separate way.

There were some happy vacations, too. For Ann's fifth birthday, the family of four went to Palm Beach, where a photographer captured the girl building a sandcastle. A year later, they traveled to Venice, where the girls raced the boys across the city in gondolas.

But these good times were always punctuated by Peter's return to his professional work in the fall and winter months. Ann would cry and cling to his leg with all her might until Maryon pried her away. For days, Ann would then sulk around the apartment. She had no other playmates, spending most of her time flicking marbles or gazing out the window as peers ran through the streets with ice skates or sleds on their backs. Thinking her rather pathetic, Maryon tried to enroll Ann in private academies. But Ann never lasted long at these places, for she couldn't get along with the other children. This left Maryon no choice but to hire governesses and tutors. Private schooling, too, proved difficult, for Ann always seemed defiant, refusing to do the tasks she was assigned. When scolded, she'd run for her room and clutch the china doll Peter had purchased for her on one of his trips. Realizing her daughter would do anything for this object, Maryon began to remove the doll until Ann behaved the way she wanted. Sometimes, she threatened that Ann would never see Peter again unless she acted like a good girl. "Why would he want to come home to a child who is rotten?" she'd ask.

In the summer of 1920, Peter's health worsened, and he had to have his appendix removed. This procedure did not resolve his problems, and by the following summer, he'd grown too weak to pick up his daughter or even leave their apartment.

Though Maryon felt sorry for him, she wasn't willing to stay home and be his nurse. While her husband limped around their apartment, she became friendly with a manager of the Ritz Hotel— the twenty-four-year-old Baron Robin d'Erlanger, who hailed from an area southeast of London. Most of this man's landowning family members still lived in England, but the aspiring artist preferred to cavort with the bohemians of Paris than to stay in the boring English countryside. Curious about this *flâneur* lifestyle, Maryon began to accompany the baron to his favorite spots around the city. Soon after, she began inviting the baron and some of his young friends up to her place.

The American nurse she'd hired to care for Peter did not approve. The fifty-year-old Elizabeth Kelly once came on shift to find Maryon, the baron, and the baron's friend Captain Rupert Higgins drinking and carrying on outside Peter's room while he tried to rest. When the captain grew more boisterous, stumbling around and knocking into the furniture, Kelly demanded that he leave.

"Leave?" the baron protested. "I think he should stay and you should be dismissed instead." His friend cheered at this suggestion.

"They are my guests," Maryon intervened. "They'll stay as long as I please."

The nurse narrowed her eyes at her. "But your husband is not well. Have you no concern about him?"

Maryon refused to be insulted. "Take her out this instant," she instructed the baron, who stood and moved toward the nurse.

"No," said Kelly, backing away from him. "I won't allow this. What you're doing is disgraceful."

The baron seized the nurse by the arm and dragged her toward the door. "My things!" she protested.

"Someone will send them in the morning," Maryon assured her.

Maryon had no choice but to rehire the woman a few days later, when Peter developed pneumonia and she couldn't find another English-speaking nurse to tend to him. Again, Kelly made her disdain plain. She told Peter's physician what had transpired, forcing Maryon to explain herself. "She was being overprotective," she said. "Mr. Hewitt was sound asleep through it all."

A few weeks later, Peter's condition turned dire, and he was transferred to a hospital, where lung specialists could consult on his case. Maryon took Ann to see him one last time, then shooed the girl away to speak privately with Kelly, who was there to look out for any needs.

"This will help him," she whispered, revealing a small vial of liquid. "It will make his last days less miserable." Maryon had gotten the potion from the baron, who claimed the pain reliever was widely used in Eastern cultures. Not wanting to know more, she'd accepted his explanation.

"I'll do no such thing," Kelly protested, ordering Maryon away from the bed.

"You'll do as I say," Maryon replied. "I am paying your salary."

Still, Kelly refused, and Maryon went away. The baron was waiting for her outside.

On August 23, a hospital worker sent for Maryon in the middle of the night to say that the end was very near. This time, she arrived alone, sitting with her husband and holding his hand until he took his last breath.

Across the globe, the press mourned Cooper Hewitt's passing. Few "achieved more in the realm of science and invention, and won more prominence in lines of thought and endeavor than any man of his generation," the *Salt Lake Tribune* wrote. "The range of Mr. Hewitt's mind was extraordinary. It embraced economics, physics, mechanics, electricity, and chemistry."

After gaining its bearings, the American press chalked the sixty-year-old's death up to Maryon's charms. "The kisses of this youthful bride of his seem to have been too joyous a shock for a man of Mr. Hewitt's age to endure," read a column in the *San Francisco Chronicle*. In other words, Maryon's sexuality had killed Peter. Though meant in jest, the comment articulated a serious concern, first raised by nineteenth-century physicians and now echoed by social reformers in the twentieth: Passionate women threatened to weaken the male sex by spreading venereal disease or sapping them of their energies. The Maryon Andrewses of the world (low-class, ill-reputed women) were going to kill off the Cooper Hewitts (well-bred, noble men) at a time when the country needed to bolster its human resources.

Panic about diseased, low-class women had prompted the federal government to apprehend thirty thousand women and incarcerate fifteen thousand of them found to have syphilis between 1914 and 1918. Officials claimed to be preventing the women from infecting US troops, who already had high rates of venereal disease. Many of the detained women had committed no crime, such as prostitution; they had simply ventured too close to a military base while walking alone or wearing too high a hemline.

Peter's private nurse agreed that the amorous Maryon was to blame for his death, but not because of her relations with her husband. "She was in love with another man," Kelly told a New Jersey court. "I am afraid she may have killed her husband to be with this new one." In an affidavit, Kelly explained that Maryon had approached her at Peter's deathbed to give him some unknown substance. She believed Maryon had administered the liquid to her patient at a later date when no one was around to observe her.

Nurse Kelly had been subpoenaed to testify in a New Jersey court, where the Hewitt siblings had filed a motion to dismiss the scientist's last will, executed in Paris within a month of his death. In the will, there was a generous and somewhat unusual provision allowing Maryon to keep her share of the Cooper family trust upon remarriage. This clause led the Hewitt siblings to suspect that their brother had been manipulated while not of sound mind. They also claimed that their brother did not have the legal right to bequeath parts of the Cooper trust, since their grandfather had directed for the funds to be held only for "two lives." According to them, this provision included Cooper's daughter, Amelia Cooper Hewitt, and her son, Peter Cooper Hewitt. The term could not extend to any of Peter's heirs.

Shortly after learning of Kelly's affidavit and the New Jersey lawsuit, Maryon and the baron—who were now living together in Paris—contacted the nurse to demand that she withdraw her statement. "If you don't, I will crush you," Maryon threatened. "I have evidence that could have you locked up. You'll spend years in jail and then live in poverty."

When the nurse refused to comply, Maryon and d'Erlanger went to the American ambassador in Paris and falsely claimed that Kelly had stolen Peter's scientific papers and sold them to the Japanese government. To their surprise, the ambassador refused to take action. They then went to the French newspapers with another claim: Kelly had taken Maryon's jewels on her way out the door.

Maryon knew this narrative would prove credible, as she'd hired an investigator to look into Kelly's background. He didn't have to look far to find that the nurse was wanted for theft. Four years previously, a Manhattan banker who'd hired Kelly to care for his influenza-stricken son claimed that she'd taken his wife's diamond wedding ring from the dresser in the infant's bedroom. Kelly had denied the charges, and because there was little evidence against her, she'd been released. Just one year later, she was re-implicated in the crime after she gave a pawn ticket for this item to a woman in exchange for a $175 loan to go abroad. When Kelly failed to pay the loan, the woman redeemed the ticket and took the diamond to Tiffany's. The shop's jewelers had immediately recognized the bauble as the one belonging to the banker's wife. But by this point, the nurse was somewhere in Europe.

Just as Maryon expected, the American newspapers swiftly connected Kelly to this old crime, and the New York police arrested her. "I'm innocent!" the nurse declared. "The woman is conspiring to frame me and distract from her own crimes."

A New York court sentenced Kelly to three years in "the Tombs," a municipal jail in Lower Manhattan. From her cell, she continued to speak against Maryon and d'Erlanger. "If only I can get to Paris and push a civil suit against them for what they've done, I will startle the country," she told a reporter. "I do not intend to stop until I have exhausted every possible effort to express this frightening conspiracy that has been formed to discredit me."

In case anyone believed the condemned woman, Maryon engaged the attorney representing Peter's estate in the proceeding between her and the Hewitt siblings to quell the public's suspicions about the possibility of foul play in Peter's death. The much-respected man told the newspapers that Nurse Kelly's accusations were "preposterous." He further alleged that Peter's will had *not* been executed under duress, as the inventor had corresponded with him about the changes. But he couldn't produce this correspondence when pressed to do so.

Columnists shifted their attention from Maryon's possible involvement in Peter's death to the equally intriguing prospect of her tumbling from society's upper echelons to the lackluster middle class. Many news readers, like Louis and his wife, itched to see Maryon humbled to the status of her birthright. These critics were disappointed when she prevailed in court against Peter's siblings. Her attorney, L. Barton Case, proved that Peter had full ownership and control of the share of the Cooper trust designated in the will. This attorney's success was probably due to his determination to keep Maryon in Europe and off the stand. If she had testified in person, she certainly would have been asked about extramarital affairs. And if all of her skeletons came tumbling out of the closet, the judge may not have ruled so favorably.

But the Hewitt siblings were not prepared to surrender. Peter's brothers and sisters next attempted to disqualify Ann from inheritance on the grounds that she was only a love child and not a legitimate issue. Another of Maryon's attorneys, Edward Blanc, defeated the siblings on this point, proving that Peter and Maryon's subsequent wedding legitimated the child. "While New Jersey law does not provide rights to children whose parents married after their conception, humanitarian legislation in nearly all other states does," Blanc maintained. The attorney further claimed that defending Ann's legitimacy was morally imperative. "It's not that my client wants the money, though she is rightfully entitled to it. She merely wants to protect the girl from growing up with a stain on her name."

In the end, the feud over Peter's estate shamed the Cooper Hewitt family far more than Maryon. Peter's siblings were mortified that their brother, a respected and educated man, had been seduced by a society pet, who was now dragging the family name through the mud. Even after the court ruled in favor of Ann's legitimacy, they refused to acknowledge the girl. But Maryon barely blushed about the incident and proceeded to marry her baron. She figured she could live with bad press, if it meant getting what she wanted.

While not extraordinarily wealthy, Maryon's fourth husband offered something that no previous one had: a title. The prestige of a title so attracted wealthy women that, a few decades previously, over four hundred American heiresses had moved to Europe to gain one. "Dollar princesses" often sacrificed extravagant lifestyles in the United States to move into drafty, dilapidated houses in the countryside of a foreign country. They used family money to revive these crumbling estates in exchange for the power and status that derived from the monarchy. Abroad, they had a lifelong guarantee of importance; there was no need to compete in the type of cut-throat social environment Mrs. Astor had established at home.

Incidentally, "baroness" was not the only title on the table for Maryon. When she married d'Erlanger, she forfeited another name of high stature—that of "leading lady." The Shah of Persia had invited her to become the highest-ranking woman in his harem. After Peter's death, the shah had followed her around Paris in his limousine, attending all the same parties she did. Some claimed that Maryon declined his offer only because she was unwilling to brave the competition among the shah's other lovers. Why else would she turn down a man who was ready to shower her with rubies, emeralds, and sapphires?

But concubine life was simply not for Maryon, as she told the press: "The shah is a dear boy, but I was not made for the sultana of an oriental harem. My freedom means too much to me." It seemed neither Pedar Jr. nor Ann would have prevented Maryon from taking up the offer, if she had found it appealing. Her son was nearing the age of his majority, and Ann had been sent to the Swiss sanatorium.

The baron took Maryon on a tour of Europe, introducing her to a coterie of artists and other important people. This new milieu enchanted her, and, as with the Newport crowd, she didn't hesitate to establish a name for herself among it. Sometimes she even played tricks on higher-ranking persons to give herself an advantage. When Prince Umberto visited the Lido Casino in Venice, where she and the baron were staying, she spent a large sum to have the casino converted into a doge's palace for a grand ball. The prince delighted at the splendor and to learn that the baroness had prepared a surprise for him at midnight. On the stroke of twelve, a beautiful woman entered the doors of the ballroom to dance solo on the floor. The prince adjusted his glasses to peer at this belle and then signaled for the audience to applaud. A moment later, he sent an envoy to Maryon's suite to inquire about the woman.

"I call her Monna d'Elta," the baroness responded.

"Ah, an Italian!" the prince exclaimed upon hearing the news.

Maryon corrected him, saying that the woman was an English stage-dancer in a dingy Liverpool cabaret. She'd taken a liking to the girl and taught her how to dance and play the harp, enabling her to trick even the discerning eye of the prince. Those close to Umberto demanded that the baroness apologize for the affront. She laughed at the suggestion.

A little while later, a group of talented entertainers came through the doors and made their way to the floor in front of the prince's royal box. A handsome man in Renaissance costume led the troupe. Impressed, the prince forgot the recent slight and sent another envoy to Maryon's suite to ask about the entertainer. He wanted him to perform for his friends back home.

"He?" Maryon's eyes twinkled. "Oh, he is Antoine, my Paris barber."

The royal party hastily left her suite, and the prince did not make further contact before departing.

After a few months on the party circuit in Europe, Maryon realized that she could not sustain her lifestyle on an artist's income. So she and her husband returned to New Jersey to petition the courts to increase the annual amount issued to Ann from the Cooper trust. They demanded $35,000 per year, saying the current $12,000 was simply not enough to support the girl in proper style. (The average worker in the city earned less than $3,000 per year.) The baroness testified that she herself lived on $250,000 per year.

No one doubted her calculations. Some recalled the time Maryon had shown off a diamond-studded anklet designed, but not paid for, by Baron d'Erlanger while stepping off a boat from Europe a few years ago. She had still been married to Cooper Hewitt at the time. The woman had glided down the gangplank, lifted the hem of her dress, and shaken her foot. Reporters had flocked to inspect the object. So had customs officials, who raised their eyebrows anytime jewelry was carried in an unusual way. The authorities, however, had quickly concluded that anyone trying to smuggle stolen goods into the country would not act as ostentatiously as this woman did. One of the reporters asked Maryon when she had taken up the fashion. "Take it up! I originated it," she'd scoffed.

The baron and baroness's trip was productive. The New Jersey courts allowed an increase in spending for the child the papers dubbed "the poor little rich girl," and the newlyweds returned to France. "For a while, life was one grand merry-go-round of gayety and gambling," the *Daily News* later recounted. But Maryon quickly grew bored of the husband who had no income. She complained to friends that her spouse cost her $50,000 a year.

"I've never met a man who required so much in clothes and up-keep," Maryon told friends. "The figure is even higher considering the income I gave up to marry him."

"Income?" her friends asked.

"That's right! I forfeited half of my inheritance from Peter's family trust to marry the young fool. When Peter died, the fund was estimated to be almost one and a half million dollars. One-half of my two-thirds share is almost half a million." In addition to this, Peter had left another several million in assets.

Her friends paused. "But that money will go to little Ann now. It's not as if the trust reabsorbs it."

Such reassurances didn't assuage Maryon, who was beginning to realize that she would have to go through the New Jersey courts for every penny of Ann's beyond the allotted maintenance. The baron and baroness began to live apart when d'Erlanger relocated to London in 1923. Maryon was not bothered when her husband had affairs; she took a few lovers herself. It was the baron's public rebuke of her that proved a tipping point. D'Erlanger put a notice in the English newspapers that he would no longer be responsible for her debts, some of which had been printed in the papers. "Just for that I won't pay his bills anymore," Maryon declared.

She soon divorced the baron. After thirty-nine months of marriage, he had cost her roughly $12,500 a month—$400 a day, or $17 per hour.

Still, Maryon walked away from the union with a smirk. His family in England agreed to give her $85,000 in exchange for never using the family name again. If they knew any better, they might have saved their money. She was bound to remarry and acquire another name.

In 1924, Maryon and her daughter returned to the United States. Now ten years old, Ann had received only sporadic schooling. None of her governesses and tutors stayed for very long because of her inattention—and because Maryon fired any staff whom she perceived to be judgmental of her habits. If a governess raised her eyebrows or shook her head when she thought her mistress wasn't looking, she was out on the street with her trunk within the hour.

Ann's beloved Nini was an exception. The French maid had been dismissed because of something the little girl herself did. Often, when Maryon and the other maid, Eugenie, were out, Nini allowed

Ann to wander into her mother's dressing room to try on her big hats in the mirror. One day, Ann grew very bold and tried on a frothy dinner gown. When the chiffon ripped, she called for Nini, who came running in and spanked her. As soon as she did, the maid took the girl in her arms and rocked her, promising that she wasn't angry. The maid wept more than Ann did over the punishment. When Maryon returned home later that afternoon, the maid confessed to the damage and was told to pack her things.

That evening, when Eugenie came to tuck her in, the maid refused to tell Ann a bedtime story. She said she didn't have time for such silliness when there were chores to do. Ann went to Maryon and revealed that she had been the one to ruin the dress. She begged her mother to let Nini come back. Furious that she'd been tricked, Maryon refused. When Ann continued to plead, she plucked the girl's prized doll from her arms and threw it in the garbage.

In New York, Maryon developed another intolerance: staff who filled Ann's head with stories about the habits of the working class. After all, she had no intentions of taking her daughter to ride the Wonder Wheel or peer at dwarf men on Coney Island.

"But there are lions and tigers," Ann once begged.

"They have those at the menagerie."

"There's the Eiffel Tower and Big Ben."

"They're just small-scale reproductions. Why do you want to see those silly fakes when you've seen the real things?"

Ann crossed her arms. "Well, I want to have my palm read."

At this, Maryon paused. "I suppose that's not an awful idea. I'll arrange for someone to come to the apartment."

When a silk-robed, bangled woman arrived at their penthouse with cards and crystal, Maryon took the first turn. She rolled her eyes when the psychic promised true love in the near future. All she cared to know was if her fortune would grow.

It did. Just a few years later, Maryon married a successful lawyer by the name of George W. C. McCarter. Like husbands past, McCarter was accomplished and came from a reputable family. He was the son of Robert H. McCarter, the former New Jersey state attorney general, known around the country for his work in the Hall-Mills murder case. That high-profile case involved the murder of an Episcopal priest and a woman in the church choir believed to be his mistress. Edward Hall and Eleanor Mills were shot in the back of the head, then positioned to lie under a crab apple tree as if embracing. Their heads were tilted toward each other, and the woman's hand was placed on the man's thigh. The crime scene contained torn love letters and Hall's calling card. Prosecutors charged the minister's wife and three brothers with the crime, but the defense team, which included McCarter, managed to get all of the defendants acquitted. Over three hundred reporters packed into the courtroom to hear McCarter and his opponents spar throughout the thirty-day trial. In 1926, no criminal court case had received such extensive media coverage.

By the third decade of the century, the press had dramatically transformed in ways that impacted the coverage of sensational figures like the Hall-Mills victims and Maryon. The tabloids established in the late 1890s had now thoroughly whetted the public appetite for "yellow journalism," leading more respected publications to imitate their tactics. Even the *New York Times* now emphasized sex and crime; used bold, catchy headlines; and printed plenty of photographs to enthrall readers. The *Times* editors had also learned from the tabloids that they could sell more papers by developing single stories and squeezing them for all they were worth. Given her beauty and the many scandalous claims made about her, Maryon was prime grist for the mill.

Media coverage of Maryon actually died down during her final marriage, even as her behavior caused her to be expelled from the many social clubs where McCarter had long been a member. She often became so stupefied from drink that she had to be carried out the door. Other diners expressed shock, particularly chiding Maryon for behaving that way in front of her "moron" daughter. (Maryon always introduced people to Ann by saying, "You'll have to excuse my daughter. She's not quite right." They didn't question her on it.)

Most of the news about Maryon during this time related to court filings for unpaid debts. In one case, the filer, confused by all her married names, listed her as "Jane Doe." In another, the high-end fashion house Nicole de Paris accused Maryon of owing $10,000 for silk stockings, hats, and other confections. Forced to appear before the New York Supreme Court, Maryon insisted that most of the charges were for items that she never ordered. She claimed that she purchased a few pieces (mostly for Ann), but the business sent a limousine to her address with numerous other treasures. As she was indisposed when the parcels arrived, she could not refuse them.

"Ordinary women tried to imagine a New York store sneaking in and dumping ten thousand dollars' worth of unordered finery on them," a writer observed in a 1934 profile of Maryon, following her eventual divorce from McCarter and resumption of the Cooper Hewitt surname. (Once single again, Maryon saw no reason not to reclaim her link to the revered scientist.) While portraying Maryon as entitled, the *San Francisco Examiner* writer nonetheless couldn't help but be awed by his subject. "It is doubtful if any woman ever married more first-class, grade A, highly desirable husbands than Mrs. Maryon Andrews-Bruguiere-Deming-Hewitt-d'Erlanger-McCarter," the author began. "How does one woman manage to draw five aces out of the matrimonial deck?" He went on to describe Maryon's various assets, including

her wittiness, her beauty, her clothing, and her lineage. He seemed
to believe her claim that she was once a southern belle whose
family was respected, if not overly wealthy, before migrating to
California. Rather than dismissing these attributes as the trappings
of a superficial society, the author admired Maryon, reminding
readers that she was a "self-made woman who was poor when
she started collecting husbands." He marveled at the fact that she
"bloomed" after each marriage transaction, echoing a columnist in
Goodwin's Weekly who once likened the name-changing Maryon to
a creature "emerging from a sort of chrysalis." And another, in the
Daily News, who observed that, like music, Maryon goes "'round
and 'round and 'round. Where she comes out always remains to
be seen."

Maryon fascinated journalists like this one for the same reason
that she provoked their disdain: because she managed to constantly
improve herself. She did not stand in the street and wait for
money to fall from the sky—although this actually happened to
some lucky individuals in New York. (After tripling his wealth
with a single stock trade, a man once threw a fistful of greenbacks
out a tenth-story window of the Plaza Hotel, delighting three
schoolboys on their walk home.) Rather, Maryon took steps to
augment her circumstances the only way available to a woman in
the early decades of the twentieth century: by marriage. She may
have developed affection for some of her spouses, but each union
was clearly a business venture. This attitude enabled her to move
on from each failed marriage without a care in the world. As a *San
Francisco Examiner* columnist cheekily wrote after the dissolution
of her fifth marriage, it was "all right for men to love her and leave
her—provided they left her plenty."

Ann's mother was no less shrewd than the entrepreneurs who
transformed American society with their ambitions and inventions.

Jay Gould and J. P. Morgan had speculated on real estate; Maryon speculated on men. John D. Rockefeller had worked his way from a stable boy to an oil tycoon; Maryon worked her way from a humble family to a titled millionaire. Like these men, she did not make her money honestly or without inflicting any harm, which would become especially clear when her crimes against her own child were made known to the nation. But unlike these celebrated figures, she was perceived to be disruptive from the moment she entered the social scene. In a world in which one's family greatly determined one's station, Maryon's ambiguous origins stirred rage. How could people keep Maryon in her place, if they didn't know for certain what her place was?

By portraying Maryon as a coquette who seduced a smart man before finally annihilating him with her charms, the press reinforced the paranoia surrounding socially mobile women. Nurse Kelly may have stirred this paranoia when she suggested foul play at the scene of Peter's deathbed. But it mattered little to the press whether or not Maryon had a hand in her husband's actual demise. As far as the press was concerned, she was already responsible for the honorable scientist's downfall. Her beauty had distracted him from his nobler pursuits, and the world was going to suffer for it. *That* was the story.

Although she never let such criticism influence her pursuit of partners, Maryon paid close attention and tried to use the same narratives against others. Both privately and publicly, she characterized her child exactly as the newspapers had long characterized her: stupid, spoiled, and sexed. Maryon deeply resented Ann, not only for drawing Peter's devotion, but for reminding her of her own lowly origins. Haunted by the true circumstances of her birth, she saw in her daughter the younger self she desperately wanted to erase—the one who didn't know how to sit up straight or hold a conversation with a perfect stranger, and whose eyes sometimes crossed when she grew tired.

But Maryon's efforts to control her reputation ultimately proved in vain, as the "backwards" traits she had long tried to hide were eclipsed by the far more atrocious caricature of her that developed with the trial in 1936.

PART II:

WOMANHOOD AND EUGENICS
ON TRIAL

7

AN ACCIDENT

On February 21, 1936, an ambulance was called to the Hotel Plaza in Jersey City, where a guest registered under the name Mrs. Jane Merritt was found unconscious. It appeared that the woman had taken an overdose of a sleeping potion.

"She was in bed," a nurse explained to the doctor who arrived on the scene. "I tried to wake her, but she wouldn't open her eyes. I found this in the linens." She held a bottle of a liquid narcotic for him to see.

"What is her condition?" the physician asked. "Epilepsy? Diabetes? Heart problems?"

"None of those."

"Why did she hire you?"

"She told me that she was suffering from a nervous breakdown. She was frightened to go anywhere or be alone."

The ambulance transported the woman to the Jersey City Medical Center. The driver rang the bell the entire way, as he always did for people hailing from the Plaza. The woman was admitted to the hospital under the name the hotel concierge provided to the operator. The concierge also told the operator what little he knew of the guest: She was visiting from Boston and planned to stay at the hotel for only a few days. She was prone to terrible headaches and was also recovering from an illness, and so required absolute calm and quiet. She left instructions that no one was to disturb her in any way—not with breakfast or the newspaper or an offer of housekeeping. Her nurse would look out for any needs.

While convalescing in her private room at the medical center, "Mrs. Merritt" received a visit from the deputy chief of police.

"You know that attempted suicide is a criminal offense?" this authority asked.

The woman nodded, dabbing her eyes with a handkerchief.

"I'm afraid that means I'll have no choice but to bring you to court when you've sufficiently recovered."

The woman nodded again.

"What is your address?"

After recording the information that the woman provided, the officer put his notepad and pencil in his pocket and crossed his arms. "You know, it's funny...because there's no Jane Merritt listed at that address."

The woman looked out the window.

"Are you Maryon?" the officer asked, taking a step toward the bed. "Maryon Cooper Hewitt?"

"That is my name," the woman said faintly.

Deputy Chief Charles Wilson had with him papers from California officials asking him to arrest Ann's mother and hold her for extradition to California. The papers, signed by Judge Sylvain Lazarus in San Francisco, had reached New York Police Headquarters by airmail earlier that week. "It appears to the satisfaction of the court that mayhem has been committed and that Maryon Cooper Hewitt and two others did commit it," Lazarus had written. The judge had set bail for $10,000 in property or $5,000 in cash. He had also provided two addresses where Maryon might be found. With this information, New York police had contacted local authorities in New Jersey to aid in their search.

Shortly after learning of the fugitive, the Jersey City Police Department received an anonymous tip about a woman in the hospital who'd attempted suicide. It was the wanted woman, according to the informant. This led the deputy chief to Maryon's bedside.

Wilson later told reporters that Maryon was cooperative, offering her real name and answering all of his questions. "She claimed to have taken the narcotic accidentally," he explained. "She was in the habit of taking a sleeping potion and simply forgot that she had already dosed herself on the night of her episode. Her private nurse verified this fact." Of course, it was up to the courts to accept or reject this explanation, Chief Wilson added. The officer also assured reporters that the local charge against Maryon would not stand in the way of California's extradition demand: "A charge of mayhem is obviously more important than one of attempted suicide."

Upon learning that the California papers had been delivered and that his client was in the hospital, Maryon's attorney vowed to fight extradition. "She will furnish bail, and then I will start testing the validity of the complaint," William V. Breslin told a local reporter. "Unless the complaint is signed by the daughter, I will fight it."

Breslin didn't believe that an unsigned criminal complaint held authority in other states. He also thought Maryon's condition ought to be considered. Surely none of her physicians would think it safe for her to travel in her current state. The attorney reiterated that Maryon's overdose was accidental, attributing her error to the suffering unduly caused by her daughter: "I hope this tragedy brings home to Ann Cooper Hewitt what she is causing her mother to go through."

The criminal and civil cases in California were surely taking a toll on Maryon. The woman had been on the brink of a breakdown ever since boarding the train in San Francisco almost a month ago. While the Pullman sped over the Rocky Mountains and the Midwest plains, Mrs. Cooper Hewitt sat in her private car, wringing her hands and snapping at any train workers who disturbed her thoughts with an offer of a drink or playing cards. In the past, when she'd found herself in legal quandaries like this one, she'd only needed to pull out her checkbook to make the problem go away. But that wasn't going to work this time. She'd already pleaded with her daughter's attorney when he first demanded an accounting of her expenditures in December, signaling that a civil case was coming. "What you're doing is very foolish," she'd told Russell Tyler. "But I'm prepared to pay you a generous sum in exchange for withdrawing the request."

Tyler had refused. She'd then dialed the operator and asked to be connected to Ann. She'd figured she could talk some sense into her daughter. But Ann had refused to accept the call.

So as Maryon sat in her hospital room in late February with charges pending, her mood went from despondent to furious. She had originally been the one to retain Tyler, asking him to handle a few of Ann's affairs, such as overseeing investments made with her inheritance. And now he had turned against her. She hoped the news of her condition would at least bring him a pang of remorse. Ann, too.

Upon arriving on the East Coast in January, Maryon had met with both her New Jersey and New York attorneys, Breslin and Aaron Sapiro, to hash out a plan for both the criminal and civil suits. She had also coordinated with them to issue her own statement to the press. All three agreed to reveal that Ann was a menace to society by virtue of her sex drive. Maryon was merely protecting her daughter—and society—from the consequences of the girl becoming pregnant, they planned to say.

Maryon didn't know it, but her case rested on proving that Ann was not merely sexed, but *over*-sexed. In the decades since Maryon had first been scrutinized for her own sexuality, norms had transformed. Many social authorities had come to accept the fact that they couldn't prevent young people from having sex outside of marriage and that, contrary to Victorian sentiment, sex was a natural part of life. They realized that suppressing sexuality within marriage only undermined that institution. To better protect marriage, authorities instead decided to guide men and women to indulge in "normal" (monogamous, heterosexual) behavior with the goal of marriage and children—and to prevent those who strayed too far from this standard from becoming parents.

Fortunately for reformers, a new cultural icon had emerged that perfectly embodied the revised feminine ideal: the flapper. The skirt-wearing, jazz-listening, bob-haired woman who appeared on magazine covers and in popular literature signified the social recognition that the "gentler sex" was gaining, while also encouraging women to stay in their place. The flapper was a sexual creature, but her sexuality was believed to be part of her maternal feeling. She pursued men in dance halls and public spaces because she desired to settle down with one of them and have babies.

But Ann was no flapper, according to Maryon. Her sexual drive was far too strong to be rehabilitated into anything resembling normal. The day after Mrs. Cooper Hewitt had met with her attorneys, Breslin and Sapiro called reporters to the steps of the Bergen County Court House in Hackensack, New Jersey. There Breslin made an approved statement: "My client has done everything in her power to give her daughter, Ann, a good education, and bring her up as a normal child. But Ann's behavior has resulted in her being dismissed from one school after another. She was never able to make friends at any of these institutions because she behaved so inappropriately, bragging to her peers about her money. She also has a severe sex complex, which led her mother to worry that she'd become pregnant out of wedlock. The sad fact is the girl is feebleminded. In no way is she fit to become a mother."

The attorney suggested that there was no telling what Ann, who only ever thought of gratifying her whims, might do with a wailing infant if she found the demands of parenthood too onerous. She might drown the baby in the bathtub in a fit of rage. Or she might leave the poor thing at a foundling hospital already overpopulated with unwanted souls. There was simply no possibility of a good outcome. Breslin added another point directed at Ann: "When all the facts about her daily life are known, it will be clear to the court that my client was acting with her child's best interests in mind." With this, he was hinting to the heiress that her mother wouldn't hesitate to air the details of Ann's dalliances.

Maryon had in her possession Ann's diary, which was full of entries detailing the girl's riotous, carefree life. He assumed that if the girl had any wits, she would realize that this item was missing and revoke her claims before any of the pages were read in court— or worse, transcribed in newsprint.

Sapiro had then taken his turn, accusing Ann of misrepresenting the financial gains his client would obtain because of the procedure. "The will is very clear," he said. "It provides that if Ann dies without issue, the entire estate goes to the Cooper Union Institute in New York, subject only to Mrs. Cooper Hewitt's rights of income during her life." In other words, Maryon would not inherit Ann's entire share of the estate, as the plaintiff charged. Never mind that she could petition the courts to access this money, as she'd done many times before. With her daughter declared feebleminded, she could easily make the case that Ann required ongoing medical care and oversight of her affairs.

Breslin and Sapiro had offered a foil to the sex-crazed Ann, who couldn't be trusted with a child: the virtuous, self-sacrificing Maryon. To portray the woman's maternal devotion, Sapiro had explained that Maryon had protected the girl's legitimacy years ago when the Cooper Hewitt family tried to exclude her from the will. When the millionaire's siblings had claimed that Ann was merely a love child, Maryon had successfully convinced the courts that the couple's subsequent marriage legitimated Ann. "Why," the attorney asked the gathered members of the press, "would Mrs. Cooper Hewitt endeavor to include Ann in the will, in which she was the only beneficiary, if not for her extreme devotion to her child?"

The physician present at Ann's birth, Dr. I. L. Hill, had corroborated this story, claiming in an affidavit that the sickly infant he delivered in Paris might have died if not for the painstaking attention her mother gave her. As Breslin put it: "If Mrs. Cooper Hewitt wanted to get the entire estate for herself, she would have let Ann die long ago. She kept the child, born two months prematurely, alive only by superhuman effort."

Maryon's thirty-one-year-old son, now living in New York and California and going by the name Richard Bruguiere, had also come to her aid. The man had filed an affidavit challenging his half sibling's claim that she lived as a pauper. "Ann lives in an expensive apartment in San Francisco and owns a dozen evening gowns, forty pairs of shoes, and thirty hats, thanks to our mother, who has dressed her in style since she was a babe in arms," he'd written. Bruguiere had added that Ann had her own car and chauffeur and that she often traveled in special railroad cars to ensure the privacy of her pet dogs. According to him, Ann's life was not impoverished in the slightest, and their mother had always shown nothing but love to her.

Maryon knew that Richard's affidavit had put a wedge between him and his father, as her first husband supported Ann in pursuing her lawsuit. She'd learned that, after asserting her independence, Ann had hired a secretary to assist with her financial and personal matters, and it was none other than Bruguiere's twenty-one-year-old wife, Josephine Marie Slavish. Pedar and this woman (wife number five) lived quietly on an artist's income, as the sixty-two-year-old had finally forsaken medicine. When Ann told her assistant why she needed a full accounting of her money, both of the Bruguieres were enraged. Maryon's attorneys had suggested that they then conspired with Tyler to bring the lawsuit. Maryon was inclined to agree, believing Pedar had never forgiven her for losing interest in him years ago.

Richard wasn't the only one to testify regarding Ann's privileged life. A private shopper claimed that Maryon spent no less than $35,000 a year on the heiress's clothing. "I was instructed by my client to purchase only the finest coats of ermine and chinchilla for the plaintiff," the woman wrote. "Who would do this for a child she disdained?"

In the affidavit she'd filed herself before fleeing California, Maryon had asserted that, despite her giving Ann every possible advantage, the girl was deeply, irreversibly damaged. She was prone to bronchial trouble and other maladies. "If Ann became ill, it would be twice as hard with her as for a normal child with the same illness," she'd explained. "Even a slight cold would become a serious thing with her. When she later grew up and had chicken pox it was one of the most severe types, bringing the kind of fever that usually has a fatal ending. I was only able to nurse her back to health with prayer and round-the-clock attention." As a result of her deficiencies, Ann required constant medical care throughout her adolescence. This, coupled with the cost of Ann's education and clothing, explained the deductions from the girl's trust fund.

Maryon admitted that she gambled, but insisted that she had never used Ann's money for it.

It was during this time, Maryon had asserted, that Ann's sex addiction was made known, as she was found sleeping in bed with a boy of the same age at an institution. This occurred a few years after Maryon had caught Ann masturbating as a toddler. The first incident, Maryon had excused. She didn't want to believe her daughter's ways. But the second revealed to her that her daughter was absolutely deranged.

To further demonstrate that Ann was feebleminded, despite her best efforts, Mrs. Cooper Hewitt claimed that Ann had refused to be educated, misbehaving at one institution after another in order to be expelled. "Ann has never cared for anyone who could teach her or help her get along in life," she told a newspaper. Maryon also cited the intelligence test performed by the state psychologist shortly before the procedure. According to Scally's notes, Ann had poorly responded to the questions about American history. As a result, she'd been classified as a "high grade moron." Mrs. Cooper Hewitt noted that the two doctors agreed with this assessment, as they'd already publicly stated.

Maryon didn't know it, but with the label of "moron," Ann had actually tested higher than two other clinical categories: idiot and imbecile. According to the state-sanctioned intelligence test that she'd been given (the Stanford-Binet test), the heiress had a mental age of eleven. The state applied the term *imbecile* to those with a mental age between two and seven, and *idiot* to those with one under two years. These clinical categories had been supplied by psychologist Henry Goddard, whose intelligence rubric (little more than a civics test, privileging those with knowledge of American history) provided the basis for the Stanford-Binet, created by Stanford psychologist Lewis Terman and used to diagnosis Carrie Buck.

Goddard had adapted his classification system from one made by French physician Théodore Simon and French psychologist Alfred Binet. Simon and Binet had created their system to help educators identify areas of need among intellectually disabled students. When Goddard revised the rubric in 1909, and then when Terman revised Goddard's rubric in 1916 to create the Stanford-Binet, the two men had another motive. They wanted to enable medical professionals to identify defective persons in order to prevent those persons from proliferating their traits. Terman revised his predecessor's work only to make the exam more widely applicable, thereby allowing medical professionals to pathologize more of the population. By the time the Stanford-Binet was applied to Ann in 1934, over nine million adults and children had been tested with it or its progenitor, revealing alarmingly high rates of morons among certain populations. When one researcher administered a slightly modified Stanford-Binet to US troops, he found that 47 percent of whites and 87 percent of African Americans (who still had no access to public schools) had a mental capacity below that of a thirteen-year-old.

Goddard believed that "morons" like Ann constituted the greatest danger to society, since those with a mental age between eight and twelve years could often pass as normal. Disguised in educational and occupational settings, these individuals could find mates and pass down their deficiencies to future generations. To prevent this, the psychologist maintained, the "moron" population needed to be identified and segregated. Goddard had developed the clinical term *moron* from the Greek *moronia*, meaning "foolish," to carry scientific weight and arouse public concern about individuals in this primitive phase of development. *Idiot* and *imbecile* were already in the lexicon.

Of course, the psychologist's rubric and the Stanford-Binet test adapted from it allowed diagnosticians considerable discretion in determining who was feebleminded. Goddard explicitly encouraged authorities to factor in traits such as unwed motherhood, prostitution, homosexuality, unemployment, and alcoholism. Like other eugenicists, he believed "immoral tendencies" signaled genetic flaws.

The psychologist articulated this idea in his popular 1912 book, *The Kallikak Family: A Study in the Heredity of Feeble-Mindedness*, which traced the deficiencies of 143 feebleminded people to a single ancestor—a tavern girl. Goddard maintained that the man whose affair with the tavern girl led to so many defective persons was of good stock himself. (Like Peter Cooper Hewitt, he was merely seduced by a trickster woman of inferior class.) The patriarch was married to a high-class Quaker woman with whom he produced hundreds of upstanding citizens over several generations. To convince readers that negative traits, just like positive ones, could extend for many lifetimes, Goddard included doctored photographs of the supposedly defective family members. Appealing to racial biases, the photographs portrayed individuals with darkened hair and eyes and enlarged facial features.

It never occurred to Maryon to attribute Ann's defects to family genes, as Goddard would have. After years of telling people she was of noble birth, Maryon had nearly come to believe this herself. Instead she and her attorneys blamed Ann's defects on her premature birth, just as the physician who delivered her did. Hill had testified, "Such a [premature] birth frequently causes complicated problems in the nervous system and produces instability and functional difficulties. That resulted with Ann, and she has been characterized by a definite underdevelopment in which her mental age is far behind her physical age." While pointing toward a different somatic origin of Ann's troubles, Hill nonetheless reiterated the notion that physical, intellectual, and sexual defects were interrelated.

Maryon also implicitly suggested another reason for her daughter's degeneracy in her affidavit: the fact that Ann ran around with working-class men. "About four years ago while living in Riverwood, Ann became infatuated with a chauffeur," the woman had written. "He persuaded her to prepare to run away with him, and that encouraged Ann to write long letters to him." Unfortunately, Maryon couldn't produce these letters as evidence, as they "were of a character which justified their immediate destruction." Some contained locks of Ann's pubic hair and "a great many references to things which should not be written about it." Maryon purported to have paid thousands of dollars to the man in exchange for the letters. She did so to "break up the infatuation" and save her daughter from a life of sin. But it was too late. "Ever since that incident, Ann merely gravitated to other men in uniform," Maryon explained. "I once had to drag her, kicking and screaming, out of a bellhop's room. I've also pulled her off the lap of a Negro porter on the train."

By suggesting that a low-class man had brought out Ann's baser traits, Maryon unknowingly appealed to the "degeneration theory" articulated by psychologists like the German-Austrian Richard von Krafft-Ebing, who believed that servants and household workers introduced perversion into respectable homes. According to "degenerationists," wellborn individuals like Ann could revert to a more primitive state when corrupted by people in a lower state of evolution. When this occurred, the individual had become insane, and a doctor needed to intervene. There was nothing a family member or even a priest could do. This way of thinking had prompted many parents to send "adrift" daughters to reformatories or public institutions in the late nineteenth and early twentieth centuries. At such facilities, women could receive treatment, including sterilization. Some medical authorities insisted—falsely—that reproductive surgery was curative, ridding the body and mind of errant sexual urges.

At the Jersey Medical Center following her attempted suicide, Maryon was fortunate to find her physician sympathetic to her situation. "It's no wonder that you've had a nervous breakdown," Dr. William Doody told Maryon, shortly after Chief Wilson had departed. The physician explained that he'd closely followed the news of Ann's lawsuit, including the false report that Mrs. Cooper Hewitt had sailed for Europe. (Someone had claimed to see a woman resembling Ann's mother in the New York harbor area with two large trunks.) "I didn't think you would do such a thing," Dr. Doody assured Maryon. "I know you must be eager to resolve this matter and repair your relationship with your daughter. It sounds like she needs someone to look out for her."

"You're quite right about that," Maryon said. "It's a shame more people don't see it that way."

"In time, they will," the physician promised. "Once all the facts are laid bare."

Mrs. Cooper Hewitt smiled. It didn't surprise her that a medical man understood the urgency of Ann's sterilization. Over the years, not one physician had ever questioned her about her daughter's defects.

"The good news is that you will soon have a chance to defend your name," Doody continued. "Your prognosis is excellent, and I'm planning to release you tomorrow morning."

This, however, didn't suit Maryon one bit. She couldn't bear to be in public after her "accident," as she preferred to call it. She knew that reporters would hound her for statements and take photographs without her permission. Those sympathetic to Ann might even accost her. Furthermore, the warrant for her arrest and extradition had just been presented in the First Criminal Court in Jersey City. The authorities of that court wanted her to appear for a hearing on the matter in a few days. There was no way she could physically or mentally prepare herself so soon after nearly dying. She told Dr. Doody that she feared for her life, as well as her sanity.

"I'm afraid it's too soon," she explained. "I'm still so weak. And the thought of newspapermen trampling me at the courthouse—it frightens me! It makes me feel the way I did the other night."

If Dr. Doody hadn't had any doubts about the accidental nature of Maryon's overdose, he did now. The physician listened carefully as his patient related the psychological strain she'd been under for the last month. He scribbled notes, nodding throughout her story and raising his eyebrows at certain moments—for instance, when Maryon told him that her ex-husband may have plotted with her daughter to sue her for money.

Of course, she omitted certain details, such as the fact that the operating physician second-guessed the procedure after it was complete. "She seemed perfectly capable to me," Dr. Boyd had remarked to Maryon while Ann recovered at the hospital. "Before the surgery, we talked about Roosevelt's upcoming visit and the International Exposition in San Diego. She didn't strike me as moronic at all."

But Dr. Doody didn't note any of the discrepancies between her story and that of the newspapers. He simply promised to take good care of her.

Maryon smiled opening the *New York Times* the following morning. A story reported that she'd taken "a slight turn for the worse" since being admitted. Her physician was quoted saying that his patient was now on the "serious" list at the medical center and that she would be unable to leave the hospital for at least two weeks. There was no possibility of her attending court that week.

When the new court date approached a few weeks later, Dr. Doody announced that Maryon had taken "another turn for the worse." This time, he explained, his patient had a heart and intestinal condition that was aggravating her illness. She was now in a "*very* serious condition." Consequently, the extradition hearing would have to be delayed again.

In the meantime, Breslin assured the public that Maryon would comply with extradition if the New Jersey courts ruled to cooperate with California. But he planned to present a brief at the rescheduled extradition hearing explaining his client's condition.

For the next few weeks, reporters petitioned the hospital for updates. Dr. Doody fed them comments authorized by Maryon. As the extradition hearing approached again in late March, the physician said that Maryon had suffered yet another relapse, this one characterized by difficulty breathing. "She is in a highly nervous and irrational state, and her condition is critical," Doody told anyone who inquired.

The extradition proceeding would have to be postponed once more.

8

A NEW ANN

Back in California, Ann learned of her mother's attempted suicide the same way the rest of the nation did: on the front page. A few days after her mother's near-death, the *San Francisco Examiner* published an article titled "Sterilized Girl's Parent Faces Battle for Life." But unlike most Americans, she questioned the bolded headline.

She'd snapped the paper shut, only to reopen it a few moments later, reading of her relative's supposed perilous state with as much awe as indignation. It was just like her mother to divert attention to herself, she thought. And it was incredibly clever of Maryon to commit a crime in New Jersey, embedding herself in that state. "You little weasel," the heiress said aloud as she read what actions California authorities would now need to take to extradite her mother.

When Tyler telephoned later that day to ask if she'd seen the news, she told him she wasn't convinced her mother had truly attempted the deed.

"But there's a toxicology report," he countered.

"If you think Mother isn't capable of fixing a doctor's report, you haven't been paying attention," she said.

Ann was furious with her mother for going to such lengths to evade punishment. When filing her lawsuit, she'd expected Maryon to put up a fight for the sake of both her reputation and her bank account. But she'd never imagined that Maryon would feign a suicide attempt just to defend her interests.

Ann's misjudgment, she was beginning to realize, stemmed from a deep naïveté about the extent of her mother's plotting—a naïveté that dated all the way back to the days when she was convalescing. When she first began to hear the hospital nurses speak in hushed voices around her, she'd wondered if her condition was more serious than they were letting on. She'd thought perhaps the operating doctors had found something gravely wrong inside her—and that her mother hadn't visited because she was too broken up about it to face her. When she began to piece together what the doctors had done to her, she'd wondered how they could do such a thing without her or her mother's permission. It hadn't occurred to her that her mother could be responsible for something so vile. Then she'd heard one of the nurses remarking about Maryon's courage: "I can't imagine it was easy for her, but it was the right decision. God bless her." At this, Ann had rolled over and buried her face in her pillow, biting down on the cotton to contain her sobs.

But still, she'd continued to underestimate her mother's conniving, presuming that Maryon had simply taken advantage of her appendicitis to have her sterilized. Only after giving more thought to her situation did she realize her mother must have fabricated the medical emergency. Maryon had probably mixed something in her drink at the Coronado to cause her stomach pains. One of her nurses stirred this suspicion, remarking that she was lucky her appendix didn't burst in the four days between her symptoms presenting and her surgery. Ordinarily, she said, people couldn't wait that long to have the inflamed organ taken out. There was also the fact that Tillman never once looked at Ann's abdomen, simply taking her mother's word about the appendicitis. As details churned in her mind, Ann had grown sick. But when her mother finally came around for a visit, she'd pretended not to know a thing. She needed time to plan her next move.

When she'd conferred with the Bruguieres after moving out of her mother's apartment on her twenty-first birthday (the moment she could access her trust fund on her own), she'd become even more convinced that her mother had been plotting well in advance of the surgery. "Mother has always prevented me from having friends," she'd said, "but the last few years, she's become more aggressive about it. It's as if she wanted to prevent anyone from challenging her claims about me."

Ann had told the couple about an incident at the Coronado around her twentieth birthday. The hotel manager and hostess had found out that the day was approaching, and knowing that her mother wasn't planning anything, they'd begun to arrange for a party. It was going to be the first real celebration since her father's death. The staff had sent for flowers and cards and invited other young people residing at the hotel. It was supposed to be a surprise, but one of the workers blabbed to Ann. Not thinking, she'd run upstairs to share the news with her mother, who loved parties. Maryon had immediately grabbed the telephone to summon the hostess and manager to their suite.

"I want you to understand that I'm no pauper," she'd snapped. "I don't want your charity or your damned hospitality. Get out of here and mind your own business!"

There'd been no party. Afterward, the hotel staff looked at Ann with pity when she passed. Not wanting to enrage her mother, they addressed her with a formal tone.

Then there'd been the girl she'd met in their San Francisco

apartment building. Ann told the Bruguieres the neighbor had come to their suite for tea on two occasions. Ann liked her very much and wanted to know her better. One night, Maryon woke Ann sometime after three in the morning to dial a number for her on the telephone. She was too inebriated to do so herself. Ann recognized the number as belonging to her acquaintance, and her eyes welled with tears.

"Please, no!" she had begged her mother.

"Ann, obey me at once."

When she refused, Maryon struck her over the head with the receiver and kept trying to place the call herself. Ann crept down the hall, praying her mother would continue to fail. But Maryon finally got the numbers right, leaving Ann to quietly sob as she listened to her mother tell the person on the other end terrible lies about her. She never visited with the girl again.

Ann had written about the incident in her diary. Her mother later confiscated the item and tore out the pages, demanding that she record another reason for the friendship ending. It wasn't the first time Maryon had done something like this. She'd also forced Ann to write entries of wonderful times at parties that she'd never actually attended.

"What about that blue-eyed gentleman you met at dinner the other night?" Maryon had once asked, looking over Ann's shoulder as she doodled on the blank pages. "Didn't you dance with him?"

"I don't know what you're talking about," Ann had responded.

"Well, what if you had danced with him?" Maryon had persisted. "What would you have whispered in his ear? There's nothing wrong with using your imagination."

When Ann was a child, Maryon had compelled her to write a note to the trustees of her father's estate, saying that she was being well cared for in France. Maryon had dictated the entire letter and instructed Ann to sign it, claiming that she'd send her daughter back to an asylum if she refused. Ann never learned if the letter was sent or why exactly her mother needed it—only that there was a great divide between her experiences and those her mother wished to present to the world.

As she sat in her apartment, stewing over her mother's alleged accident, she began to worry about the book she'd left behind on the day she'd abandoned their home.

She and Maryon had just had their terrible fight. Ann had confronted Maryon with her suspicions that she was trying to steal her inheritance. Her mother had dismissed the idea: "You're crazy, Ann. It's a good thing your father isn't here to see what a dimwit you've turned out to be."

"Don't you dare bring my father into this!" the heiress had fumed.

"Why not? He'd be mortified to see who bears his name."

Ann had stormed to her room and thrown a trunk on the bed, filling it with garments and shoes, while her mother screamed obscenities over her shoulder. In her haste, she'd packed only necessary items, leaving behind her diary.

It didn't surprise her that Maryon claimed to have lost the letters she'd confiscated from the chauffeur in New Jersey, for they had accurately recorded her romantic life, as well as her mother's abuse. It would be clear to anyone reading them that Ann hadn't thrown herself at the driver, as her mother purported; she'd simply grown close with him because he was one of the few persons in her life who didn't talk down to her.

All of Ann's life, Maryon had introduced her as being some kind of imbecile. After this, new acquaintances would speak to Ann in the same voice they'd use with a six-year-old. At sixteen years of age, when the chauffeur in question began to work for the family, she was old enough to go out on her own and set the record straight. But she and her mother no longer had cards to get into any of the establishments where her stepfather, George McCarter, paid dues. So, having nowhere to go and no companions to invite to the house, Ann had begun to ask the chauffeur to take her for drives. Cruising the suburbs of Jersey City, they'd talked about everything from motion pictures to the stock market. After a while, things grew more intimate, as the letters reflected. And there *was* talk of her leaving town with him someday. But this was mostly to rescue her from the abuse she endured at home, not because she was pining for the man.

When her mother had paid for the chauffeur to stay away, Ann had thought about running off on her own. She was tired of her mother standing in the way of her being friends with anyone. This was why she'd never succeeded in school—not because she was ornery, as her mother claimed. At every new institution, Maryon would begin by explaining to the faculty that her daughter was below average in brains. Naturally, the teachers believed this and talked about it among themselves. It wasn't long before the pupils picked up on the chatter, calling Ann names. The heiress sometimes retaliated, such as by boasting of her father's wealth and accomplishments. She couldn't help herself. A girl had to have a comeback, didn't she?

Ann's attorney assured her he would refute all of Maryon's charges regarding her character, revealing her to be a bright young woman who only had the misfortune of being raised by a violent, self-indulgent mother. Fortunately, over two hundred people had written to Tyler offering to testify for her—or rather, against Maryon. On top of this, many medical persons had agreed to assist her case. One of them was Dr. Lawrence M. Collins, senior resident physician of the New Jersey State Hospital. The physician had examined Ann in November 1934, several months after the infamous procedure. "I found her perfectly normal in every respect," Dr. Collins had written in an affidavit in January. "Her demeanor was quiet, orderly, agreeable, and cooperative. She was not antagonistic or evasive in any way. There was no expression of delusions or hallucinations. She was a delightful young lady."

This expert added that Ann had "a good grasp on the recent and remote past" and a wide range of intellectual interests. In addition to enjoying art and music, she could write fluently in French and converse in Italian. Ann also impressed the physician with her literary habits: "She's read books on Shakespeare, Napoleon Bonaparte, Marie Antoinette, King Lear, Dante's *Inferno*, and the works of Charles Dickens." If there were *any* intellectual deficiencies, Collins claimed, these were due to the fact that Ann was neglected by her mother for most of her childhood. "My belief is that this young girl has been conditioned during her early formative years by an unwholesome environment," the physician testified.

Nurse Grace Wilkins, who had attended Ann before her operation, corroborated this story. Wilkins had explained that she had been hired to look after a mental case but formed an entirely different opinion about the situation. "Half an hour after I saw the girl for the first time, I knew that here was no insane person," the nurse wrote in her own affidavit. "I observed three months of abuse of her by her mother. She was kept in pajamas upstairs. Her letters were censored. So were her telephone calls."

Wilkins also testified about a remark that Maryon made after securing funds from the Hewitt estate to pay for an unspecified medical procedure for Ann. "She said, 'Now that the covered wagon has arrived, we'll go out and celebrate.'" The nurse explained that she was initially confused by the comment. "At first, I didn't even know what she was talking about. Who celebrates a medical procedure, except for a lifesaving one? But Mrs. Cooper

Hewitt kept calling her daughter an idiot, which led me to believe this was no tonsillectomy or anything like that. I began to sense that Mrs. Cooper Hewitt was preparing to do something very bad to Ann."

Wilkins had assured the court that she never clinked champagne glasses with Maryon over Ann's circumstances.

The woman hired to care for Ann after the operation had also condemned her mother. Nurse Sarah Bradford testified that she'd been hired to replace Wilkins simply because Mrs. Cooper Hewitt didn't like that Wilkins and her daughter had grown so close. More than once, Maryon had walked in Ann's room to find Bradford comforting her tearful daughter. The nurse claimed that Maryon had explicitly instructed her, "I don't want Ann to leave her room, nor to be disturbed by visitors. She's not well." She added that Mrs. Cooper Hewitt "did not conduct herself as a normal mother would." She was "cruel and inhuman," and she frequently hosted all-night parties during which she became intoxicated and threw herself at whatever man happened to be standing closest.

This witness further claimed to have read a story in the newspapers about a similar scenario in Paris, when Ann's father died. Bradford told a reporter, "The story suggested that people were partying in the room while the poor man was dying, and I thought 'Oh my. She's gone and done it again.'"

When speaking with reporters himself, Tyler compared Maryon to a black widow spider, who was fully willing to kill and devour her child if it would benefit her. He also made a point to refer to Maryon by all of her married names: Bruguiere-Deming-Hewitt-d'Erlanger-McCarter. Although in court documents, he had no choice but to use only the Cooper Hewitt surname, her legal one.

Angry as she was about her mother's latest effort to sway public opinion against her, Ann smiled to think how her and Tyler's boldness must surprise her mother. She could count on one hand the number of times she'd so forcefully contradicted Maryon. The first time, she'd been only ten years old, standing in her mother's dressing room while Maryon prepared herself for an evening out. Knowing that her mother took great pride in her looks, and angry that she was going be left behind again, Ann had snorted, "You look terrible."

She'd caught her mother's off-guard expression in the mirror before it transformed into a sneer, and Maryon turned toward her. "You're hideously ugly, Ann. And no amount of jewels could ever fix you."

"Well, I suppose the apple doesn't fall far," Ann had said, turning and darting out of the room toward her own. Though Maryon was right at her heels, she'd managed to slip in and bolt the door behind her.

"Take it back, Ann," her mother had shouted, slamming her fists against the door. "Take it back this instant!"

But she'd held her ground, blockading the door with every pound of her small frame and basking in the unfamiliar feeling of pleasure coming over her.

Thinking of the case she and Tyler were building against her mother, Ann experienced a similar sense of satisfaction. But no matter the outcome of the civil or criminal suit, she knew she had an undeniable way to triumph over her mother—by finding peace and contentment without her. For months now, she'd been living on her own and surrounding herself with people who showed affection, such as the Bruguieres. She'd been painting, which she'd loved to do ever since the baron let her play with his colors and brushes years before. Perhaps soon, she'd go back to school, where she'd finally be able to thrive.

Ann made a point of remarking about her plans when speaking

with reporters, knowing the details would work their way to her mother. She had also stopped bleaching her hair, after years of doing so for Maryon's sake. That way, when her mother came across a photograph of her, the message would be loud and clear: She was doing things her way now, and there was absolutely nothing Maryon could do to stop her.

9

FUGITIVE PRISONER

Just as Maryon was beginning to think she had the press's favor, she opened the newspapers in her private hospital room to find herself referred to as "a fugitive prisoner." It seemed that a few smug reporters were beginning to suspect her of orchestrating her illness. "How dare they," she fumed.

The past few months had been the most strenuous of her life. As she'd confessed to Dr. Doody, she really had been driven to end it all that night at the Plaza.

That evening, Maryon had instructed her nurse to leave the hotel suite on an errand so she could have a private moment to call Breslin. Both of the California doctors and the psychologist had been in court that day to give testimony, and she hadn't been able to wait to see her counsel in person the next morning to learn of the proceedings. Over the phone, Maryon was told that Mrs. Scally had performed exactly as anticipated. The psychologist had explained that she had fixed Ann's mental age around eleven years old, admitting that, had Ann applied herself more persistently to the exam, she might have scored a few points higher. However, she was certain that the girl would never develop intellectually beyond the level of a high-grade moron. But then the judge had pressed

Scally on her methods, demanding that she give him the same test. The alienist obeyed, and the man jotted down his answers on a piece of scrap paper. Scally reviewed it and then told him, "Your mental age is twelve years old."

"Hm. I thought it was nearer eight," the judge had said, much to the amusement of the crowd. When the courtroom quieted from the laughter, he'd added, "This whole thing is just too silly for words."

"This incident may have put doubt in the mind of the court regarding the reliability of the test," Breslin had admitted over the phone. "If the court decides that Ann is not feebleminded, then the procedure can hardly be justified."

It didn't matter that the operation occurred while Ann was still a minor, Maryon's attorney further explained. If the court found any doubt regarding her mental capacity, both she and the doctors could be convicted of mayhem. The penalty for such a crime could easily exceed a decade. This was to say nothing of the civil case, in which the plaintiff's burden of proof was even lower.

The hearing in California had concluded with an order that both Drs. Boyd and Tillman be held for trial and a sharp warning from the judge, which Breslin read to his client over the phone. "There is nothing in the record to show that this girl has ever been committed to an institution as an idiot. Thus, her sterilization does not come within permission of California law," Lazarus had written. "It concerns me to think how carelessly the doctors and the girl's mother may have acted in this case. The necessity and the desire to bear children is something not idly to be interfered with."

Maryon knew that if the doctors were tried for mayhem, it was only a matter of time before she would be, too. So she'd asked Breslin to make contact with Ann's attorney. She thought perhaps he would entertain her offer to settle the matter if it came from one of his peers. She was ready to give Tyler whatever he wanted.

"He's serious about this," Breslin had responded. "I don't think he can be bribed to do anything he thinks unconscionable."

"Come on now. Everyone has a price."

"Not this time."

Not wanting to hear another word, Maryon had replaced the earpiece in its gold receiver. Then she'd retrieved a nail file from her beaded clutch and begun to shape the tips of her nails.

Maryon wondered whom the prosecutor would call to testify at the doctors' trial. She hoped not Florence Slavish. Maryon had once remarked to her former paid companion (and the sister of Pedar's current wife) about her intent to have Ann get the procedure. "Ann's a nut. I'm going to have her operated on and tell her it's appendicitis," she'd said. If she was lucky, the bat had since died.

Mrs. Cooper Hewitt also fretted about the prosecution getting hold of Elizabeth Kelly. The English nurse in Paris had caused enough aggravation at Peter's estate proceedings. The last thing Maryon needed was for the woman to get on the stand with her wild notion about a conspiracy behind Peter's death.

The baron's second wife in London presented yet another problem. She claimed that, before dying in 1934, d'Erlanger had told her all sorts of negative things about his ex-wife—for instance, that Maryon neglected little Ann's schooling. He'd purportedly said that when Maryon finally did send Ann away to a school, she didn't even bother to investigate the institution; she simply took the recommendation of a representative of Peter Cooper Hewitt's trust company.

"He often spoke of the young girl, of whom he was extremely fond," the current Mrs. d'Erlanger had told the English newspapers, which were now on the story. "My husband would say, 'It's a tragedy Ann was never allowed a proper education. Given an opportunity, she would have had a brilliant career. There's nothing wrong with the girl, but she's a simple child because she's never been taught anything. Therefore, she can't grasp the meaning of things.'"

The widowed baroness had also taken the opportunity to refute the years-old claim that Maryon supported her husband during their marriage, saying, "She didn't pay a cent for his upkeep."

Maryon gritted her teeth over press like this. Why were the newspapers reprinting this woman's opinions? The baron's wife had never even met Ann, and therefore, anything she claimed the baron said was hearsay. Maryon was just as mad about the many strangers coming forward claiming to have known her in a previous life—and not the southern aristocratic one of which she often spoke. The latest to do so was an old-timer from the Nob Hill district in San Francisco. "She was a plain girl. Her father drove a horse car, and her family lived over a grocery store," the man told a newspaper. "Her only gift was a supreme degree of 'it.'" By this, the informant meant "shine."

That much was true, Maryon had thought. She'd always had a sparkle unlike any other girls her age.

Worries about the impending trial had taken hold that night in her hotel room. She'd imagined the doctors being taken away in handcuffs. Soon after, she'd have to stand trial herself and then be thrown in a cell with some pickpocket or check forger. Even if she managed to spend only a few years in such a place, thanks to her legal advisers, Maryon could never live with the headlines. She would always be the heinous woman who had sterilized her daughter. She could forget about finding a male companion, let alone marrying again. Of course, this meant that Maryon's finances would never improve. She didn't know how she could possibly afford to pay her daughter half a million dollars if the courts ordered her to do so. For that matter, she didn't know how she could pay her current bills. Without any further income from the Cooper trust for Ann's upkeep, she would have to rely on the small amount of maintenance provided by her divorce settlement with McCarter. There was virtually nothing left of her own part of the Cooper Hewitt inheritance. Maryon blamed Elisha Dyer for that. Her stockbroker had made a handful of bad trades before she finally fired him.

Nursing apprehensions about her fate, Maryon had found a bottle of potassium bromide among her things and made her way to the bed. As she'd drifted off to sleep, she thought how nice it would be for the nurse to find her looking like one of the girls from the pictures—her golden locks splayed across the pillow and a perfectly manicured hand resting on her chest. Perhaps a sympathetic reporter would write that she exited the world as beautifully as she moved through it.

Maryon had not been pleased to awaken in the psychopathic ward of Jersey City Medical Center with a doctor shining a light in her eyes. But at least Dr. Doody understood her need for a suite more befitting of someone of her station. Her new room had velvet drapes, which opened to a view of Manhattan on the horizon. It had two seats for visitors and a gold-framed mirror for her to see her reflection. Most important, it was out of the way of curious eyes and eavesdropping ears. If Maryon had learned one thing over the past few weeks, it was that no one could be trusted. Already an anonymous hospital source had gabbed to the press about her. Maryon had asked for a little salt with her dinner and then read about it in the newspaper the next day.

Even in the corner wing of the ward, Maryon required her attorney to speak in whispers to avoid being overheard by bribed hospital staff. She also refused to accept any phone calls, though her deluxe room had its own telephone. The authorities in California were tenacious, and there was no telling whether or not the wires had been tapped.

One morning, when Maryon had been at the hospital for over a month, Breslin came to say that Assistant District Attorney Fourtner believed reports of her illness were exaggerated. The prosecutor claimed to have had his suspicions even before the newspapers on the East Coast began to refer to Maryon as a "fugitive prisoner." Breslin told his client, "He called me this morning to say that he is ready to send officers to New Jersey with an extradition demand. I'm afraid he means it."

This left Maryon no choice but to confer with Doody once more. When the physician made his rounds that afternoon, she suggested that he listen to her chest for pneumonia. She said she was certain that an illness was developing.

The next day, the newspapers reported the pending infection.

Maryon remained in this condition for several more weeks, during which time two businesses filed suit against her for unpaid invoices.

"You must settle these at once," Maryon instructed her attorney. "Before others get the same idea."

"You mean there are others?" Breslin asked.

Maryon ignored the question.

"How many others?"

"Just take care of them," she said.

Meanwhile, authorities in the West were growing increasingly impatient with her absence. In late March, the court had convened to demand her extradition. Justice seemed to be closing in on her, and she couldn't claim illness indefinitely.

But much to her delight, the New Jersey authorities refused

to comply with the demand. Judge Anthony Botti in the First Criminal Court in Jersey City claimed that his own state had claims against Maryon—she'd been charged with a suicide attempt and also had a complaint against her related to the civil suit that Ann had filed. The heiress had demanded in New Jersey court that the United States Fidelity and Guaranty Company provide a full accounting and pay her $150,000, the approximate amount the company had bonded her mother to protect Maryon against lawsuits related to the misuse of funds from Ann's estate. The company now claimed it could not fulfill Ann's requests without first obtaining a response from Maryon.

Maryon's East Coast legal troubles saved her again in April, when the California governor requested her extradition to his state. "After careful consideration, I feel obliged to deny the requisition of the State of California for the extradition of this fugitive at this time," the New Jersey governor responded. "This is based upon the existence of the demands of New Jersey upon the accused." Governor Hoffman advised the authorities in California to file a detainer against Maryon. Such a detainer, he explained, would reopen the question of removing Maryon to California as soon as she was released from charges in New Jersey.

In June, the Fidelity insurance company settled the $150,000 bond, concluding this strand of the civil case. As Maryon expected, Ann's attorney immediately went to the press to clarify that the settlement in no way impacted the $500,000 suit against her for damages related to Ann's sterilization.

Knowing she was nearing the end of her rope, Maryon finally left the hospital ward in June to be arraigned on the charges against her. The press had a field day. Before her town car came to a full stop in front of the courthouse, reporters had scribbled notes on her wardrobe—a dark-blue coat with a black chinchilla collar and a black veil. When she stepped out of the car with the help of two nurses, one reporter even leaned down to observe the design of the gold threads on the house slippers she was wearing.

A police lieutenant shooed the men aside so Maryon had a clear path up the courthouse steps. With a nurse supporting her on each side, the trembling woman made her way inside. In the courtroom, another horde of reporters filled the first rows. A tripod was positioned directly in front of the witness stand. Maryon was peeved to see it. She had petitioned Judge Botti to forbid photographers in the courtroom, but he had apparently dismissed her request.

When it was time for her to stand before the bench, Maryon let her two nurses guide and support her. The judge peered over his glasses with a look that suggested both pity and disdain. Then he set bail of $1,000 for the attempted suicide charge, to be heard by a grand jury on September 24 of that year, and $2,500 for the fugitive charge. No one from California was present. The authorities in that state probably didn't think the hearing would actually take place, and so hadn't arranged for anyone to attend.

Breslin immediately posted the bonds and requested permission for his client to return to the hospital as a voluntary patient. Later that day, Dr. Doody issued a statement about Maryon: "I am happy to report that Mrs. Cooper Hewitt is now completely recovered. Following the shock of the poison, she was stricken with pneumonia, peritonitis and had developed a neurosis. At present, she suffers only from weakness. She will be discharged in a few days."

Arraigned and no longer perceived to be an immediate flight risk, Maryon could now live outside of the institution. The next day, she left the hospital in an automobile with a few friends. A police officer blocked vehicles attempting to follow her to her destination. Reporters asked Breslin where his client was planning to reside, but Maryon's attorney refused to disclose her whereabouts.

Nearly six months had passed since Maryon had first filed an affidavit asserting her innocence and fled California. All this time, she'd followed the case through the newspapers and her attorneys, who reported on any activity as soon as they learned of it. But none of these sources provided a comprehensive picture of the unfolding criminal suit, as the dynamics of the case had shifted in ways that hadn't been made known to the public.

From Maryon and her attorneys' vantage point, the mayhem case appeared to hinge on whether or not it was lawful to forcibly operate upon someone in private practice. Of secondary concern was the fact that Ann was a minor at the time of the operation. The sterilization laws in California did not provide for either of these circumstances. Precisely for this reason, and unbeknownst to those on the East Coast, the counsel for the two doctors had appealed to Paul Popenoe and Ezra Gosney. After reading Gosney's published remarks on the Hewitt case in the *Pasadena Star-News* in February, the doctors' attorney had learned that both men were integral to California's sterilization program.

The two eugenicists had agreed to consult with the defense, not because they wanted to protect Boyd and Tillman from jail time, but because they wanted to protect the larger practice of involuntary sterilization. With these figures strategizing behind the scenes, the mayhem case was quickly transforming into a defense of the flailing eugenics movement.

10

PLOTTING

"California's famous sterilization law has nothing to do with the Ann Cooper Hewitt case," Gosney declared in the *Pasadena Star-News* on February 5, 1936.

Having followed the news related to Ann's case for nearly a month, the president and founder of the Human Betterment Foundation could see that the public was growing increasingly curious about existing sterilization laws in his state, and he wanted to avoid scrutiny of these statutes. He explained in the *Star-News* that the law requiring the state to provide a court order for sterilizations only applied to persons committed to state institutions. And thanks to that law, he couldn't help but note, ten thousand flawed persons in California had been sterilized since 1901—nine hundred in the last year alone.

While he distanced the Cooper Hewitt case from sterilizations occurring in institutions, Gosney nonetheless expressed his wish to see the two doctors prevail in court. Noting that there was no law *against* sterilization in private practice, he concluded that Ann's sterilization was legal. He saw no reason why consent was necessary to perform such a procedure. After all, he wrote, "A feebleminded person who cannot manage his own affairs cannot give a valid consent for his own sterilization." In these cases, it was always the parent or guardian who volunteered the patient for sterilization. From his perspective, there was no such thing as involuntary sterilization.

Gosney admitted that Mrs. Cooper Hewitt may not have acted with totally benevolent intentions. The fact that she was poised to benefit financially suggested this. But regardless, there was no need to throw the baby out with the bathwater. "Many cases are on record in the courts in which an heir or beneficiary has murdered a relative in order to get the life insurance, but no one proposes because of this fact to abolish life insurance," Gosney reasoned. It would be especially rash, given that the Cooper Hewitt case was the only negative case involving sterilization known across the nation. "In the entire history of official sterilizations in the United States, covering thirty-six [sic] years, we have never known of a wrong done to any individual," Gosney claimed.

In fact, dozens of individuals had filed civil lawsuits after being involuntarily operated upon, including in his own state of California. However, these plaintiffs had not been successful in pursuing monetary damages or changing statutes, allowing eugenicists to dismiss them.

Whether or not Gosney's remarks succeeded in shaping public opinion about sterilization in the early phase of Ann's case, they had managed to catch the important eyes of I. M. Golden, the attorney for Drs. Boyd and Tillman.

On May 23, 1936, a little more than two months before the physicians' criminal mayhem trial commenced, Golden wrote to Gosney's colleague Popenoe, seeking his counsel regarding his clients' defense. The attorney explained the details of Ann's operation in private practice, included a copy of Mary Scally's report of Ann's mental examination, and then posed the following question:

"Upon the basis of this report, and assuming it to be true (the patient not being an inmate of a public institution), in your opinion was it proper to sterilize her by removing the fallopian tubes, as a matter of medical and scientific procedure?"

In a postscript, Golden added, "I forgot to mention that the entire operation, including the removal of the fallopian tubes, was with the consent of the girl's mother." Wanting to assure Popenoe of his own favorable position to sterilization, he added that, as chief deputy district attorney of San Francisco and then as the judge of the superior court of the city, he'd gotten "some idea of the havoc that is wrought by the reproduction of mental defectives."

But much to Golden's surprise, Popenoe initially declined the request. In a reply dated three days later, the eugenicist expressed agreement with the decision of Mrs. Cooper Hewitt and the two doctors to sterilize Ann, writing, "I suppose we should all answer negatively the question of whether such a woman as you describe would be a desirable mother." However, he regretted that he could not testify. Not being a medical expert, he feared his opinion would not carry enough weight in court. "I am neither an M.D., a psychiatrist, nor a psychologist," wrote Popenoe, whose "Dr." title derived from an honorary degree. "My own field is in heredity, and that is, I believe, not particularly the issue in this case...If the prosecution is going to do as much damage as possible, they might easily weaken the value of my testimony to you by inquiries on these points."

Popenoe added that he had conferred with Gosney on the matter. His colleague agreed that Popenoe would be "more of a liability than an asset." Nonetheless, Popenoe assured Golden that he could find well-known and experienced psychologists and psychiatrists in the community to attest to Ann's idiocy. He provided the name of a Dr. Olga Bridgman, who was both an MD and a PhD.

Popenoe wasn't entirely forthcoming in his letter. There was another reason why he preferred not to testify in the mayhem case, unrelated to his perceived qualifications: Both he and Gosney still hoped to distance Ann's sterilization from that of the inmates in state-run hospitals, fearing the negative press could impact the noble work that they had been doing for decades.

But Golden refused to accept no for an answer. On May 28, the defense attorney wrote to Popenoe, "I am strongly inclined to the opinion that there are certain phases of this matter in which you could be very helpful, even though you are not either a Ph.D. or an M.D." He identified those phases as having to do with the value and widespread use of sterilization. Golden assured Popenoe of his authority on this subject, writing, "By reason of your concentrated study on the subject of mental defectives and that of eugenics, you are probably in a good position to know whether sterilization is desirable in such cases; that is to say, you have a factual knowledge just as an historian has." Golden noted that the "ordinary surgeon is not [as] well qualified to speak" on the value of sterilization, which he intended to uphold in court.

This time, Popenoe acquiesced. In his response, the eugenicist invited Golden to meet in his Pasadena office, where all of the foundation's records were stored. He also referred Golden to Dr. Ludwig Emge of San Francisco, a gynecologist and expert on the sterilization of females. While maintaining that he was not an ideal witness, Popenoe was invested in the outcome of the case and ready to provide Golden with the resources he needed to prevail in court. In his opinion, Ann was no different than the asylum inmates whose sterilizations he promoted through his professional work. He didn't need to meet the woman to know that she was a moron and that she would make a terrible mother.

Gosney, too, agreed to lend a hand. He accepted Golden's

request to collaborate with a hired expert, Dr. Philip Gilman, the president of the San Francisco County Medical Association, to craft a sophisticated argument for the use of sterilization in private practice. Specifically, he would demonstrate, at Golden's urging, that such medical procedures did not require an order of the court and that they were socially beneficial. Although the defense attorney only cared to see that his clients were acquitted, Golden recognized the need for a broader defense of sterilization. "What I am going to try to prove," the lawyer reflected, "is that it is well, both for Society, for the individual and for the family group, that morons be sterilized."

On June 5, Gosney provided a full report reflecting on private-practice sterilization from a legal perspective, which would be developed by Gilman into talking points for Golden to use in court. It didn't take long for Gosney to write, as he had already given considerable thought to the question. Facing criticism from within and beyond the scientific community, Gosney had theorized that voluntary operations performed in private practice might constitute the next phase of eugenic programs in America. The leaders of the American Eugenics Society agreed with his assessment. The previous year, the society had urged its members to push surgery among non-institutionalized individuals who seemed unwilling or unable to provide their children with a proper intellectual and moral education. That same year, the society's president, Ellsworth Huntington, published *Tomorrow's Children: The Goal of Eugenics*, which similarly encouraged private practitioners to sterilize patients who seemed unlikely to rear respectable offspring.

With this same frame of mind, Gosney believed that Maryon's maternal shortcomings could strengthen the defense's case. Rather than excusing Ann's defects, they validated them. Therefore, he advised Golden, there was no need to defend her character.

If Gosney and Popenoe had initially been reluctant to become involved in the case, they now realized that the high-profile drama could do much more for eugenics than keep it on life support. In addition to expanding the practice of sterilization beyond the institutional setting, the case promised to modernize the criteria used to qualify individuals for involuntary sterilization. By shifting emphasis from heredity to the home environment as the cause of degeneracy, the case could allow eugenicists to dodge the scientific scrutiny that was currently dogging the movement.

In letting go of "defective genes" as a reason for sterilization, Gosney and Popenoe would have to admit that family pathology was not an exclusive problem of the poor classes, who had long been targeted by their sterilization campaigns—it could result from any poor domestic environment. The eugenicists would also have to avoid *overtly* targeting entire populations, such as epileptics or immigrants. However, these moves offered distinct advantages. By insisting that decisions related to sterilization needed to be made on a case-by-case basis, Gosney and Popenoe could distinguish their efforts from the goings-on abroad. They could condemn Hitler's race-based programs and continue carving into people at home. In essence, what had started as familial discontent could help to usher in the second phase of eugenics if Popenoe and Gosney had their way.

11

THE WIZARD

Sometimes, when he couldn't sleep, seven-year-old Peter Cooper Hewitt would slide his small feet into the slippers beside his bed, creep down the grand staircase, and quietly exit the back door of his family's mansion on Lexington Avenue. Behind the house, there was a stable with a workshop in the rafters. The boy would feed each horse a carrot to keep his secret and then climb the ladder to his little factory, full of tools and random contraptions that he was in the process of building or taking apart.

Peter's grandfather, who occupied the southern half of the Lexington Avenue mansion, had installed this space for him and his siblings. Peter Cooper knew the value of tinkering and encouraged the little ones to be inventive with whatever objects they found at hand. When one of his grandchildren asked for a toy seen in the pages of *St. Nicholas* magazine, the old man would say, "I won't buy it for you, but I'll give you the tools to make it." It was important to Cooper that his kids and grandkids learn a trade. That way, should they ever lose their fortune, they could earn an income. Peter Cooper Hewitt and his two brothers—Edward and Erskine—learned to engineer all sorts of goods, while their three sisters—Amy, Sally, and Nellie—learned to sew, cook, and keep house. Cooper's proviso put Peter early on the path to success, while also providing him and his siblings with many enjoyments.

In their workshop, Peter and Edward once rigged up a telephone to communicate with Erskine, who was quarantined in his room with scarlet fever. They'd gotten the idea for this object when Alexander Graham Bell had come to the thirty-five-room house seeking their legendary grandfather's opinion about his invention. Long after the man left, Peter and Edward had talked excitedly about methods to reproduce the thing. They'd sketched and re-sketched the receiver, transmitter, coil, magnet, and diaphragm, and then taken these drawings to bed when sent. The very next day, the boys succeeded in re-creating Bell's telephone. They ran the wires for the telephone under the hall carpet and pleaded with Erskine's nurse to pull them up to their brother's bed. She agreed and even held the receiver to the ear of her flush-faced patient, who beamed when he heard his siblings' voices, clear as a whistle. The experiment had worked perfectly.

When a doctor came to see Erskine a few days later, he marveled at the children's innovation. The physician even held the object to his mouth to greet the two boys on the other end, whose eyes widened before they burst into a fit of laughter. Peter and Edward next ran the wire across the street to the home of their friend Tim Mills. They managed to hold several midnight conversations with their chum before a lineman noticed the wire and took it down. It was the first house-to-house telephone in all of New York.

The house on Lexington Avenue was known as the site where engineering men came to have their dreams fulfilled or dashed. Men visited the house before going to the US Patent Office. If they impressed Peter Cooper with their creations, they could pave their own way. They might even gain the millionaire's financial backing, as Samuel Morse did with his telegraph. Morse so enthralled

Cooper that the two later collaborated to lay a telegraph cable across the Atlantic Ocean, enabling President James Buchanan and Queen Victoria to greet each other across the watery divide. But if they failed to stir his interest, men might as well chuck their beloved objects into the sea. Christopher Latham Sholes did exactly this when his host failed to appreciate a mechanical machine he was building for the purpose of printing letters. The typewriter was not developed until many years later.

The house on Lexington Avenue was also the site of many lively dinners and parties, where artists, poets, businessmen, and heads of state gathered. Peter's favorite among these was the Norwegian artist Ole Bull, who once entertained them into the wee hours of the morning. He'd walked up and down the house playing his violin, trailed by the six Hewitt children singing along to tunes like "Home Sweet Home" and "Coming Through the Rye."

In this intellectually stimulating environment, the future father of Ann Cooper Hewitt developed a love for science that would distinguish him in his own right. Here, and at his family's bucolic estate in New Jersey, where the mines had supplied iron for every war since the Revolution, Peter learned to probe and improve the world around him, eventually impressing the public with his handy inventions and not just his surname.

Unlike Ann, whose childhood was lacking in so many respects, Peter had every conceivable advantage: race, sex, health, wealth, family name, and the adoration of society and the press. He also had in his favor a culture that increasingly turned to science to explain worldly phenomena once the purview of religion, economics, or other disciplines. After the Civil War, industry was booming, and people put faith in the scientific and engineering fields perceived to be launching the nation into the modern age. And although they remained devout, fewer Americans regarded fortune and misfortune as acts of God. Instead, they turned to fields like biology and medicine to understand what it was about people that made them rich or poor. Before his daughter became prey to it, such unquestioning faith in science helped to put Peter on a pedestal.

Peter attributed his achievements to the work ethic his father ingrained in him. Abram Hewitt had incessantly reminded Peter and his siblings that he and their grandfather had worked their way up from humble to distinguished households. He told his children that he'd only eaten meat on Christmas Day and worn clothes made with wool baize cloth. His meager wardrobe had prompted his schoolmates to call him "Baizy," a nickname that he'd never forget. Determined to rise above these hardships, he had consumed every printed fact within reach and earned a scholarship to study at the prestigious Columbia University. There he'd reaped his rewards. He met their uncle Edward Cooper and agreed to tutor him, visiting the family's Lexington mansion and seeing their mother, Amelia. The first time he met her, she was still wearing her hair in braids. Then one day, she appeared in full bloom, and he couldn't keep away. He soon proposed.

At this point in his retelling of the story, Mrs. Hewitt would invariably interrupt, "I was never quite certain I would marry him till I walked down the aisle to the altar."

After wedding the daughter of Peter Cooper, Abram never wanted for anything. Still, he'd refused to be idle, even though it meant being away from his family. He believed there was dignity in hard work. Abram was absent for much of Peter's youth, serving for nearly a decade in the US Congress and then as mayor of New York City. The Democrat defeated Theodore Roosevelt for mayor by campaigning on the promise to close gambling houses and other unsavory places around the city. "We need to clean up New

York and restore it as a reputable place for its citizens and visitors," Hewitt urged. The people agreed. They believed the millions of opportunity-seeking German, Irish, Russian, and Slavic immigrants coming to the city had brought with them depravity. Such hostility toward these foreigners inspired some New Yorkers to propose expanding the current law prohibiting "undesirables" (Asians) from entering the country. If they were going to protect against disease and drink, and preserve the opportunities supposedly available to all who worked hard, they needed to keep America American.

While her husband represented the great state and city of New York, Amelia Hewitt devoted herself to maintaining the family's properties. At the Ringwood estate, she added plush blue upholstered furniture to improve the ambience at the musicales and recitals she hosted for the family's many guests. She hung the paintings of Thomas Cole and other members of the Hudson River School to reflect current trends. And she made sure that her children received the best governesses money could buy. But besides overseeing her children's moral and intellectual education, as Victorian mothers were expected to do, Mrs. Hewitt largely left them to their own devices. She believed children should find their own amusements, apart from the world of grown-ups. Consequently, Peter and his brothers had great freedom to act unruly.

The Hewitt boys were known to ride sleighs down the front staircase and out the front door at the Lexington Avenue house, knocking down anyone in their path. They also had a reputation for pranking their family's many visitors. One of the boys' favorite tricks was to wind a fine silk thread around the lamppost in front of the mansion and then thread it through a crack in the parlor window. From just inside the window, they lowered the thread to tip the hat from the head of a passerby. With even greater skill, the boys could snap the cigar out of a man's mouth without letting him see or feel the string. If the string touched his nose, the man was bound to proceed up the walk and ring the bell. When this happened, the boys quickly broke the thread and closed the window to eliminate the evidence before a servant called for them to explain themselves.

Once, during a big snowstorm in the city, the boys dropped a giant snowball on top of a drunken man from their perch on the flat roof of their gymnasium behind the house. (Believing a sound body was essential to a sound mind, their grandfather had acquired gymnastic rings, a horizontal bar, and a flying trapeze for them.) When the individual dug himself out, he was sober enough to get a policeman, who came to arrest the boys. But as usual, the Hewitt sons were crafty and hid under the gymnasium floor where, years before, they had discovered a trapdoor in the floorboards, which opened to a space wide enough for several adolescent bodies. Anytime they saw or heard the police approaching the house, which occurred rather often, they fled to this refuge and held their breath until they heard no more footsteps overhead. Mrs. Hewitt knew very well what her boys were up to and even played along. She often sent inquiring authorities to the gymnasium knowing they would never find her children.

The neighbors eventually learned not to bother involving the police in petty matters. If they found a broken window or pulled doorbell, they simply had the damage repaired and billed Mrs. Hewitt. The lady paid the invoice without question.

In this permissive environment, Peter developed the attitude that the world largely existed for his amusement. There was little he couldn't do or have. Far from being rebuked for this opinion, he was encouraged by the press—that was, until he laid claim to passion and a profession. Peter symbolized the values that members of the press held dear. At a time when record numbers of unwanted immigrants were populating northern cities, Peter represented the virtuous American breed perceived to be in peril. At a time when industrial urbanization was forcing hundreds of thousands into poverty, Peter signaled both the promise of science and technology, and the great wealth to be had by those who rolled up their sleeves. And at a time when middle-class white women were beginning to yearn for greater livelihood outside the home, he and his first wife symbolized the stability that Victorian gender norms offered.

In 1887, the twenty-seven-year-old Peter married the twenty-year-old daughter of millionaire banker Frank Work in a fashionable ceremony at Grace Church on the corner of Broadway and 10th Street. Just like Peter's mother, Lucy supported her husband's scientific pursuits by encouraging him and staying out of his way. She'd long been told that intellectual men like Peter were prone to "neurasthenia" (fatigue, headache, and irritability from performing intense mental labor) and that if she flaunted herself when he came home, her husband might grow weak.

Though she didn't inquire about the technical details of his experiments, Lucy proudly told dinner guests about the research he was conducting in his laboratory in the tower of Madison Square Garden. Once, when she shared that her husband was experimenting with an X-ray machine recently invented by Wilhelm Conrad Röntgen in Germany, the dinner party decided to get into their cabs and drive to the tower see the marvel. Peter turned on the apparatus and asked which lady would like to go first. When no one volunteered, Lucy stood in front of the fluoroscope, and guests oohhed and ahhed at the image of her ribs and steel corset on the screen. Another woman stepped up to take her turn. This one, dressed in a beautiful satin dress, stood exactly as Lucy had done, but instead of awe, the other ladies burst into laughter. The screen revealed that the bones of her corset were twisted and misshapen.

She demanded to know what they found so humorous, but her company refused to explain.

It wasn't the only time a dinner guest was humiliated by some technology in Peter's laboratory. Once, the inventor's friend Dr. Robert Abbe brought a tube of radium from France to show off its strange properties. One of these was the ability to make diamonds fluoresce in the dark. When Dr. Abbe turned off the lamps in the room, a woman brought her diamond ring close to the tube. Immediately the ring glowed. Another guest brought forth her own ring, which consisted of three very large diamonds. When she held it close to the tube, only the middle jewel lit up. There was a hush among the crowd, and soon after, the lady and her husband rose to return home. It was rumored that they fought the whole way, with the woman threatening divorce unless her husband replaced the paste jewels with real ones.

This woman's embarrassment paled in comparison with Lucy's, when Peter was arrested in 1890. When the inventor and his party exited the theater on the night in question, they found their carriage blocked by a cabman and his horse. Cooper Hewitt asked the saddled man to back his horse up and allow his wife and her friends to enter their vehicle. The cabman refused, and so Peter seized the horse by the bridle. This prompted the cabman to rise in his seat and whip him over his back. The ladies gasped, while Peter hopped onto the box and broke his cane over the cabman's head. The two men began to exchange punches and insults, while crowds quickly formed. A police officer came upon the scene and placed Peter under arrest. Despite the indignant protests of theatergoers, the newspapers reported, the officer "brutally handled" Peter, dragging him to the 30th Street station house and abusing him with foul epithets along the way. At the station house, the officer locked Peter in a cell without giving him a chance to speak.

James D. Townsend, one of Hewitt's friends, appeared, having witnessed the scene and protested the handling of his chum. He'd demanded that the officer hold Peter by the arm, rather than the collar, and that the officer transport him via cab or streetcar, rather than on the sidewalk. Both of these demands were ignored. At the station house, Townsend tried again to defend his friend. "You have no right to detain this man," he told the officers. "I insist on speaking with the sergeant this instant!"

The officers laughed.

"Do you know who my father is?" Peter tried. "Abram Hewitt, the former mayor of this town and one of its most revered citizens. He'll be outraged to learn how your police force treats members of the public."

"I don't care if you're an Astor or a Vanderbilt," said the arresting officer. "I'd have run you in all the same."

Abram Hewitt soon arrived at the station. The former mayor immediately secured the release of his son and filed charges against the policeman for the "unwarranted treatment." He outwardly assured the sergeant that he did not consider his son special. Rather, he was pressing the complaint on the grounds that this kind of treatment was liable to be received by anybody, if he didn't intervene.

The incident provided fodder for conversation in clubs and hotel lobbies for the next week. Diners were indignant about police methods, while busboys snickered at the thought of Peter Cooper Hewitt being dragged, kicking and screaming, down Madison Avenue on a Saturday night. It wasn't often that a member of the upper class was held to account—even briefly—for deeds that would sink others, especially once experts began to conceive of criminality as an inherited trait. Noble families relied upon pardons for their lawbreaking members to protect the clan's reputation.

When the excitement died down, Abram took the opportunity

to raise another matter with his son: Peter's seeming lack of business application. The elder Hewitt was somewhat depressed by the fact that Peter spent many secluded hours in his den in Madison Square Garden without having anything tangible to show for it.

"Peter, my boy. What are you doing up in that tower?" the gentleman asked at the dinner table one evening.

"Making a lamp," Peter replied.

"What kind of a lamp?"

"An incandescent one."

"Hmph!" said Mr. Hewitt, raising a napkin to his lips. "I hope you're not wasting your time."

Lucy pretended to be uninterested in this conversation, though she was eager to hear her husband's reply. Only three years into the marriage, the two were already beginning to lead totally independent lives, and some of the women in her circles had begun to whisper. It was one thing to have distinct interests and hobbies, but quite another that she and her husband barely crossed paths.

"I think not, sir," said Peter without looking up from his plate.

Peter continued to pass his days in his tower while his wife spent her time with other society ladies, attending luncheons and organizing charity balls. In a room reportedly "no larger than a Harlem flat," Peter worked in overalls to rival the invention of Thomas Edison. Beneath him, in Madison Square Garden, roaring crowds gathered and dispersed for horse shows and bicycle races. But Peter could hardly hear them over the humming of his machines.

Hewitt's goal was to produce light without heat, proving wrong the many scientific men who declared cold light impossible. In 1901, after years of plodding, Peter came down from his tower with a glass tube in his hands and a grin on his face. He took the object to the Engineers' Club on West 21st Street to show his peers what one newspaper described as a "large thermometer with an electric wire at each end." In it, heat melted mercury into vapor, transforming the electricity into light. The lamp's bluish-white flame was bright enough to light the street for one hundred feet. That evening, those standing outside the club were awed when a radiant beam suddenly appeared, illuminating the pedestrians and carriages before them. According to one reporter, some onlookers thought it was the Second Coming.

The newspapers described the invention as groundbreaking and the scientist as a genius humanitarian. "Peter Cooper Hewitt looked around to discover the most inefficient branch of mechanical science, the one in which there was the greatest field for improvement," a *San Francisco Call* writer wrote. "He decided that the manufacture of light was the most backward department of modern engineering activity, and he set out to improve its condition."

This reporter had the honor of touring Hewitt's laboratory to get an idea of Peter's mysterious work habits. The experience convinced him that the inventor was cut from the same cloth as the sage of Arthurian legend. "The room was such as Merlin might have occupied. Dark hangings covered much of the wall space; from the ceiling hung festoons of electric wires, tangled and twisted like the creepers of a tropical forest; and here and there stood reflectors and brackets of unfamiliar shape." In such an environment, the reporter explained, "it was not difficult to imagine Peter Cooper Hewitt in the role of a magician, and indeed, that gentleman's somber clothing, with white only at the throat and wrists, lent reality to the illusion." Another reporter observed that the elevator boys in the Madison Square Garden tower referred to Hewitt's laboratory as "the wizard's den." In his hideaway, Mr. Hewitt didn't even interrupt his experiments to go outdoors for lunch or tea;

he could save himself forty minutes daily by having his food and drink delivered.

There was just one problem with Hewitt's lamp, as one of the authors above noted—it had a ghastly effect upon human beings. It had no red rays (to allow for greater efficiency), and this distorted an individual's complexion. "Even the most beautiful woman in New York becomes a hideous sight under the rays of a Hewitt lamp," a newspaper explained. "The human flesh loses its tints. The reddest lips become blue, and the face and hands turn purplish yellow with dark blue blotches. It is as if the corpses of a morgue suddenly sat up and talked and acted if they were still alive." Another publication printed, "If a man wishes to know how he'll look when he's dead, all he has to do is study his face in the Looking Glass under the light of the Hewitt lamp. Under this magic, light oak furniture appears light green, and brown wallpaper becomes gray. The whole color scheme of the universe is upset by the rays Mr. Hewitt has discovered." If the image-conscious Maryon had been a fixture in Peter's life at this point, she certainly would have urged him to rectify the problem before taking the invention public.

It soon became clear that Hewitt's lamps would never work in a department store or an artist's studio, let alone a private residence. In an interview with a reporter, Peter insisted that people could work around this issue. "All you need to do is cover the sample with red silk colored with rhodamine dye. The rays lose their ghastly effect at once. They are still far more brilliant than those from an Edison lamp." He added that he would soon improve upon the technology, obviating the need for silk screens and perhaps even enhancing the glow of human beings. "It is within the range of possibility that, by means of these color effects, a woman of forty may be made to look like a girl of twenty. The light of the future is one generated by vapors."

An Englishman realized the commercial potential of the current technology. George Westinghouse understood that a vapor lamp without red rays cast little shadow and didn't strain the eyes, in addition to emitting little heat and not requiring wires. These features could transform industrial spaces, he intuited. Soon after Hewitt's invention reached him in London by boat, Westinghouse cabled the inventor to say that he would finance the product. He also helped to secure fifteen patents for the technology. In 1902, the two men formed the Cooper Hewitt Electric Company to produce and sell the new lamps to factories across the country. The money from this venture would grow Peter's wealth well beyond his inheritance.

One year after he debuted his mercury-vapor lamp, Columbia University awarded Hewitt an honorary doctorate for his achievement. After the much-publicized hooding ceremony, his reputation grew. No longer only the grandson of Peter Cooper, he was now an accomplished inventor himself.

"My light is better and cheaper than daylight," he matter-of-factly told a *McClure's* reporter in his looming tower. Peter sometimes came across as boastful, before persuading his guests of his brilliance.

The reporter scratched his head. "How is artificial light better than natural light?"

"When the human eye focuses upon an object—any object—it involuntarily exercises its muscles for different colors. If the color is predominantly red, the eye focuses to that—or to blue, if that is the predominating color. But where the colors are pretty evenly balanced, the eye will focus from one to the other from instant to instant. Daylight contains a number of colors—red, yellow, green, blue—and so it requires constant labor. This causes fatigue and is very hurtful to the eye."

The reporter hurried to scribble down these points.

"All right," the interviewer acquiesced. "But how is your lamp cheaper? Daylight costs nothing."

Peter stood and walked to the window, peering at the many buildings below. "Have you ever tried to build a big office building in the city?" he asked with his back turned. "When you face the problem of building a skyscraper in which every room must have an adequate supply of daylight, you are appalled by the amount of space you have to sacrifice in order to achieve that end."

The reporter declared in his story that Hewitt's lamp was indeed practically and economically superior to the sun. He also quoted Peter as saying of his youth and early adulthood, "I was always planning and contriving, and was never satisfied unless I was doing something difficult—something that had never been done before, if possible."

Other writers similarly portrayed Peter as a daring frontiersman, a member of a species that distinguished America. What other nation could boast the likes of Benjamin Franklin, Eli Whitney, Thomas Edison, Peter Cooper, and Henry Ford?

Sometimes, people remarked to Peter that he was fortunate to have the means to persist with his vapor experiments for so long. Had it not been for his private wealth, they suggested, the project might have been abandoned years ago.

"That is not true!" Peter invariably corrected. "I have always had to make my laboratory pay as I went along." He did not clarify how he made his laboratory pay or what external gifts, if any, he received.

Throughout his life, Peter earnestly desired to identify as a self-made man, as his father and grandfather had always been regarded. Contrary to many other Gilded Age elites, who claimed to be inherently virtuous and, therefore, deserving of their many advantages, he yearned to prove himself to the public. Peter understood that, since its beginnings, America had idealized the men whose potential seemed to lie within themselves, rather than in their material or social conditions. Benjamin Franklin was such a man. The quirky polymath had risen above his humble boyhood in a candle shop to found a nation, explain electricity, invent streetlamps and bifocals, and transform a wide range of scientific fields. Abraham Lincoln, Andrew Carnegie, and John D. Rockefeller embodied the same spirit of ingenuity and determination, according to Peter.

But of course, all of these men were full-fledged, rights-bearing citizens; and Carnegie and Rockefeller had made much of their money by creating monopolies within their respective industries, poorly paying workers for long shifts under unsafe conditions, and unethically trading on the stock market, earning the nickname "robber barons." Peter failed to appreciate these realities. Though his views were more egalitarian than those of his peers, he was still somewhat oblivious.

The press mainly described Hewitt as a man who achieved great things *despite* his station, implicitly agreeing that character transcended economic and political circumstances. "Once in a while, it is given to the sons of the rich to ride out of the ranks and distinguish themselves in the field of might," the *Detroit Free Press* wrote of Peter's scientific accomplishments. This newspaper suggested that Hewitt might have rested on the family haunches and counted his money, were it not for his drive to make use of his talents for the betterment of humanity. Others remarked that Peter forsook a life of leisure to honor his namesake. Both he and his grandfather had been named after the apostle in whom Christ had entrusted his kingdom; and like the revered disciple, both had proven themselves to be fearless leaders of men.

No doubt, press like this was good for business. Shortly after

Peter's discovery was broadcast to the world, photography and film studios swiftly disposed of their old forms of lighting to make way for "Hewitt lamps." In the era of black-and-white film, the color of a photographer's light made little difference—the quantity was all that mattered. Peter's vapor lamps could be found on nearly every Hollywood set and in most blue-collar workplaces until the 1910s, when another incandescent form of lighting was developed.

By this time, he had built upon his lamp technology to create a three-pound rectifier (an object used to convert high voltage into direct current), replacing the seven-hundred-pound ones currently in use. He also developed a mercury-vapor interrupter, which produced rapid interruptions of currents, to improve wireless telegraphy. Hewitt won the prestigious Elliott Cresson Medal of the Franklin Institute for these children of his lamp.

Peter had also created a hydroplane motorboat, which rose and planed on four small wing-shaped hydrofoils that extended from the hull below the waterline. The gliding craft did not cut the water, but scanned the surface to allow for higher speeds. Hewitt demonstrated a speed of thirty-eight miles per hour in the Long Island Sound and then claimed he could soon attain one of more than one hundred miles an hour. Coming on land to speak with gathered reporters, the inventor pulled up his goggles and promised, "I'll bring London within thirty hours of New York."

Peter's father was no longer present to witness his achievements. The former mayor had died of intestinal problems in 1903, two years after Peter debuted his lamp. At least, before he passed, Peter had the chance to justify all those hours sequestered in his laboratory.

Abram's death delayed the grand unveiling of a private theater in the Lexington Avenue residence, constructed by Amelia, Lucy, and Peter's two unmarried sisters, Sally and Nellie. The theater was built to host hundreds of guests for amateur theatricals.

Before her marriage to Peter, Lucy had delighted New York and Newport crowds with her singing, dancing, and acting abilities. She had attended Alva Vanderbilt's infamous ball in 1883 in a Joan of Arc costume that so impressed a society photographer present that he commemorated her two years later in a *tableau* (a static live scene with one or more models). The artist named Lucy the "Maid of Orléans," and the moniker stuck among certain crowds.

When Peter began to drift away from her a few years into their marriage, Lucy encouraged her mother-in-law to build a stage within the family mansion. Here the women could host theater parties and play the popular game *tableaux vivants*, in which participants held a pose for thirty seconds while players tried to guess the scene from literature or art from which it derived. High-society women adored this game, as it allowed them to display their erudition and embody a new, and perhaps socially unacceptable, identity.

Amelia and Lucy hired an architect to fulfill the vision. A few years after Abram's death, the Hewitt women finally showed off their creation, inviting three hundred society persons to a program featuring Lucy and other actors in Guy de Maupassant's *Histoire du vieux temps*. The stage resembled an 1830 boudoir, and Lucy pranced across it in powdered hair and a rose-colored brocade gown with hoop skirts trimmed with lace. In the play, her character reunited with a count who had swept her off her feet forty years previously, before she married a marquis and became a widow. Perhaps Lucy revealed something to herself with that role: that she could survive—and even thrive—following the end of a marriage.

Over the next few years, she extracted herself from New York society, hosting and attending few charitable balls and making frequent solitary trips to Europe. The philanthropic world Lucy left behind dramatically transformed, as distinguished families started to rethink their charitable interests. By the beginning of the second decade, the Harrimans, Kelloggs, Carnegies, and Rockefellers were beginning to believe that their charity was exacerbating the social problems it was meant to resolve. After all, the poor were still poor, and the crippled still crippled; only now, there were greater numbers of poor and crippled persons.

This anxiety was not new. In the late 1700s, English economist Thomas Malthus had published a landmark theory on the nature of poverty, in which he argued that generosity to the poor was limiting the food supply and worsening social relations. In 1850, English philosopher Herbert Spencer reinforced Malthus's view when he declared that it was better to allow for the "survival of the fittest" than to uplift diseased, impoverished, and uneducated persons against the laws of nature. The wealthy families in the Hewitts' circles didn't suggest letting vulnerable populations suffer and die, only preventing the "unfit" from reproducing. Gregor Mendel's newly rediscovered laws on heredity made it possible to identify these individuals—or so they thought.

According to these elites, it was time for philanthropy to reflect the latest scientific developments. "From now on, our charity must be governed by science and rational analysis, not sentimental impulses," they declared. "Giving indiscriminately to the poor, as we have done for years, is wasteful and inefficient. We must cure evils at their source." Eugenics promised to eliminate social ills and, therefore, the need for charity altogether. If the rich supported researchers such as Charles Davenport and Harry Laughlin, there would soon be fewer alcoholics, criminals, and prostitutes on the streets and more Billy Sundays.

Ever since Andrew Carnegie's 1889 essay "The Gospel of Wealth," the rich had taken for granted that it was their moral responsibility to engineer society though their philanthropy. In that influential essay, Carnegie had argued as much, without once acknowledging how the mechanisms of unregulated industrial capitalism created an unprecedented disparity between the rich and poor, engendering the need for wealth like his to be wisely redistributed in the first place. Two decades later, it did not occur to the moneyed families financing eugenics that they and their ancestors had created many of the social problems now requiring radical reforms by blowing open the gap between the "haves" and the "have-nots."

Neither Lucy nor Peter ever became involved in eugenics. When his wife exited high society, Peter continued to devote his energies to his career. And, after 1911, to the beautiful woman who waltzed into his life—the one who would make him a target, and not only a beneficiary, of the gatekeeping society in which he lived. By seeming to unbridle the scientist's passions, Maryon revealed that elites like Peter had a duty to uphold the virtues of the upper class, whether they wanted to or not. The fate of the nation was at stake.

12

LOVE OR THE LAMP

Rumor had it that Peter hadn't been to Newport in years on the day he met Maryon Andrews. According to the newspapers, he simply decided one day to drop in and look the place over when she appeared before him like a magnificent light from the heavens, totally reordering his universe.

Naturally, his friend Reginald Vanderbilt was peeved when Peter stole Maryon for himself. He refused to speak to the inventor when they encountered each other at parties. Reginald wasn't the only friend Peter lost; many of Peter's fellow inventors snubbed him over the affair, thinking it a cruel repudiation of the wife who had long supported him and his pursuits. "Poor Lucy," they said. "She's graciously tolerated his obsessions, and this is how he repays her?"

Peter didn't mind losing a few chums, as it meant he could spend more time with Maryon. While abroad with his lover, Peter learned that his mother had died at the family's Ringwood home. She was eighty-two years old. Soon after, he endured an even greater shock: He was going to become a father.

When Maryon returned to her flat after sharing the news, Peter went to his study and opened a book on thermodynamics. When it didn't quiet his mind, he returned it to the shelf and took down a volume on magnetism. The pages of this text, too, failed to placate him, and so he began to fiddle with the glass tubes on his workbench. In his absentmindedness, he broke one of the tubes and gashed his thumb. He required two stiff drinks to fall asleep that night, and he'd already consumed champagne at dinner, upon Maryon's insistence. "Let's toast to baby," she'd said, filling their flutes.

For the next few months, Peter fretted about the prospect of parenthood. He didn't worry about the demands of the job— few men of his era did. Rather, what bothered him was the fact that becoming a father would shift the triangular dynamic among him, Maryon, and Lucy. Peter had a feeling that Lucy knew about Maryon and that she had found a way to live with the fact of her existence. But he wasn't sure that his wife could tolerate a mistress *and* a love child.

When little Ann came along, and he saw her for the first time in New York, Peter momentarily forgot his worries. The pink-skinned bundle was more precious than any earthly wonder he had ever considered. He examined the swirls on her feet and curled the dark ringlets on the nape of her neck around his finger. He admired the almond shape of her eyes and the tiny lashes that framed them.

Peter became concerned when Ann didn't gain much weight, still fitting in his palms at three months of age. Sometimes, when Maryon was out of the room, he would ask the nurse about the baby's feeding schedule. He didn't dare to inquire about it in front of Maryon; she would take offense at the suggestion that she was poorly supervising Ann's care. His mistress had many gifts, but maternal instinct didn't seem to be one of them.

When Maryon returned to France in the New Year, Peter considered writing to Lucy in England to tell her that he was leaving her. This would put an end to his constant fretting about the press exposing the affair—and also allow him to better observe Ann. But before he could act on this idea, he needed to finish his experiments with his oscillator. He had connected the gas and vapor device with electrical apparatuses to transmit wireless messages. Once he perfected the telephone receiver, enabling it to catch and amplify sounds for the human ear, he could present it to the public. No sooner had Peter announced his success in the *New York Times* than he received a call from President Woodrow Wilson's advisers asking him to serve his country. Realizing that America faced an existential crisis like never before, he couldn't say no.

Peter made frequent trips between Paris and New York so he could offer insights about the impact of developments in aviation upon warfare. In an extensive piece printed in the *Detroit Free Press*, he predicted that aeroplanes like the one he'd engineered would soon steer themselves and drop explosives on targets half a thousand miles away. There would be no limit to the chaos and destruction when weapons could move though sea and air. Hewitt believed this reality would ultimately bring the citizens of the world to their senses. "Civil populations will insist upon a war-less world," he said. "People will find themselves so incensed as to force a peace between their warriors." Hewitt's hopes for global unity would dwindle, and he'd eventually embrace the nationalist sentiment sweeping postwar America.

Lucy also felt called to serve her country. Peter's wife left her Gramercy Park mansion and boarded the *Kaiser Wilhelm II* to organize and oversee the Cooper Hewitt military hospital in Paris. On the transatlantic vessel, she dined with Supreme Court justice Oliver Wendell Holmes, whose opinion in Carrie Buck's case would indirectly shape Ann's fate.

Perhaps it was witnessing the realities of war that provoked Lucy to make major changes in her personal life. In December 1917, eleven months before the war ended and five years after learning of her husband's infidelity, Lucy returned to the United States to file for divorce. In the beginning of Peter and Maryon's romance, she'd seriously doubted that the affair would last. She'd even laughingly remarked to a friend, "Not even fascination of this tramp will keep him away from his beloved paraphernalia." But Ann's birth had changed the situation for her, as Peter suspected it would. Lucy didn't care to uphold the pretense of being Mrs. Cooper Hewitt any longer.

Peter learned of her intentions by telegraph while in Paris. He immediately put on his hat and hurried to Cartier's jewelry shop, where he asked to see the biggest diamond in stock. "That'll do," he said, seeing the sparkler.

When he slid the gemmed ring on Maryon's finger, the woman held out her hand and paused to consider her answer. "It's me or the lamp," she finally told him. "At least for the first two years."

Peter assured Maryon that he would devote himself to her—not only for two years, but for the rest of his life. Satisfied, Maryon agreed to travel with him to America to respond to Lucy's filing and then marry.

Once they returned to Paris, Peter allowed his young bride to take him to every party she fancied. The tall, gangly inventor even permitted Maryon to teach him the fox-trot, which he, in turn, taught Ann. A photographer captured one of his lessons with Maryon and displayed the image in the pages of a local newspaper, evidencing the American scientist's complete about-face. Peter winced at the thought of Lucy coming across the picture as she took her morning tea. At least he and Maryon took care to avoid the establishments his ex-wife was known to frequent.

But there being only so many fine restaurants in the city, it was just a matter of time before Peter ran into his old wife while with his new one.

One afternoon, the concierge at the Ritz Hotel received two phone calls for dinner reservations for a Mrs. Cooper Hewitt. On the second phone call, Monsieur Paul reminded the lady to whom he was speaking that she'd already placed her request. "No, sir," she said. "It only occurred to me a moment ago that I'd like to dine here tonight."

Monsieur Paul put the receiver down and considered the situation for a moment before the horror of it occurred to him. He decided to seat the former Mrs. Cooper Hewitt on the Rue Cambon side of the dining room and the current Mrs. Cooper Hewitt at the Place Vendôme entrance. With one hundred feet between them, the ladies wouldn't notice each other, he presumed.

But there was a mishap that evening, and seating for several dinner parties had to be rearranged. Tables were moved here and adjoined there. After all the shuffling, the two Mrs. Cooper Hewitts found themselves seated at the same table with the scientist between them.

Monsieur Paul listened with his mouth agape as a maître d' recounted these details the next morning. "What did they say?" he asked.

"Nothing at all," said the maître d'. "The bride went pale. The first Mrs. Cooper Hewitt went frigid. Her guests whispered."

"And what about Mr. Hewitt?"

"He just grinned awkwardly."

A society writer in the *El Paso Times* noted that Maryon left for Vichy the very next day, while Peter returned to his laboratory in New York. "Just what happened between the newlyweds after that fateful encounter is not known. But the fact remains that the promised first two years of gay life in Paris have been cut short,"

Barbara Craydon reported. Craydon delighted in the possibility that Peter was once again devoting himself to his experiments. "Has Peter Cooper Hewitt, Millionaire Inventor, Been Recaptured by Science Since His First Wife and His Second Met in a Paris Restaurant?" she asked in a subheading. The story featured a sketch of a man at his workbench, while a beautiful woman tried to pull him by the hand in the other direction. The moral couldn't be clearer: A man could have either romance or a profession, but not both.

In the writer's words, "When a man is wedded to science, when he has made great inventions, when he stares longingly at electric rays…marrying a woman is like tempting Providence." That's precisely what Peter did in wedding Maryon. But now, thanks to the awkward encounter in the Ritz Hotel, he might be going back to his wizard's den.

After the publication of Craydon's profile, rumors grew of a split between Maryon and Peter. Until he died in 1921, the scientist was troubled with questions about his marital life. On trips to New York, he couldn't go out to dinner in the city without someone approaching to express sorrow about the estrangement. He grew increasingly impatient with these busybodies, huffing and snapping his newspaper open to obstruct the sight of them.

The gossip mill churned even faster when the *Daily News* told of a "scene" alleged to have taken place between Peter and Maryon in a Parisian hotel, where the inventor became irate with his wife's amorous ways. "Tired of her flirtations with young society men, he used forcible means of showing his displeasure," the story related. The author didn't mention Baron d'Erlanger by name, but several Americans in Paris understood this gentleman to be the one in question. They had seen the Ritz Hotel employee escort the inventor's wife to dinner and the opera when Hewitt was known to be in New York. To stir readers' intrigue, the story captioned a photo of Maryon, "AN ESTRANGEMENT?"

In response to this news story, Peter told a prying newsman in Manhattan, "Such rumors are without foundation and utterly untrue. I have just received a cable from my wife, who is presently vacationing in Venice with our little girl, Ann. I plan to meet them there as soon as I resolve some business matters here in this city."

Peter's frustration with the reporters circling his marriage was soon eclipsed by worries of his declining health. Despite his weakness, he made it to the United States in October 1920 to vote for Republican senator Warren G. Harding in the presidential election. Though he'd been a lifelong Democrat, Peter liked Harding's promise to put "America First," which meant keeping the US out of the League of Nations to maintain diplomatic power. Peter may not have realized it, but a vote for Harding was a vote to expand a range of social programs meant to protect and uplift the American race, some of which Wilson had supported. Upon taking office, Harding declared his support for immigration restrictions, anti-miscegenation laws, involuntary sterilization, and other existing eugenic measures to "improve" human heredity. From Harding's perspective, the political realities of the twentieth century signaled the urgency of a "fit" citizenry—one that was white; mentally and physically sound; and middle to upper class.

Encouraging other nations to follow this lead, Harding's newly assembled state department invited dignitaries across the world to attend the Second International Eugenics Congress in New York in September 1921. Here authorities spoke about the need to eliminate the unfit from the population and to encourage the breeding of persons believed to have descended from good "stock." They referenced marble busts of perfectly proportioned men and women as evidence of sought-after physical traits.

Cooper family friend Alexander Graham Bell presided over the conference.

But by the time the American Museum of Natural History opened its doors to a standing-room-only crowd of conference attendees in Upper Manhattan, Peter Cooper Hewitt was in the ground in Brooklyn. He'd been buried in the family plot of Green-Wood Cemetery, after dying in Paris of complications from pneumonia and having his remains repatriated.

Following a ceremony in Grace Church, the same place where Peter had married Lucy thirty-four years earlier, mourners had walked with the family to the final resting place. There pallbearers had lowered the casket, covered with leaves and a heap of Easter lilies, into a pit. Peter's widow had kept her head bowed throughout it all. Every time Maryon peered out from her bonnet, she'd caught Edward and Erskine Hewitt giving her an evil glare.

In death, Peter Cooper Hewitt cemented his saint-like status. The newspapers commended him for his mind and the noble purposes for which he'd used it. "Mr. Hewitt was the highest type of man in every sense," columnists wrote. "He could have lived a life of luxury, but instead decided to follow in his grandfather's footsteps and serve humanity." All was forgiven, after all.

13

THE CRIMINAL TRIAL

On Friday, August 14, 1936, the long-awaited criminal mayhem trial of Drs. Boyd and Tillman commenced. Well before the clerk opened the doors to the San Francisco courthouse, reporters and onlookers had gathered by the hundreds, placing bets on everything from the heiress's wardrobe to the outcome of the trial.

Ann did not disappoint, arriving that first day in a tailored satin dress and matching pillbox hat. As soon as her chauffeur opened the car door and a jeweled heel extended to the pavement, the crowds swarmed around her. "Ann, what do you expect to happen?"

"I expect that justice will be served," said the young woman, releasing the arm of her driver to smooth the wrinkles from her skirt.

"And what is justice to you, Ann? A maximum sentence of fourteen years?"

"That's not for me to decide," said the heiress, straightening her shoulders as photographers angled for shots. "But I have full faith in the court to deliver the appropriate punishment."

"What about your mother? Have you spoken with her?"

"I haven't spoken with Mother since I moved out of our apartment about a year ago," said Ann.

"So you don't know her whereabouts?"

Ann looked around for her attorney, remembering that she'd promised not to answer any questions without Tyler at her side. "I don't have a clue where or with whom Mother is. All I know is that she's not where she's supposed to be, which is here in California, answering for her crime."

"Do you believe your mother may make another attempt on her life?"

"Mother has always tried to avoid reckoning with the things she's done to people. But I pray she won't take such extreme measures again. I only wish for her to answer for what's she done."

"So you won't blame yourself if she succeeds?"

Ann winced, before taking her driver's arm again and pressing through the crowd.

Once inside, she spotted Tyler in the bench behind the prosecution, where she'd been promised a seat. She walked toward him with her chin high, pretending not to notice as heads turned and fingers pointed. A few minutes later, a clerk escorted the two physicians to the table where I. M. Golden and Harry McKenzie, the trial lawyer appointed to assist Golden, were shuffling papers.

Ann marveled at the grins on each doctor's face and the ease with which they awaited the proceedings, exchanging thoughts and chuckles. Tillman, especially, looked as though he didn't have a care in the world. This led her to wonder if they knew something she didn't. Had her mother taken action to influence the outcome of the trial? She knew for a fact that Maryon had recently tried to lure Tyler away from her. Was it possible that she'd tried to sway the judge, too?

When Judge Raglan Tuttle entered the courtroom, she scanned his face for evidence of something sinister. But all she saw was a man who seemed emboldened by the scene before him, sitting as tall as he could and clutching his gavel with an air of self-importance.

The first task of the day was to select the jury. One by one, Golden and McKenzie managed to strike mothers from the panel, just as Tyler had told Ann they would. "They'll want to weed out those who might be sympathetic to your situation," he'd explained.

"That hardly seems fair," the heiress had replied.

After several hours of interviewing candidates and whispering to each other, Golden and McKenzie were finally pleased. They had nine men and three childless women. The main proceedings could begin.

Assistant District Attorney August Fourtner, who led for the state, began by calling medical persons to establish the fact of Ann's operation. The first was a surgeon, Dan Delprat, who claimed to have examined Ann in January 1936 to confirm that she was, indeed, sterile. Then an X-ray specialist took the stand to verify his colleague's findings.

"There was no doubt about it," said the second expert. "Her fallopian tubes had been removed."

"And did you find that strange?" asked Fourtner. "That the organs had been completely removed?"

"Well, ordinarily, female sterilization involves cutting and tying the organs, rather than taking them out."

"And what did you make of that? At the time?"

"I thought, 'Gee, I suppose someone wants to make doubly sure that she can't become a mother.'"

Fourtner paused, surprised that neither Golden nor McKenzie objected to his line of questioning. He then called Irwin Wallace, the anesthetist who attended to Ann before the operation.

"You administered the analgesic to subdue Miss Hewitt, correct?" the prosecutor began.

"That's correct."

"And for what purpose did you believe you were subduing the patient?"

"To prepare her for surgery."

"And what surgery was that?"

"Sterilization."

"You're certain it wasn't for another surgery?"

"I'm certain."

"Did you know that the patient was also about to undergo an appendectomy?"

"I don't recall. But it was clear that sterilization was the primary reason for operating."

"Thank you," said Fourtner, returning to his seat.

When McKenzie stood to cross-examine this witness, Ann expected him to refute the man's conclusions. But he did no such thing. Instead he asked Wallace about her sex complex. The expert gasped before answering, "I wouldn't know about that."

"You mean you didn't know *why* the patient had been volunteered for sterilization?"

"Not exactly, no."

"Do you know why most women her age undergo the procedure?"

"I suppose it is because their family members request it."

"And did you know that, in this case, the patient's mother had requested it, after trying for years to rehabilitate her from an addiction to sex and masturbation?"

Ann leaned over to Tyler. "What is he doing?" she whispered.

"Planting seeds," was the reply.

The heiress crossed her arms. Then Tyler cleared his throat, and she returned them to her lap, remembering that she wasn't to show any disdain for the witnesses. Sadness or hurt was all right, but not anger, Tyler had instructed.

"As I said, I didn't know why the surgery was requested," said Wallace. "That's not my job."

"So you didn't know that this particular patient had tried to run off with her driver? Or that her mother feared her becoming pregnant out of wedlock?"

"No, I did not."

"Do you assist many patients who undergo sterilization?"

"Yes."

"So you don't object to the practice?"

"No."

"Is that because you believe it will benefit those who are operated upon? Perhaps saving them and their children from a lifetime of poverty or sin?"

"In many cases, yes."

"And have you ever asked any of your patients what their wishes are, as they prepare for the procedure? Or do you trust the authority of their physicians and the family members who volunteer them?"

"I've not asked any of them," Wallace admitted.

"That'll do," said McKenzie, returning to his seat.

Ann looked at Tyler again.

"What they're doing," he explained, "is making the case that only medical experts can identify mental states. They'll say it can't be left to just anyone to decide the severity of a person's intellectual deficiencies."

"So only their opinion holds weight? It doesn't matter what my friends have to say about me?"

"Precisely," said Tyler.

"And they're going to allow that? They're going to let them say whatever they want about me?"

"Don't worry," said Tyler. "The prosecution has a plan."

Next the state introduced the affidavits submitted by Drs. Boyd and Tillman in January. They intended to note the discrepancies between the doctors' stories and Ann's. As Tyler had explained to Ann the day before, they planned to reveal that Mary Scally's psychological exam was perfunctory, as the doctors had already agreed to operate upon Ann.

"And the jury will see it that way?" she had asked.

"Well, there is the matter of payment, too. The jury will find it suspicious that they each received such extraordinary sums. And the timing is curious. Your surgery took place just months before your majority, while your mother still had a say in your affairs."

But when the court clerk read the affidavits, it seemed to Ann that the documents only provided an opportunity for the entire courtroom to collectively turn and stare at her. She could feel the heat in her cheeks as the clerk read Tillman's words: "I felt completely justified sterilizing Ann both from a moral and scientific standpoint. After all, the young woman had been labeled a high-grade moron." There were snickers throughout the courtroom. "Mary Scally is a psychologist," the clerk continued, "who is qualified to discern mental states. There was no reason to question her conclusion. I also happened to know Ann well, having observed her for a period of six months both as her physician and a friend of the family. She was unreliable, easily influenced, untruthful, and dangerously over-sexed."

Laughter erupted, and Ann glared at Tillman, thinking of one time the round-faced man had come to their apartment to visit her mother. Maryon had been indisposed, and, not wanting to be scolded for being inconsiderate of their guest, Ann had tried to sit and exchange niceties with him. But rather than talking about the weather, the physician had been keen to know what sort of man attracted her. He'd been told Ann liked working-class men—was that true? Was it also true that Ann had lost her virginity to a bell-hop? When Ann avoided his questions, he leaned over and tucked a curl behind her ear. "You're too pretty to give yourself to just anyone, Ann," he'd whispered. Just then, her mother had emerged from the down the hall, and he'd cleared his throat. "So, Ann, I hear you're an avid painter. I wouldn't mind taking a look—I'm an artist myself."

Ann had gone to her room and slammed the door, only to face her mother's wrath the next morning. "I've lost my patience with your ill manners, Ann," Maryon had fumed. "You've always been possessive of me, but I won't allow your behavior to stand in the way of my own happiness."

The clerk continued reading Tillman's statement: "I believe it is an injustice to all concerned to allow the feebleminded to bring children into the world. I would have taken the same action if it were my own daughter."

The heiress couldn't stand to hear another word. She thought of turning and walking out of the courthouse right then and there, but she'd promised not to create a scene—not to do any-thing that jury members might perceive as erratic. So she forced herself to remain composed as the clerk finished reading Tillman's statement and then Dr. Boyd's, which reiterated the same points. Both men admitted to receiving payment for the procedures, but maintained that there was nothing unusual about the amounts. And because they hadn't physically taken the stand, the state had no opportunity to cross-examine them. The jury had received both men's carefully crafted statements without either having to undergo questioning.

When the court recessed for lunch, Ann began to approach the prosecution's table, before Tyler grabbed her arm. "No, Ann."

Then, in a hushed voice, "This is a criminal case. You can't be seen to be collaborating with the state."

So she'd gone outdoors, meeting hordes of reporters on the street.

"Ann, what do you think of the trial so far?"

"I think it's clear to all that a vile crime has been committed."

"Are you planning to testify this afternoon, Ann?"

"If I'm called."

"And what will you say?"

"I'm going to tell my story is all."

But when she took the stand later that day, Ann fumbled when trying to tell her side of things. Her nerves overcame her, and she suffered three paroxysms of coughing. The first fit didn't gain much notice; the judge merely told the bailiff to bring her a glass of water. The second one, occurring only a few moments after the defense began to cross-examine her, caused the crowd to whisper. Then Dr. Tillman muttered something under his breath, and the men surrounding him laughed.

She recovered herself long enough to answer a few questions about Tyler and the Bruguieres, whom McKenzie was trying to implicate in a conspiracy against Maryon. The defense attorney wanted to show that his clients were merely caught up in the plot.

"Miss Hewitt, why did you go to your mother's ex-husband after you learned of the operation? Why not a friend?"

"Mr. and Mrs. Bruguiere are my friends. And I had no one else I could trust with my secret. Mother saw to it that no one liked me."

"I see," said McKenzie. "And how did they take the news?"

"They were horrified, as anyone would be. They said they'd known Mother was shameless when it came to money, but they never imagined she'd do something so awful."

"And what did you advise you to do?"

"They said I ought to get an attorney."

"And what did you say to that?"

"I told them I already had one."

The defense attorney paused. "Could you state his name for the record?"

"Russell Tyler."

"And he's present today?"

Ann looked at her attorney, who nodded at her. "Yes."

"When did you hire this man to work for you?"

"Well, my mother arranged for him to handle some of my affairs. That was a few years ago, I think."

"So he was your mother's attorney?"

"Originally, yes."

"Which means this man presumably had knowledge of your mother's assets."

Ann glanced at Tyler again. "Probably so, yes."

McKenzie paused to allow this fact to resonate with the jury. "All right. When you approached Mr. Tyler about this matter, were you alone?"

"No."

"Who was with you?"

"My friends, the Bruguieres."

"Do you always bring friends along when tending to legal affairs?"

"No," said Ann, feeling the tickle in her throat return.

"Then why did you involve them?"

Ann began to cough. "Because I was scared," she managed to say. "I wanted support."

"And you think the Bruguieres were there to support you—and not to spite your mother, with whom Mr. Bruguiere has an unsavory history?"

The heiress took a sip of water. "Yes."

"And now you're suing your mother for half a million dollars?"

"That's right."

"Is that what the Bruguieres told you to do?"

As Ann began to cough more rapidly, Judge Tuttle leaned toward the witness stand. "Yes or no, Miss Hewitt?"

But Ann had succumbed to another fit and was unable to answer the question.

Chatter spread across the courtroom, and a light flashed, even though photographers had been prohibited from using cameras during testimony. Ann observed Tillman grinning at her.

"That's enough," said Tuttle, smacking his gavel. "I'm going to recess for the weekend. We will resume on Monday morning. Miss Hewitt, I trust you'll rest over the weekend?"

The red-faced heiress nodded and hurried away from the stand and down the aisle, Tyler at her heels.

When Ann returned to the stand on Monday, she redeemed herself. She'd spent most of the weekend rehearsing her statements before a mirror. "The defense is perfectly correct in stating that there has been a conspiracy," she calmly told the court during Fourtner's redirect. "They have failed, however, to correctly identify the conspirators." Ann then told of the coordination between her mother and doctors, which resulted in her unknowingly having the operation. As she related the horrific moment when she'd realized what had been done, she thought she caught a sympathetic glance from two of the ladies in the jury box.

But her testimony didn't move the judge. "Remember that conspiracy requires the commission of a crime," Tuttle instructed the jury. "Therefore, we must first determine that one was committed."

It was becoming clear to Ann that Judge Tuttle did not look as kindly upon her as Judge Lazarus had in January. She suspected that, despite his pretense of impartiality, he'd allowed the press coverage to influence his opinion of her before the trial had even begun. Even those reporters who defended her couldn't help but inject patronizing comments about her appearance and childish personality. The *San Francisco Examiner* had written, "Ann is definitely no beauty, but has the humorous charm of a good-natured, changeling elf." An elf! Was it any wonder that so many people sided with her mother, when even her allies regarded her as subhuman?

Headlines dubbed Ann the "Duped Girl," in reference both to the surgery she unknowingly underwent and to the alleged conspiracy among her, Tyler, and the Bruguieres. "They think I'm stupid!" she'd complained to Tyler. "They all believe Mother's lies."

"Don't worry, Ann," her attorney had said. "We'll set them straight."

While on the stand, Ann also testified about her mother's neglect and abuse, corroborating trial witness Anne Lindsay's claims that Maryon had a drinking problem, among other bad habits.

"It's unfortunately true what my nurse said. Mother had a terrible fondness for the bottle. When I was very young, and we were living in France, she'd leave me alone in our apartment to go out to parties. My maids used to jabber about her in French. I knew enough of the language then to pick up that they were very disapproving."

"And did you ever accompany your mother to these parties?" Fourtner asked.

"When I got a little older, I did."

"And what happened on these occasions?"

"I saw for myself how recklessly she behaved."

"Did she ever become violent?"

"Well, one night Mother was very drunk, and we went downstairs for dinner. She saw two men we knew and insisted on dancing in front of them. She was wearing this negligee kimono thing, which could have been modest if she'd sat in one place. But she had to show off on the dance floor, and the garment flapped open. People began to point, and so I chased her down and begged her to sit with me. She pushed me to the ground and told me to mind my own business."

"Were there other times she harmed you?"

"Yes," said the heiress, peeling back a white glove to reveal cigarette burns on her forearm. "On more than occasion, she treated me as her ashtray. She also used to slap me for being courteous to waiters or other people in the service industry."

"Oh?"

"She accused me of flirting if I smilingly asked a porter to bring me a glass of water."

"How would she have preferred for you to ask for it?"

"She wanted me to snap, 'Get me a drink!' That's how she spoke to servants."

"All of them?"

"Well, no," said the heiress, remembering a key part of her testimony. "Mother had a fondness for certain working-class men."

"But she's said the same of you," said Fourtner with feigned surprise.

"That's because Mother felt that way about workingmen and so naturally she expected me to."

"So she encouraged you to pursue men in uniform?"

"She encouraged me to at least toy with them."

"Can you be more specific?"

"Well, she once pushed me to leave a note for a waiter she found attractive," Ann explained. "She wanted it to say where we were staying in the city. I told her no, but she could do so if she liked. She said, 'All right.' But it turned out she used my name instead. I learned this when the man came to our hotel looking for me."

As the questioning continued, Ann found herself talking more freely about her mother's abuse than she ever had before. And she didn't have the slightest remorse for it.

When, at last, Fourtner concluded his questioning, Golden cross-examined Ann. In lieu of challenging the heiress on her salacious claims against Maryon, the attorney refocused the conspiracy charges upon her, Tyler, and the Bruguieres. This time, he went so far as to suggest that the three parties intended not only to extort Maryon for half a million dollars in damages, but to push her to end her life. "Mrs. Hewitt has tried to commit suicide and for many weeks lay near death," he told the jury. "If she had died, all the income under the Hewitt estate would have gone to Ann. Just think about that for a moment."

When Tyler took the stand for the prosecution to testify that Maryon had offered him a generous sum in exchange for dropping the civil case against her, Golden interrogated him on the same subject.

"What exactly are you purporting Mrs. Cooper Hewitt said to you?" Golden asked, crossing his arms in front of the witness.

"She said, 'What will it take to make this problem go away? I should think $10,000 would do the trick,'" Tyler replied.

"And what did you say?" asked Golden.

"I quickly disabused her of the opinion that she could manipulate the case."

"I see," said Golden. "So the girl offered you more than $10,000?"

"Excuse me?"

"How much did Miss Hewitt pay you to file the civil suit?"

"That's none of your business!"

"Was it a handsome sum?"

Tyler slammed his fist on the table, rousing the jury. "My fees are none of the business of the court. Just as your fees are not."

"All right," said Golden, raising his hands to signal he would drop this line of questioning. "Then let me ask you this. Why did you shift your attention to Ann's affairs? You were hired to be Mrs. Cooper Hewitt's attorney."

"I fail to see the relevance of this question," said Tyler, glaring at prosecutors Brady and Fourtner for not raising an objection.

"Just answer the question, Mr. Tyler," said Judge Tuttle.

"As the court already knows," said Tyler, looking back at Golden, "it was Maryon Cooper Hewitt who initiated my work for Ann. She asked me to handle a few matters related to Ann's estate."

"Hmm," said Golden, drumming his fingers on his chin and turning to face the jury to observe their reaction to his next question: "Was this about the time you learned Miss Hewitt was to inherit a large amount of money from her father, the late inventor?"

"Objection!" Fourtner finally intervened.

Golden raised his hands again. "That is all, Mr. Tyler."

After several more days of testimony, most of which rehashed the well-known content of previously filed affidavits, the twelve people in the jury box appeared to be stumped. One side asserted Ann's innocence and the other her deviance. One asserted Ann's intelligence and the other her imbecility. One associated sterilization with lawlessness and the other with order.

But these individuals' opinions were never solicited, as Judge Tuttle dismissed the case. "This is a useless expenditure of public funds," he declared. "The prosecution has completely failed to make a case against the defendants. The evidence is simply not meritorious enough to be given to a jury." According to the judge, sterilization in California was not a crime; therefore, mayhem had not been committed, and there had been no conspiracy to commit it.

Both doctors wept from their seats at the defense table, while Fourtner vehemently shook his head and declared the court's action "all wrong." Ann did not betray a single emotion. When the gavel struck, the heiress simply stood and walked out of the courthouse. Her driver was waiting on the street, ready to speed her away from reporters demanding her reaction to Tuttle's move. But once the vehicle turned the corner, she stomped her feet and began to scream.

In a written opinion, Tuttle elaborated that there was no proof of any bad faith in the case. "The most that can be said," he claimed, "is that there were suspicions and innuendoes, which certainly would not sustain a verdict against defendants." The judge disagreed with the prosecution that the timing of Ann's sterilization (occurring within a year of her twenty-first birthday) was meaningful. He claimed, "The law makes no distinction between a case where the minor is nineteen years of age and where the minor is five years of age." From a legal perspective, "both are under the identical disability so far as consent to an operation is concerned, and the parents or guardian have the same power to consent in each case." If this reality leads to situations that are unjust, "then the remedy is with the legislature and not the courts."

Brady and Fourtner immediately implored the court of appeals to reopen the case, claiming Tuttle had conducted the trial in "a disorderly fashion." One week later, on August 28, 1936, their appeal was denied. Popenoe and Gosney, who had been quietly following the case in the newspapers, slapped each other's backs. On August 29, Popenoe wrote to Golden, "May I join my congratulations to the flood of them which I am sure you have been receiving, for your smashing victory which the appellate court seems now to have made complete."

Golden accepted this praise with a note explaining that though the case wasn't fully closed, he was confident he'd prevailed. "Since you wrote, the District Attorney has made an application to the Supreme Court for Writs similar to those which were denied by the Appellant Court," Golden explained. "But in my opinion, the Supreme Court will likewise deny his application."

He was right. Later that day, the California Supreme Court refused to reopen the mayhem case.

There was not a single protest, riot, or even op-ed written to criticize the decision. In fact, locals expressed agreement with the use of surgery to protect traditional family values. The author of a weekly column in the *Los Angeles Times Sunday Magazine* noted an increase in public support for sterilization after the trial. Fred Hogue commented, "I find there is a growing interest in a more extended enforcement of State sterilization laws. This increasing interest comes chiefly from women, most of whom are mothers."

Hogue claimed to have received many letters from women confiding their sympathies and reporting concerns about certain women in their community who had no business rearing children. The writer published some of these letters, such as one from a thirty-one-year-old reader who wrote, "I am amazed in this day and age right-thinking people let imbeciles have children. Why, and when will a law be passed to stop this?"

Emboldened by the case's outcome, Popenoe sent hundreds of copies of the court decision to private physicians around the world. So did F. O. Butler, the director of the Sonoma State Home. Judge

Tuttle's ruling had basically authorized sterilization as a medical solution to domestic environments deemed lacking. In doing so, the ruling lessened the burden of proof to demonstrate a woman's unfitness for motherhood, while also distancing sterilization efforts from the race-based programs developing in Germany. At the time of the trial, authorities acting on behalf of the state had to produce evidence of disease or degeneracy based on one's family tree or intelligence tests, albeit very skewed ones. Going forward, they only needed to establish that a woman had a morally bankrupt mother; it followed that she would become such a mother herself.

Popenoe wondered if the shift in criteria would actually help authorities to focus on working-class and minority women, such as Mexican Americans, who often had no apparent disabilities but were long believed to be reckless breeders. Just two years before Ann's case made headlines, he'd observed that such women in California had, on average, 5.2 living children, few of whom were of "superior quality." With a new rubric for establishing feeble-mindedness, authorities could simply cite a minor offense, such as truancy, and the number of one's siblings to make a case for sterilization.

Also, in denying that mayhem had been committed, the case might have actually affirmed individuals' right to sexual pleasure, Popenoe thought. Prior to 1936, legal scholars had struggled to apply the definition of mayhem (the "unlawful and malicious removal of a member of a human being or the disabling or disfiguring thereof or rendering it useless") in sterilization cases because they couldn't pinpoint the primary purpose of the female sex organs. If the organs' primary purpose was reproduction, these scholars reasoned, then a case of mayhem could indeed be made. However, if the organs' primary purpose was gratification of sexual desires, then there was no case for mayhem. Which was it? Though

Golden hadn't specifically intervened in this debate during the trial proceedings, his victory for the defense suggested that pleasure was a right of all and procreation a privilege of the certain few.

This meant that now more than ever, eugenicists needed to emphasize societal interests over individual ones. Rather than simply claiming that sterilization was protective or even curative, they needed to stress the impact to society when defective individuals reproduced.

But for all its immediate and potential impact, there was one thing the mayhem trial of 1936 didn't do: let Maryon Cooper Hewitt off the hook for the criminal charges brought against her. In fact, after the case against the two doctors was dismissed in August, the San Francisco district attorneys were more determined than ever to extradite the woman from New Jersey to stand trial on conspiracy to commit mayhem. As far as Brady and Fourtner were concerned, Ann's mother still needed to pay for her odious crime.

PART III:

___

THE AFTERMATH

Undated photo of Paul Popenoe of the Human Betterment Foundation. *(Paul Bowman Popenoe Papers, American Heritage Center, University of Wyoming.)*

Eugenics Society Exhibit (1930s). *(Image from Wellcome Library. Creative Commons 4.0. Public domain.)*

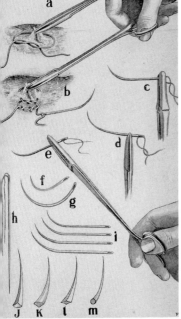

A sketch of salpingectomy surgical techniques. *(Originally published in E. C. Dudley's* The Principles and Practice of Gynecology: For Students and Practitioners *[1904]. Wikimedia Commons. Public domain.)*

A 1910 postcard of the Sonoma State Home complex, where inmates were forcibly sterilized. (*Scanned from the personal collection of Alex Wellerstein. Public domain.*)

Peter Cooper Hewitt holding his mercury-vapor lamp in 1900. (*Library of Congress. Public domain.*)

Lucy Work in Joan of Arc masquerade costume in 1885. (*Wikimedia Commons. Public domain.*)

A *San Francisco Call* story on Peter Cooper Hewitt's celebrated lamp. "A Light Better Than Daylight." *(Published January 26, 1913.* Chronicling America: Historic American Newspapers. *Library of Congress. Public domain.)*

"Mrs. Maryon Hewitt McCarter of San Francisco and New York, wealthy and socially prominent, was sued for $500,000 by her daughter, Ann Cooper Hewitt, 21-year-old Heiress on Jan. 6, 1936 in San Francisco. Miss Hewitt in the suit alleged her mother had an operation performed to prevent the girl from becoming a mother in order that Mrs. McCarter would not lose the benefit of a $10,000,000 trust fund." *(AP Photo.)*

Ringwood Manor, New Jersey, home of the Cooper Hewitts. *(Photo taken as part of Historic American Buildings Survey. Library of Congress Prints and Photographs Division. Public domain.)*

A profile explaining scientist Peter Cooper Hewitt's attraction to his second wife, known to be a flirt. "Why Brainy Men Often Marry Frivolous Wives." *(Published September 16, 1919. Richmond Times-Dispatch. Public domain.)*

A profile of Maryon and Peter Cooper Hewitt suggesting that the scientist must choose between passion and a profession. "Love or the Lamp?" *(Published September 19, 1920. El Paso Morning Times. Public domain.)*

A story on Ann's contested legitimacy, following Peter Cooper Hewitt's death. "Awful Shadow That Menaces Baroness D'Erlanger's Daughter." *(Published June 17, 1923. Detroit Free Press. Public domain.)*

"Ann Cooper Hewitt, left, is shown in court where she testified on the sterilization operation she says was performed on her by trickery, Jan. 23, 1936 in San Francisco. Municipal Judge Sylvain J. Lazarus will decide whether criminal charges shall be filed against the heiress' mother, Mrs. Maryon Hewitt McCarter, and two physicians. At the right is Anne Lindsay, the girl's nurse." *(AP Photo/ RJF.)*

"Ann Cooper Hewitt is shown here being sworn before testifying before municipal judge Sylvain J. Lazarus, on the sterilization operation she says was performed on her without her knowledge or consent in San Francisco on Jan. 23, 1936. Judge Lazarus will decide whether criminal charges shall be filed against the Heiress mother, Mrs. Maryon Hewitt McCarter, and two physicians named in the case." *(AP Photo/ RJF.)*

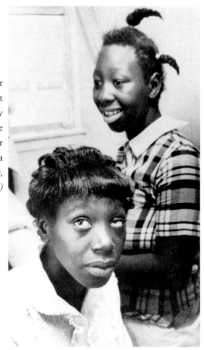

"Minnie Lee Relf, 14, left, and her sister Mary Alice, 12, who have had a suit filed in their names claiming that they were sterilized without their knowledge or consent, show reporters their bedroom in the family's apartment in a public housing project in Montgomery, Ala., June 28, 1973." *(AP Photo.)*

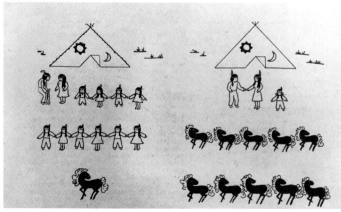

A page from a 1974 Department of Health, Education, and Welfare pamphlet encouraging sterilization of indigenous readers living on reservations. The page suggests that readers can grow richer if they have fewer children. *(Wikimedia Commons. Public domain.)*

A 1977 anti–forced sterilization poster by artist Rachel Romero. *(Library of Congress Prints and Photographs Division. Public domain.)*

Eugene Gordon, "Women's Strike for Equality," August 26, 1970. *(Photography ©New York Historical Society.)*

14

BURYING THE STERILIZED HEIRESS

A few days before her father died in 1921, Ann had stood by his bedside, holding her doll in one hand and his palm in the other. The little girl in braids made a promise to her father: that she would devote herself to finding a man just like him.

"Someone who has got brains and not just a pretty face. Will you find a man like that, Ann?" Peter Cooper Hewitt had asked.

The little girl nodded.

"Someone who has got integrity and a work ethic, and not someone who is going to rest on his laurels because he is married to a rich girl. That, too, Ann?"

Ann nodded again.

"And someone who can carry on my scientific experiments. There is so much more to do—so much more to give to the world. I can't bear to think of my plans collecting dust. Will you look for a man who can fulfill my visions?"

Ann had said yes, and her father reached to cup her cheek.

"That's a good girl," he'd said.

A few moments later, Ann's mother had come in to the hospital room and shooed her away from her father's bedside, ordering her home with Nini. The girl and her nurse had walked the few blocks to the family apartment in silence, with the nurse looking down every so often to see that Ann was holding herself together.

After she ate her supper and was tucked into bed, Ann waited until she heard Nini close the door to the guest room of the apartment. Then she sat up, tossed the blankets from her lap, and tiptoed to her father's study. In the drawers of his desk, she found stacks of papers—official-looking documents that she couldn't read and drawings of strange-looking lamps, engines, and other contraptions. She selected one of a giant aeroplane, folded it to one-quarter its size, and took it back to bed, where she slipped it under her pillow and cried herself to sleep.

Fifteen years later, Ann had ten thousand men to choose from. That's how many prospective suitors mailed her letters after the doctors' criminal trial in August. The majority of them had return addresses listing the United States, Europe, or Canada, though one had been stamped in China and another in Palestine. Ann's infertility didn't seem to bother these far-flung men, many of whom offered Ann a quiet, modest life in their hometowns. The heiress shared a few of the letters with a reporter, who came to her San Francisco apartment in September to interview her about the outcome of the mayhem case.

"Here's one from a man in Salt Lake City," said Ann, holding a paper before her. "He says he is twenty-six years old and a college graduate. He's sorry for me and wants to give me love and a home. H-O-M. Why, he doesn't even know how to spell!"

Ann tossed the missive aside and retrieved another. "Here's one from a man in Florida. He asks me to bring $30,000. The rest doesn't matter, he says. He only wants enough to build a house and buy a few chickens. Goodness! Couldn't he suggest anything that would make a girl a bit curious?

"Oh, you'll be amused by this one," said Ann, pulling another from the pile. "'I wonder how a man can be in love with a girl he's never seen, but I know I'm in love with you. I am a retired soldier with a small army pension. I offer you a nice quiet home in Washington with my widowed mother and me.'" She put the letter down to see the reporter's reaction. "Did you hear that? His mother!"

Ann told the newsman that she realized the majority of these men were after her money and not her. "They are proposing to marry my millions," she explained. "Still, if I come across the right man—one who loves me for *me*—I will entertain the offer. If I do marry, it will be for love."

"And what is love to you?" this reporter asked, his pen posed to capture her response.

Ann paused for a moment, then, noticing his impatience, said, "If I am slow to answer, you must be patient. You see, I usually do my thinking in French."

"Take your time," said the reporter, looking around at the apartment and making a mental note of the venetian blinds and the chrome ashtrays sitting atop every table.

"My idea of love is quite simple," said Ann. "Mutual understanding, admiration, and affection. The benefit of marriage is companionship, and I don't believe people should marry unless they have enough in common to adapt their lives to each other." The heiress paused to allow the reporter to record these details. "As for myself, I don't care if I have to wait to marry until I am thirty or until I am one hundred. I won't marry until I find a man whose interests are in common with mine."

"And what are your interests?" This writer hadn't read about any of the heiress's hobbies, other than her passion for running around with men in uniform. In the past year, Ann's sexuality had framed nearly every story about her.

"Well, I'm fond of good books, but art and music are my principal interests," she replied. "I like to paint. I enjoy landscape work, and I like to sketch with pen and ink. These things mean more to me than anything else in life. Isn't it just common sense that the man I select should have the same taste?"

"What if, by some unforeseen circumstance, your fortune were to change?" the reporter countered. "And you couldn't paint or draw. And you were forced to live a life of drudgery. What would you do then?"

Ann had been asked this question before. She was beginning to realize that most people didn't regard her as someone who deserved her fortune, especially now that she had no children to spend it on. Profiles of her often noted her extravagance alongside the fact the she could "take over a whole foundling asylum" if she wanted. But whose business was it if she'd rather spend her money on baubles than babies?

"I'd gladly go to work to augment our income," said Ann. "I have been reared in luxury, but I only want to live comfortably and with a man I love. I don't need all this," she said, gesturing toward the modern furniture in her Nob Hill apartment.

The reporter followed her hands to the furniture and then scribbled in his notebook.

"What about your mother?" he next asked. "Have you spoken to her?"

"No, I haven't," she said. "Last I heard, she was in a psychiatric ward in New York. I'm not going to fret about Mother. I have to look out for myself now."

"How do you suppose she is recovering from her near-death?"

"I'm not going to give one thought to that," said Ann. "As I said, I have my own future to consider."

In truth, Ann was worried about her mother. She had been

ever since February, when she'd learned that Maryon truly had attempted suicide. Tyler had called to explain that she'd been wrong—Maryon had not faked the event. He'd learned this from the nurse hired to accompany her at the Plaza. Ann had dropped the telephone receiver in shock. Of course she wanted justice for the wrong she had suffered; but she had never meant to cause her mother so much anguish.

While she'd told the world about her mother's incessant abuse, the truth was that there'd been some happy moments, too. She and her mother used to have great fun pretending to be other people, such as English royalty. They'd go through all the courses of a meal bantering to each other with accents and indulging their waiter's curiosity about what their second cousin, the king, was really like behind closed doors. Then there'd been the times they had pranked Maryon's suitors. Once, when her mother had decided to cut one loose, she'd arranged for her daughter to flirt with the gentleman while he waited for Maryon at the bar. Seeing the chatter under way, Maryon then "stumbled" upon them and caused quite the scene. They'd had several good laughs at the poor man's expense, their mirth growing with each bouquet he sent to apologize.

"So you don't regret pursuing your lawsuit? Even though it failed and it led to your mother's decline?"

"Not one bit."

In fact, when Ann had gotten off the phone with Tyler, she'd immediately dialed Pedar Bruguiere, her hand still trembling. She hysterically conveyed that she'd made a grave mistake. Her mother's ex and his wife had rushed to her apartment to console her. "She's manipulating you, Ann," Pedar had urged, while Mrs. Bruguiere went to put a teakettle on the stove. "She wants you to revoke your claims. Don't fall for her tricks!" Thanks to them, Ann had stayed the course and remained involved in the criminal proceedings.

After the reporter left her apartment, Ann began to smoke one cigarette after another, wondering if her mother would finally come out of hiding. With the two doctors free, she had little reason to fear a mayhem conviction for herself.

The heiress got her answer a few weeks later, when newspapers reported that Maryon had appeared in First Criminal Court in Jersey City for a charge related to her suicide attempt and one related to her fugitive status. Accompanied by her physician and her attorney, Mrs. Cooper Hewitt had kept quiet throughout the proceedings. Because no representative from California was present, the judge had postponed the case on a day-to-day basis for thirty days. He'd continued Maryon's bail and waived a hearing to await action by the grand jury. According to the papers, her mother was believed to have returned to a New York hotel, where she'd been living since her discharge from the hospital.

Two days after the hearing, the newspapers wrote that the governor of New Jersey was now in possession of papers from California asking for her mother's extradition.

Ann busied herself with painting and other hobbies until December 7, when the New Jersey governor read a statement from his assistant attorney general: "After careful consideration, I am of the opinion that Maryon Cooper Hewitt is substantially charged with crime against the laws of California, the demanding state, and that she is a fugitive from the justice of that State. It is legal and proper for the Governor of New Jersey to honor the requisition of the Governor of California for the extradition of the accused person."

But Maryon's attorney swiftly challenged the decision. William Breslin told reporters, "I spoke to Mrs. Cooper Hewitt over the telephone this afternoon and shared the sad news. I am afraid of the effect of the governor's decision upon her. Mrs. Cooper Hewitt is still a very sick woman." He further explained, "We will call her doctors, who will decide whether she can stand the strain of the long trip to California, to say nothing of the terrific mental ordeal of the case in California with her daughter present." Depending on the physicians' advice, Breslin explained, he and his client would determine whether to file a writ of habeas corpus, suggesting that Maryon was being unlawfully detained. He had absolutely no concerns about their chances of prevailing in California court. "I am confident of her acquittal," said Breslin. "Both doctors in the case out there have been acquitted, the California courts have decided that no crime is involved, and everyone knows that Mrs. Cooper Hewitt has acted in the best interests of her daughter."

While she was reading these updates, Ann's telephone rang. It was Deputy Prosecutor August Fourtner, calling to say he planned to hold his own press conference the next day. Ann thanked him for alerting her, but said she didn't want to attend. Instead, she'd read about the conference in the local papers.

"The state of New Jersey ordered Mrs. Cooper Hewitt's extradition yesterday," Fourtner told the small crowd outside the courthouse the following day. "I am ready to try Mrs. Maryon Cooper Hewitt on mayhem conspiracy charges as soon as she is returned to this state."

"But do you have a chance?" one of the newsmen asked. "You failed to convict the doctors of the same charge."

"Our case is ready, and we are anxious to start the trial," Fourtner said.

"What if she refuses to comply?" the newsman pressed.

"We have two deputy sheriffs ready to go after Mrs. Cooper Hewitt as soon as official word is received of the New Jersey action."

"What if she tries to flee?"

"We will track her down and return her to California."

Reading this exchange, Ann imagined officials bursting into her mother's apartment and taking her away, despite her protests. If her mother was as frail as her attorney claimed, she might never survive the train ride to the West Coast. She could suffer another breakdown or even make another attempt on her life. If she succeeded this second time, would Ann ever be able to live with herself?

Ann went to her telephone and dialed her attorney, telling him that she would not testify against her mother after all. She listened to Tyler sigh on the other end and regretted disappointing him, but she continued on, reading a statement that she'd carefully prepared: "In view of the existing facts and circumstances, including the claimed physical condition of my mother, I am reluctant to testify against her in a criminal proceeding at this time. I continue to ask for peace and privacy in this matter."

Upon hearing this, the prosecutors' office had no choice but to drop the criminal charges against Maryon. Without Ann as a witness, Brady and Fourtner couldn't justify putting the state to the expense of sending officers to collect Mrs. Cooper Hewitt and then trying her in court. The civil suit, however, would remain on the books.

Back in New Jersey, Ann's mother was cleared of charges of being a fugitive of justice and refunded her bail payment.

In December, a California judge declined to officially dismiss the mayhem charges against Maryon. "The charge has been filed against Mrs. Cooper Hewitt, and I feel it should not lightly be dismissed," said this authority. "I commend Miss Hewitt for her difficult decision not to testify in this case. However, that fact alone is not sufficient to close this case. I will continue the case to the summer of 1937."

Perhaps the judge hoped that Ann would come to her senses, allowing the prosecution to proceed. But Ann didn't change her mind, prompting another judge to remove—but again, not dismiss—the case from the court's docket eighteen months later. Her sympathy for her mother wasn't the only factor in her decision. Ann had tired of legal proceedings, and she longed to escape public scrutiny. Since the New Year, she had been excoriated by the press. The worst came when a satirist in the *New York Daily Mirror* had penned a poem about her, suggesting she was most upset about her mother ruining her sex life. An excerpt read:

> I'm only a sterilized heiress,
> A butt for the laughter of rubes,
> I'm comely and rich
> But a venomous bitch—
> My mother ran off with my tubes.
>
> Oh, fie on you, mother, you bastard,
> Come back with my feminine toys,
> Restore my abdomen,
> And make me a woman,
> I want to go out with the boys.

A known philanderer, Gene Fowler, had crafted this mocking caricature of Ann. Fowler's extramarital affairs often made it into print, but they didn't stop him from achieving moderate fame for his journalism and, later, his scriptwriting. It was only women like Ann who were punished for their private lives. And in her case, most of the claims weren't even true.

Fowler's attitudes toward Ann were by no means universally accepted, as the flood of marriage proposals from men around the world made clear. Many women also sympathized with the millionairess who'd testified, "I had no dolls when I was little, and I'll have no children when I'm old." That year, an aspiring actress assumed the role of Ann in the Federal Theatre Project, a New Deal program established to fund public entertainment and employ artists, writers, directors, and theater workers. The actress traveled from one city to the next, performing a poignant monologue based on the heiress's court testimony.

Much to Ann's relief, the press attention fizzled after the San Francisco district attorney announced that he was dropping the case. After nearly twelve months, she could finally walk outside her apartment for cigarettes without fear of being accosted. Still, she wore a hat to cover her face on the streets. She didn't mind sitting down to talk with someone on her own terms, but being hounded in public was another matter.

Ann was annoyed when a reporter knocked on her door in January to ask for her reaction to the news concerning Dr. Boyd.

"Dr. Boyd?" she asked.

"Yes, haven't you seen?" The visitor took a newspaper rolled under his arm and snapped it open for her to see. "Dr. Samuel G. Boyd Dead of Influenza," the headline read.

"Well, I've nothing to say about it," said Ann, closing the door. She then poured herself a glass of Pinot Noir to celebrate the news.

The heiress was even more irked in April, when a courier delivered papers related to a claim filed against her in county court. Eugene Fritz, owner of the Park Lane apartments, named Ann and her mother in a lawsuit seeking damages for unpaid rent and $25,000 to repair furniture, glass, and rugs in the Nob Hill district penthouse that she and her mother had occupied before she (and then Maryon) deserted the home. "The couches and rugs are ruined with liquor stains," Fritz wrote. "The beds and mattresses are unfit for use. There are gold-encrusted champagne glasses shattered. I have to refurbish the entire place."

A few weeks later, Ann was forced to appear before a judge in San Francisco to explain that she knew nothing about the damage and had never acted recklessly. When asked if her three Pekingese dogs had torn furnishings, she answered, "Absolutely not." As for the rent due—well, she was only a minor at the time of her occupancy. She was not responsible for mother's debts.

Thinking the former landlord had dropped her name from the matter, Ann became furious a month later when she noticed a few men following her around town and even up the elevator to the floor of her flat. She soon learned that the men had been hired by Dana Malden, head of an investigative agency in town. In August, she filed her own suit against Fritz, also naming Malden and the four assistants hired to trail her. "They've tapped my telephone wires and even those of my friends, the Bruguieres," she told the court. "I'm on the verge of a nervous breakdown."

Fritz denied the charges. "Ann Cooper Hewitt and her mother were tenants of mine in the Park Lane apartments several years ago," he responded in a pleading. "Since they moved, I have never seen Miss Hewitt and have no interest in her affairs."

When a representative of the court suggested that the spying might have been ordered at Maryon's request, Ann denied this. "My mother is in New York and has forgotten all about me," she said.

Ann was beginning to believe her mother truly had put her from her mind. When she'd refused to testify in the criminal case against Maryon, she'd thought her mother might finally make her way back west. If she was being honest with herself, she sort of hoped she would. Now that Ann was an adult, living on her own, she didn't need to fear Maryon controlling her like before. Perhaps they could be on friendly terms, meeting for the occasional lunch. But months had passed since her withdrawal from the case without any word from her mother.

Without evidence to substantiate Ann's claims against Fritz and his cronies, the court dismissed her case.

———————————

That summer, Ann turned to the Bruguieres for comfort and distraction from the events of the previous year. She even considered moving into the couple's flat, as she hated to be alone. It was in their company that she became better acquainted with Florence Slavish, the sister of the current Mrs. Bruguiere and an old companion of her mother. Tyler had solicited Slavish as a potential witness at the mayhem trial, due to her friendship with Ann and the Bruguieres, but the woman had refused to get involved. Soon after reconnecting with Mrs. Slavish, Ann began to attend her dinner parties in Oakland. At one of these, she met a garage foreman named Ronald Gay. The man with oil-stained fingers and a tool in each of his trouser pockets reminded her of her father. Gay did not care for gossip or politics; he preferred to drift to an obscure corner of his host's home to examine some neglected object, such as an old telephone or typewriter.

At Mrs. Slavish's nudging, the two began to see each other. Gay preferred taking Ann to his own favorite restaurants. He didn't like the way people at uppity places stared when he ate his food three big bites at a time or when he chewed a toothpick at the end of a meal. Nor did he appreciate reading about his scuffed boots in the newspaper after being spotted out with Ann.

"You might think of going to Bullock's to look for a new suit and shoes," Ann told him when he complained about the scrutiny.

"Now, Ann, we weren't all born with a silver spoon in the mouth," Gay replied. "I'm perfectly content with who I am. If you're not, you ought to say so."

The heiress didn't raise the subject again. She didn't want to start a fight.

Instead she allowed Ronnie to take her to neighborhoods where she'd never been, such as the Mission District. There she even agreed to eat the food of street vendors. The first time she was handed a hot dog fresh off the turning rods, she looked around to be sure no one was watching. Seeing only hipsters dancing to the beat of bongos and eclectic crowds gathering around a street performer, she lifted it to her mouth and nibbled a bite. Gay laughed and put his arm around her waist.

In October, Ronnie proposed with a modest solitaire diamond, which had belonged to his mother. As he slipped the heirloom on Ann's finger, she thought it some kind of joke. It didn't look important enough to grace the hand of a millionairess. But she still threw her arms around him and said yes.

After they shared the good news with the Bruguieres, they drove to Mrs. Gay's home in Oakland. The elderly woman was less excited, peppering them with questions.

"Exactly where do you plan to live?"

"I suppose I'll move into Ann's place for the time being," said Ronnie.

Ann nodded. She was relieved that no one expected her to move into the Gay home, where every appliance and furniture item appeared to be mail-ordered from the Sears Roebuck catalog.

Mrs. Gay then wanted to know if her son planned to quit his job.

"Of course not," Ronnie assured her. "You know me better than that."

When she went down the hall to use the toilet, Ann heard

Mrs. Gay whisper to her son, "It's too soon. You barely even know her."

Ann looked at herself in the bathroom mirror and frowned at her appearance. She hadn't bleached her hair for more than two years. Perhaps her mother was right that the dark locks made her look boyish. She reapplied her lipstick, straightened her shoulders, and returned to the living room in time to hear Mrs. Gay say that the next-door neighbors were pregnant again. Ronnie had promised her that he was content with having no children, but that didn't mean his mother would be.

On the drive back to San Francisco, Ann stayed quiet. She tried not to think about the conversation with Mrs. Gay. Ronnie loved her, and that was all that mattered.

Soon after this visit, the engaged couple traveled to Grants Pass, Oregon, to wed in a private ceremony. A county judge officiated with the groom's mother and a few friends there to witness. Ann had thought about writing her mother about their wedding plans, but decided against it. She desperately wanted Maryon to know that she'd found someone to love her, but she didn't know how her mother would respond, if at all. In the end, she figured it wasn't worth risking her happiness.

When the judge announced the marriage to the press, reporters flocked to the Redwoods Hotel, where the newlyweds were staying, and begged the two for a statement and photograph. The couple obliged.

"I'm going to live happily ever after," Ann raved, looking down at her ring finger. "I am happy for the first time in my whole life. I don't suppose you can understand what that means—to suddenly come upon joy and laughter and romance and tenderness." She turned to Ronnie, who beamed back at her.

When asked what she imagined of married life, Ann said,

"Ronnie and I are going to be ordinary people. People who never have their names in the paper. We're going to bury Ann Cooper Hewitt by pretending she never existed."

Her husband added that he would take drastic measures, if needed, to keep pests away. "My wife's got to have peace now," he urged. "She doesn't need people poking around her past. She's got to move on."

Back in San Francisco, reporters went to Pedar's house for a comment about Ann's elopement. "Elopement? I don't know if I'd call it that," the former physician corrected. "They've been dating for months. Long ago, I asked her why she was waiting, and she just laughed. I hope this will mean happiness for her." His wife added that she'd already selected a wedding gift from the department store. She, too, had known this day would come.

"Heiress Begins Life Anew; 'Happy for First Time,'" read a headline the very next day. The news story noted that the couple planned to tour the Pacific Northwest and then make their home in San Francisco. Other newspapers doubted the marriage from the start. "Can Ann Be Happy Without a Baby?" asked the *New Orleans Item.*

It seemed not. In January, after only a few months living together in wedded bliss, Gay moved back into his mother's house while the heiress remained in her fashionable apartment. After hearing both Ann's and Ronnie's sides of the story, the newspapers concluded, in a roundabout way, that Ann's infertility was to blame.

According to Ann, Ronnie was reluctant to commit. When a reporter appeared at her doorstep for comments about the split, she told the man, "He was constantly working. We didn't even take a real honeymoon because he said he couldn't leave the shop for that long. So, we never really had a chance to understand each other." Ann admitted that it was her husband's devotion to his trade that had initially attracted her. Seeing him tinker with car parts had reminded her of her father, she explained. But she quickly came to understand the dilemma of her father's first wife. "When a man is married to his trade, his wife is always going to play second fiddle. He's never going to love her the same way."

According to the mechanic, two different factors had brought the couple's happiness to an end: Ann's unwillingness to confide in him about her past and her unreasonable desire to make him her possession. Gay told a reporter, "If we ever get back together—and I sincerely hope we can work this out—it must be on a completely new basis and with a new understanding of what marriage really means. Trust." He explained that Ann was awfully sad most of the time, but she refused to talk about her feelings. She'd rather go out and forget her troubles. She'd pressured him to quit his job so they could spend more time attending parties. "That wasn't the arrangement," he'd reminded her. "I take pride in my work." The two had fought and even split in November over their differences. A mutual acquaintance had repaired the relationship, but it didn't last. "I'm going away now," Gay had finally told his wife. "But I'll be waiting for you when you change your mind about things."

Journalists interpreted this to mean that the woman reared in luxury expected her husband to escort her to social engagements. When her mate came home after a long day, Ann—who had slept until noon and then gone out for light shopping—wanted to dress him in a white tie, top hat, and tails. Perhaps if Ann had domestic duties or children to occupy her, there might have been a positive outcome. "A poor girl has to accept the fact that her husband is away working all day because, if he stays home to wait on her, there soon won't be anything to eat in the place," one writer opined. "A woman who cooks, cleans, and minds children is as tired as her man when he gets home. She isn't eager to start an argument about going places."

The Tennessean published a cartoon of Ann pushing a man in a baby carriage, alongside a story referring to Gay as a "compensation" husband. The author suggested that Ann dominated Gay to appease her "burning, unfulfilled desire" for a child to govern. This yearning purportedly began in Ann's childhood, when she'd been denied dolls to "dress, undress, and boss around in the imitation of the way her governess governed her." While her peers were being properly socialized toward motherhood, the author wrote, the little rich girl developed the feelings of a "cruelly-hurt child" that would haunt her in adulthood. For whatever reason, adoption didn't suit Ann, "nor the usual cat or dog compensation which seems to satisfy so many childless women." Instead, she sought a man to "dress...and boss around in most every other way until he fled from it all."

According to this writer, Ronnie's needs were completely reasonable—he only wanted to spend Sunday afternoons on a workbench, "trying out some inventions that were on his mind." But "Ann suppressed that desire as firmly as her mother had crushed the one for dolls." Lacking the chance to express her maternal instincts, the heiress had become psychologically abusive.

The image of the violent, childless woman was hardly new. Dating back to the ancient world, childless women have been portrayed as grotesque or even subhuman creatures who terrorize men, children, and even the earth. In Greek myth, the half-bird Harpies become beast-like and ravage the land to assuage their envy of others' fertility; and the Libyan queen Lamia becomes a child-eating monster after her children are killed and she is rendered infertile by Hera. In the Old Testament Book of Kings, a woman steals another's infant and then when brought before King

Solomon for judgment agrees for the baby to be cut in half, after her own infant dies. According to these tales, a woman is either nurturing or destroying. There is no middle ground.

Mid-twentieth-century experts elaborated on this myth by claiming that childless married women were even a danger to themselves. Those without children were prone to develop nervous disorders, as well as "emotional perplexities [that may] become serious enough to require the attention of a psychiatrist," a *McCall's* magazine writer reported in 1950. Some claimed that childless women were more likely to develop certain kinds of cancers. Fortunately, there were ways for these individuals to build "satisfying, complete" lives and protect their health, writer Elsie McCormick maintained. Florence Nightingale offered an ideal example; the childless nurse had saved countless lives across Europe by thinking of others, instead of herself. For this, she achieved a deep sense of personal satisfaction, according to McCormick at least.

But childless American women didn't have to go to such lengths, McCormick assured readers. They could simply socialize with friends and relatives with children, befriend shy youngsters, stimulate bright ones, or be a doting godparent. They could also volunteer in a children's hospital or improve their hometown. Such tasks not only benefited the community and promoted the volunteer's health, but also improved her social capital among mother circles. A "woman who does volunteer work in children's hospital wards or on recreation can barge into maternal shop talk without apology," McCormick explained. There was even something a childless woman could do better than anyone else in society: "comfort [her] friends whose children have left home and whose lives have suddenly crashed around their heads. The intelligent childless wife has learned how to deal with vacant hours and is thus in an excellent position to help her friends whose children have flitted."

By McCormick's logic, Ann's issue wasn't her infertility, but her unwillingness to apply herself to healthy forms of caregiving.

Privately, Ann did wonder if a baby might have made a difference in her marriage. "Perhaps if we'd had a little one, things would have worked out," she confessed to Pedar and his wife. "Of course, that is something that I can never realize." But she knew that her and Ronnie's childlessness was not really the problem.

When the tenth reporter came to her apartment fishing for more details, she revealed to this man that Gay had spent many nights in the living room, as he couldn't stand the sound of her crying. (She claimed to have cried often about their fighting.) She also used the opportunity to return her wedding ring. "Here, take this back to him," she said, pulling the solitaire diamond from her finger and handing it to the person on her doorstep. "It's the only thing I've got left, and I don't want it anymore. It was his mother's, so he ought to have it."

"Are you sure?" the man asked.

"I'm sure." Ann had never really liked the piece of jewelry anyway.

The man did as told, driving all the way to Oakland to deliver the heirloom.

Even after learning more of Ann's side of the story, the press maintained that Gay was innocent in the breakup. The only shortcoming that columnists admitted was the mechanic's marital cluelessness. "Mr. Gay knows how to fix most any motor element. He knows a drop of water in the carburetor can do wonders for the best of engines," a columnist for the *San Francisco Examiner* wrote. "But alas, he is not a marriage mechanic. He has no idea how to correct his problems with his wife other than to walk away." Just like Peter Cooper Hewitt, he was charmingly aloof, perhaps as a result of applying all of his brain to more important pursuits.

This popular characterization of white men as blunderers

developed in the 1920s and '30s to challenge the Victorian notion that the male species was prone to sexual aggression, requiring the female species to tame it. Social reformers now insisted that men were simply ignorant about ways to keep their women partners sexually and emotionally satisfied, and so they needed gentle instruction. (Black men, long perceived to constitute the greatest threat to white women, continued to be perceived as depraved.) The new perspective accorded women some respect in marital matters, while ensuring that men remained in control. Since men were simply buffoons, women no longer had permission to be squeamish about sex.

When Ann filed for divorce in March, citing "grievous mental suffering and temperament incompatibility," Gay didn't contest the action. The foreman merely brushed away the phrasing, saying it wasn't as though he'd tortured his wife. Ronnie told friends he was "completely fed up" with the notoriety he had received since their marriage in October. "It's rather exhausting being Mr. Ann Cooper Hewitt," he explained. "I led a pretty quiet life until I ran into this thing. I want to return to that life and be left alone." The comment greatly wounded Ann, who'd sincerely hoped the marriage would prove a fresh start.

She lost a close friend in the aftermath of the split. Because her spouse had been working all the time, she'd begun to pay a woman named Pauline Rodrigues $50 a week to be her companion. But Pauline couldn't tolerate the phone and doorbell ringing off the hook. "I'm sorry, dear. I just can't stand this chaos any longer," she said.

Ann was lonely again, but she soon got another chance at love. About a year later, the heiress met Gene Bradstreet, a bar steward at the swanky Army and Navy Club, where she often went for cocktails with Mrs. Bruguiere. The curly-haired, blue-eyed twenty-three-year-old slipped her notes with each martini he served. Ann took these home to re-read and hold against her chest, just as she did with some of her father's letters. Unlike Gay, Bradstreet was willing to go to parties and be photographed. In fact, he loved to have his picture taken. The drink maker aspired to go to Hollywood and become a film star.

Bradstreet hailed from New England, he told Ann. An ancestor of his had served as the first governor of Massachusetts in 1679. His parents wanted him to become a business executive, and he'd attended university with that aim; but on summer vacations, he'd spent all his time in theatricals. Instead of getting a traditional job as planned, he'd decided to become a ship steward and travel a bit. After doing that for a few years, he'd made his way to California.

Within months of meeting, Ann and Gene drove to Reno to be married. "You know I don't care about your money," Gene told Ann before the ceremony, which was witnessed by one hotel employee. "I prefer to be poor and make my own living, as I always have."

Ann nodded and picked up the telephone to call her bank in San Francisco. She had to arrange for $25,000 to be transferred to Honolulu, where they planned to honeymoon before settling down in Santa Barbara. Gene was going to take a break from juggling bottles to focus on his film career.

This marriage lasted exactly as long as Ann's first (three months). The greatest strain on the union had nothing to do with the bride or groom or even the press, but rather Maryon. Ann's mother died in New York in April 1939, pushing Ann to the edge of a nervous breakdown. When the young woman first learned of her mother's passing from a friend in a restaurant, she was overcome by emotion and unable to speak.

Maryon had died of cerebral apoplexy (a stroke) in her one-bedroom Beaux Arts apartment. After her body was removed to the funeral parlor, there was no one in her home to receive callers—a fact that haunted Ann. The Sunday before Maryon's death, Ann had received a telephone message from her mother. The operator had conveyed that Mrs. Cooper Hewitt regretted their estrangement and asked Ann to please call her back when she found the time. Needing time to process, Ann hadn't yet returned her call. Now she wished she'd immediately phoned.

The heiress was also tortured by the possibility that she was responsible for her mother's death. Even after her legal troubles were resolved, Maryon had never fully recovered from her attempted suicide and illness, nor from her fall from high society. She was plagued by debts and lawsuits, including one filed by a literary agent with whom she'd contracted to write her account of Ann's sterilization. Maryon never submitted the manuscript, suggesting to Ann that she truly did have regrets.

The attendance at Maryon's funeral was as slight as the *New York Times*' few lines covering the event. But Ann, who'd insisted upon traveling to the East Coast without her husband, barely noticed. She wept at her mother's graveside, suggesting to the few of Maryon's friends watching that she was, if not the ideal daughter, at least a forgiving one.

In a seventeen-year-old will, Mrs. Cooper Hewitt left all her money to her son. She justified the disparity between her children by noting that her husband's will provided for Ann. Maryon did leave furs, clothing, pictures, dressing bags fitted with gold, and household ornaments to her daughter, prompting the headline "Sterile Daughter Gets Knick-Knacks." As it turned out, the tchotchkes exceeded Richard's inheritance in value. By the time of her death, Maryon had assets totaling less than a few thousand dollars and liability of over seven hundred thousand. After the trial, both state and federal governments had sued her for back taxes, and some businesses had taken possession of her jewels to satisfy debts. Newspapers delighted in this, titling stories "Gold-Digger Dies Penniless." The fact that Ann's mother had died utterly alone also seemed to amuse writers. "Maryon Cooper Ends Belle Roll in Secluded Death," one journalist quipped. At long last, the loathed woman had received her due.

While on the East Coast, staying with an old friend, Ann developed a throat infection and a high fever, which required her to stay longer than she'd planned. During this time, she told her friend that her marriage was "up in the air." She couldn't stand to be with Gene anymore, she said. They just weren't compatible. Shortly after that conversation, she called her husband to tell him it was over. Maryon's passing had given Ann the clarity to realize how emotionally disconnected she was from her spouse.

"It was quite sudden. I never really understood what changed between us," Gene told the newspapers later that summer. "I made up my mind then to devote myself to my career in pictures. But one thing I do not want is to capitalize on any publicity that I have gained by being Ann Cooper Hewitt's husband."

In fact, Bradstreet hoped to do exactly this. He mentioned Ann's name in every audition he landed. One studio considered hiring the baby-faced actor simply to exploit the connection with the sterilized heiress. But the aspiring actor had so little talent that studio officials had to go with another candidate. Bradstreet had more success mentioning his ex-wife to potential mates. "We married because I felt sorry for her," he often reminisced. "All her life, Ann had everything she wanted when she wanted it. She never realized that there are some things money can't buy, like self-satisfaction and pride. She sometimes telephones, asking me to take her back." At this, most young ladies raised their eyebrows and scooted closer.

Ann dropped out of public sight until August 1941, when she was identified as the "mystery girl" in Tonopah, a gold-mining town in Nevada. She was seen out and about with Jack Whitaker, a six-foot fifty-year-old who had been prospecting in town for years. Shortly after local residents realized the identity of the woman in their midst, Ann and Jack married in a quiet ceremony, bought a mining property, and named it Anjax, a combination of both their first names. If it hadn't been for a photograph of the marriage certificate, readers in California might never have believed that Ann was the pretty girl in hobnail boots, Western clothes, and a sombrero hat standing alongside a man in the same getup.

The *Tennessean* profiled Ann in September with the headline "Ann Cooper Hewitt's Love for Working Men." In addition to suggesting that Maryon had been right all along (about her daughter's preference for men in uniform), the author derided Ann for her two failed marriages and her naïveté in thinking this latest union was based upon love, rather than Whitaker's need for someone to bankroll his mining adventures. "To get gold out of them thar hills, one must sink a lot of money into what may be just a hole in the ground. That would be Ann's part of the partnership," the columnist wrote. "If the land proves to be as barren as the heiress, the union is doomed," added another writer in California. It was agreed that the couple would never celebrate their second anniversary, as Ann was simply insufferable.

The marriage lasted longer than these cynics imagined. It outlasted a long snowstorm, during which the couple was forced to live on condensed milk and canned baked beans. It also outlasted Jack Whitaker's night in jail, after the miner decked a man in a saloon. The two were dining in town with friends when a guest from the East Coast remarked that he couldn't help thinking he had seen Ann somewhere before. "Don't you know?" asked another member of their dinner party. "She's the sterilized heiress." Others gasped, while Jack stood and lunged across the table at the man who blurted these words.

Columnists attributed the marriage's success to Ann's transformation. "After scrambling around on her feet all day, she comes home with her husband so dog-tired that she just wants to go to sleep," they observed. Finally, Ann had chores to render her a good wife.

The reality was that Ann hoped her third spouse would be the one to finally carry on her father's scientific mission. She had never forgotten her promise to the dying man.

At first, Whitaker entertained the idea of assuming Peter Cooper Hewitt's shoes. He let Ann show him some of the inventor's blueprints and patent applications, raising his eyebrows at certain machines—especially the ones that might prove useful on a mining property like theirs. Whitaker had always thought of himself as an amateur engineer, having invented a few devices for plucking things out of the earth. But whenever Ann suggested he take some time to read a mechanical journal or one of the books from her father's library, he preferred to take his glass of whiskey to the porch, cross his boots on the rail, and look down at the sage-covered mountainside.

After a few years, Ann grew tired of the view of the Smoky Valley. She missed the city skyline, with its angles jutting this way and that. She decided that Jack Whitaker was no Peter Cooper Hewitt, and there was nothing she could do to change that. Shortly after coming to this realization, she filed for divorce. Like her mother, she'd marry again.

15

MR. MARRIAGE

Had the case of Ann Cooper Hewitt come before him a few decades later than it did, Paul Popenoe might have categorized the heiress's sterilization as unnecessary. Rather than defending the doctors who'd operated on Ann from behind the scenes, Popenoe might have claimed that her sexual deviance could be cured with therapeutic and behavioral techniques within the context of a stable marriage—or that her alleged masturbation addiction could be channeled into a healthy sexual drive for a lifelong partner.

Following the famous sterilization trial of 1936, the mastermind behind the doctors' defense case began to focus his energies on positive eugenics (increasing reproduction among middle- to upper-class able-bodied white women). Along with Ezra Gosney, he realized the need for a tactical shift in eugenics—one that could carry the race betterment movement into the latter half of the century. In fact, even before the famous socialite came into the spotlight, the two eugenicists had created the American Institute of Family Relations, a spin-off of the Human Betterment Foundation, to promote alternative methods of uplifting the race. Rather than targeting individuals who had excessive sex outside of marriage, this institute's purpose was to ensure sexual compatibility *within* marriage through programs like couples counseling.

The institute outlasted Gosney by many years. Popenoe's colleague died in 1942, at which point Gosney's daughter liquidated the Human Betterment Foundation's assets, donating materials to the California Institute of Technology. This was all right with Popenoe. As far as he was concerned, the organization had done its part to promote selective breeding, and it was now time to focus on the other side of the eugenic coin. With this rebranding, Popenoe finally gained substantial allies on the religious right.

Couples counseling ensured that only fit people got married and that, once married, these people stayed together and reproduced—except in cases where one of the partners was physically or mentally unsound, rendering divorce an acceptable outcome. Not even infidelity provided sufficient grounds for divorce, according to Popenoe. If a woman found her husband with a lover, she ought to ask herself what she had done to drive her husband into the arms of another woman. Then she ought to swiftly redress her mistake. Every man was entitled to certain rights in a marriage: emotional security, financial security, sex, companionship, and children. Chances were, the woman had been lacking in at least one of the departments. "Do you encourage and inspire your husband?" Popenoe would ask. "Do you use his earnings wisely, rather than squandering them? Do you meet his sexual needs whenever he asks? Do you maintain a trim figure and wear smart clothing in becoming colors?" In cases where the woman was unfaithful, Popenoe wanted to know if the affair stemmed from feelings of resentment about her role within the home. If so, he'd try to persuade her to swap her academic and professional ambitions for a love of dishes and diapers, noting that college-educated women were overstuffed intellectually and starved emotionally.

Popenoe now fully devoted himself to the American Institute of Family Relations, training hundreds of church officials, youth group leaders, and other community authorities to counsel couples in accordance with his values. Fortunately for him, California brimmed with conservative-minded clergymen, probation officers, schoolteachers, nurses, and public health officials who shared his conviction that feminism and the "me generation" were going to degrade the American family if they didn't intervene.

Popenoe and his protégés also advised dating couples of their genetic risks, used personality tests to assess their compatibility, and ensured that couples were prepared to consummate the marriage. The eugenicist believed that a woman's frigidity or nervousness about intercourse could doom a marriage; fortunately, there were surgical treatments for these problems. For instance, in the case of nervousness, a doctor could cut a thick hymen (the tissue surrounding the vaginal opening) ten days before the wedding ceremony, making sex less difficult and saving a woman from having her marriage start off on the wrong foot. Daily vaginal exercises conceived by Dr. Arnold Kegel also helped. "There's no reason why a woman can't engage her Kegels while she is engaged in some of her housework," Popenoe often told clients. "By evening, her home will be sparkling, and she'll be primed for intimacy."

Over the years, the man dubbed "Mr. Marriage" claimed to have rehabilitated many "sex-crazed" women, in addition to "frigid" ones. He and his crew taught passionate women to avoid stimulation of the clitoris and to favor the missionary position, which allowed for males' "natural" aggression and females' "natural" passivity. They also retrained lesbian and bisexual women to prefer the penis and to embrace more feminine characteristics, such as modesty, meekness, romanticism, and sincerity. By the time of his retirement in the late 1970s, there were few sexual or temperamental dispositions for which Mr. Marriage didn't claim to have a fix.

After World War II, Popenoe believed a focus on restoring the family unit was especially critical, as the global conflict had allowed women to happily abandon their brooms for factory lines and filing cabinets. It had been noble of the weaker sex to step up and serve in the labor force, he said, but with the return of peace, women needed to be re-domesticated and de-skilled. Those who refused to let go of their day jobs compromised the well-being of their families and the nation. Workingwomen birthed fewer children, while also neglecting to raise morally upstanding ones, he reasoned. If America was to prevail as a world power, women needed to embrace their maternal responsibilities. Believing this, Popenoe especially disdained married women who shunned motherhood. "The wife who refuses to bear a child when health and eugenic considerations are favorable, and when her husband wants children, is refusing to meet a very important expectation," he wrote in 1952.

The marriage counselor and his cohort were not alone in thinking this, as the baby boom between 1946 and 1964 proved. After the war, white middle-class women faced increased social pressure to reproduce, as moral and medical authorities stressed that birth rates were essential to liberal democracy and world peace. Other nations, including America's enemies, were growing their human and military resources; the United States needed to keep pace or else risk nuclear annihilation.

In the decades following Ann's case, Popenoe reached millions of Americans, not singly through his counseling practice, but also through his guest publications in nationally circulated newspapers and magazines. In 1953, the California man founded and authored the popular advice column "Can This Marriage Be Saved?" in *Ladies' Home Journal*. In the pages of the much-loved magazine, he recounted the stories of actual clients for married readers' benefit and venerated white motherhood as the institution that would save civilization. The success of the column suggested that the public largely agreed with his sentiments. "Can This Marriage Be Saved?" was the longest-running column in the magazine's history, printing under other authors' names until 2014, when *Ladies' Home Journal* transitioned from monthly to seasonal issues. Before his retirement, Popenoe even collaborated with one of the magazine's editors to compile a book of favorite columns.

Over the years, Popenoe also appeared on radio and television programs, including a weekly advice show, *Divorce Hearing*, with Roswell Johnson. In this unscripted show, couples submitted disputes for the two authors of *Applied Eugenics* to resolve. Popenoe, who only left the house in a stiff white collar, was also a regular guest on Art Linkletter's *House Party*, a popular daytime talk show; and in 1950, he helped to produce the film *Modern Marriage*, based on his book of the same name about a psychiatrist who guides his depressed wife through her sexual problems. *Modern Marriage* played in over three thousand theaters across the nation. With all of his film and writing gigs, Popenoe had become a household name; and he couldn't go out in public without strangers approaching him for a handshake or an autograph.

But rumors of scandal surrounded him. Some gossip columns alleged that the man who saved marriages had a troubled one himself. His neighbors reported that a beautiful, sunglasses-wearing woman resembling Lana Turner frequented his house. In response to these charges, Popenoe explained that he counseled the blond actress in his own home to protect her privacy and that his wife was always nearby for these appointments—not that she had any reason not to trust him.

Some anonymous family friends whispered that the marriage was on rocky ground for other reasons, such as Popenoe's grueling work habits and his expectation that his wife devote herself to supporting them. In all of his married life, Popenoe had never scrubbed a dish or changed a diaper, and after years of homemaking, Betty Popenoe was tired of being his maid, these sources said. She had also never forgiven her husband for demanding that she abandon her passion (dancing) so soon after their marriage. Yet another informant claimed that political differences put a wedge between them. According to this person, Betty was a closet Democrat, and her authoritarian husband simply couldn't stand the possibility of her voting for a man as unscrupulous as Jack Kennedy. Despite the chatter, the Popenoes remained together; and until his retirement in the 1970s, the counselor idealized his own marriage as one for which youngsters should strive.

Thanks to the marriage defender's efforts to establish couples counseling as a legitimate discipline, marriage clinics popped up across the country, giving rise to the American Association for Marriage and Family Therapy, which now represents over twenty-four thousand marriage and family therapists, not all of whom embrace conservative values. After his death in 1979, Popenoe's torch passed to figures like James Dobson, an assistant at the institute, the founder of the Christian organization Focus on the Family, and host of the radio program of the same name; Jerry Falwell Sr., the evangelical who founded the political action group Moral Majority in the late 1970s to mobilize voters around conservative social values and the political candidates who espoused them; Popenoe's own son, David, who has written prolifically on traditional family values from a secular perspective; and other vocal defenders of strict sex-gender norms.

Both Popenoe and many of his predecessors rigorously resisted the "homosexual revolution" of the late 1960s and '70s, during which gays, lesbians, and other non-conforming individuals gained visibility and rights. Believing homosexuality to be "an intolerable evil that should not exist in a Sound society," the atheist Popenoe encouraged his clients to reject abnormal desires and pursue conventional relationships. He also explored methods to suppress homosexual desire, such as electroshock therapy, although it's not clear if his institute ever utilized this technology. The problem with same-sex unions, besides the fact that they threatened masculine power, was simple: They weren't productive. As such, they undermined postwar efforts to strengthen the nation through procreation.

But Popenoe did not die without witnessing major blowback to his program of positive eugenics. In the 1960s and '70s, when gays and lesbians were marching in the streets, white women also grew increasingly resistant to national imperatives. Not wanting to birth as many babies as authorities deemed necessary, they began to take legal action against hospitals standing in the way of the latest birth control technologies. Thanks to their efforts, the pronatalist agenda would finally begin to falter.

16

THE INQUEST

Thirty-three-year-old Ann had recently returned to California when she met a man named Frank Nicholson at the Sir Francis Drake Hotel in the Bay Area. The disc jockey, known to listeners as "Radio Roy," was several years her senior and already off the market. But this didn't stop the two from flirting at the bar. The married Nicholson mentioned that he'd just lost his assistant and asked Ann if she'd care for the job.

Not once in her life had the heiress ever considered going to work in an office, though she knew many women pined for such an opportunity. "Well, I don't type or take shorthand," she admitted.

"Oh that," said Nicholson, his face coloring a bit. "That doesn't matter. There's not much secretarial work in the ordinary sense of the word. It's mostly just answering calls."

"Well, I think I could handle that all right," Ann replied. She'd have to buy herself some smart-looking dress suits.

The following day, Ann visited Nicholson's Eddy Street apartment to further discuss the matter. There she met his wife, Gertrude, who took her fur and brought a cup of tea before pretending to sort letters on the other side of the room. The next morning, Ann reported to work at the radio station. It wasn't long before she found herself terribly in love with Frank.

The disc jockey felt the same way. The moment he went off the air, he'd toss his headphones, grab his jacket, and take her for a drive in his open-top roadster. Sometimes, when his wife was out of his town, he'd stay the night at Ann's apartment, and they'd listen on the radio to Frank's husky-voiced rival at another station. They shared stories. Nicholson said he'd been married before and showed her a picture of his teenage daughter, now living in Texas with his first wife.

After a few months of hiding their romance, Frank and Ann decided to go to his brother, Eugene, for his advice. He agreed that the situation could not go on. They had to sit down with Gertrude. So in the same living room where Ann had recently taken tea, the two matter-of-factly told Mrs. Nicholson that they were smitten with each other and there was nothing she or anyone else could do about it. They hadn't planned on this happening, they assured her. But alas, such were the circumstances, and the only solution was a divorce.

Mrs. Nicholson appeared to accept the explanation, not protesting or calling anyone names. Perhaps she already knew about the affair, having seen a lipstick-smeared handkerchief in Frank's coat pocket or a vanity case in his automobile. Ann had strategically placed these items hoping she would. She knew it was wrong, but she was desperate to have Frank—to be loved deeply by someone the way her father had once loved her.

The woman agreed that it would be better for her to seek the divorce and to do so quietly. With Frank's prominence in radio, it would cause a stir if he were to initiate the pleadings and then be seen with Ann. Scrupulous listeners might boycott his program, and then Frank could lose his job. Of course, this would mean that he wouldn't be able to pay his wife whatever sum the court deemed appropriate for her maintenance.

After the meeting, the disc jockey moved his things into Ann's apartment. He told Ann that his wife had threatened suicide when he packed his trunks, but he didn't think much of it. "Whenever she feels neglected or gets peeved at me, she threatens to end it all," he explained. "She's threatened it so often that I sometimes tell her to go ahead."

Gertrude was serious this time. Four days after being deserted, she was found dead of an overdose. A toxicology report found evidence of fifty aspirin pills in her stomach. Authorities might not have raised eyebrows had Frank and Ann not married the very next day. But before even alerting the deceased woman's relatives, the two lovers bounded down the aisle of a courthouse. According to the newspapers, the hasty marriage led local police to wonder, "How come the couple decided to clamber on the orange blossom special just twenty-four hours after the wife's death? And how did they obtain health certificates on the day of their marriage without a recent blood test?"

When first brought into the local police station for questioning, Ann and Frank refused to answer either question. A sheriff slapped them in jail, where the heiress sulked and Frank paced back and forth, swearing to himself. They were released with a date to appear in court for a preliminary hearing on charges of fraud. Officials suspected that they had falsified the blood tests and possibly even the health certificates needed to obtain their marriage license.

Blood tests, like sterilization, were first implemented as a eugenic measure, intended to protect "superior" persons (healthy whites) from polluting their germplasm with "inferior" traits. The blood tests required in California and twenty-five other states tested for venereal diseases like syphilis, which was believed to signal moral laxity, and certain genetic disorders like sickle cell anemia and Tay-Sachs disease, which were associated with African Americans and Jews, respectively. Though states imposed blood tests as a requirement for marriage, they didn't prohibit individuals from marrying based on results. Some states, such as Virginia, had other laws to criminalize marriage between "fit" and "unfit" persons. The Racial Integrity Act of 1924, for instance, punished blacks and whites who married. Blood tests were instead meant to encourage individuals to make eugenic choices themselves. Individuals were expected to consider their and their partner's test results and ask themselves, "Will the offspring of this union improve the quality of future generations?" According to their health certificates, Ann and Frank presented no symptoms or concerns.

While detained in the police station, Ann was indignant to learn of the pending fraud and conspiracy charges against them. "What about our honeymoon?" she asked the sheriff who had locked them in their cells.

"Honey, you'd better stay in town," said the man in uniform. "The city coroner is announcing an inquest into the motives for the suicide, as well. You're both to testify at that, too."

The couple went only as far as Sacramento, where Nicholson worked by phone to coordinate his wife's funeral arrangements. He agreed to provide the address where they would be staying in case the sheriff had to come for them.

With people gossiping about the scandal, the radio station temporarily suspended the disc jockey from his job. At first, station officials pretended not to know anything about the goings-on. When Bay Area residents dialed in to inquire about the cowboy with the nasally voice, Frank's co-workers simply said, "We haven't heard from him." But it soon became clear that the matter was not going to die down and, furthermore, that their adored personality could never emerge from the scandal unscathed. The station's listeners had come to the conclusion that, even if the jockey was innocent of his wife's death, he ought to have at least waited until after her burial before remarrying. So it was time for Frank and the station to part ways.

"We're going to be absolutely broke," Ann told reporters at the preliminary hearing for the charges against them.

"That's not true, dear. I made $16,000 last year, and you won't have to worry," her husband offered.

Ann ignored Frank. "I haven't any fortune left. All my money was to come from my husband. I'm a working girl now. That's why I was hired as his private secretary, you know."

But the heiress soon forgot her woes. On the morning of Gertrude's funeral a few days later, she was "all smiles," the newspapers reported. Before making their way to the church, she and Frank met with reporters in the home he'd occupied with Gertrude. "I'm going to have a boy," Ann told the newsmen crowding the living room. "A baby boy." A reporter who had been taking notes on the titles in a corner bookcase hurried over to hear more.

Frank put his hand on his wife's arm. "Well, Ann, we don't know that yet," he said.

Reporters glanced between the woman, dressed in black, and the man, dressed in brown slacks and a sports jacket. They made a note of Nicholson's outfit, which seemed like unusual attire for a funeral.

"No, not yet," Ann admitted. "But I've recently been examined by a doctor who said I might conceive a child. Since then, three other physicians have confirmed it."

The newsmen looked to Nicholson to corroborate this fact. An expert witness at the mayhem trial had confirmed that Ann had definitely been irreversibly sterilized.

"It's wonderful news, isn't it?" asked Frank. "All these years, she thought it wasn't possible for her to become a mother. And it turns out, by some surgical fluke, she can.

"My wife has become interested in Christian Science," Ann's new husband continued. "I've been practicing for years. With prayer, we believe she will conceive. But I suppose it remains to be seen whether it'll be a boy or a girl."

There was silence in the room before one intrepid reporter leaned forward to ask the question on all of their minds: "So is it a surgical fluke... or faith?"

"Both," said Ann, taking a sip from the glass of water in her hand.

Since meeting Frank a few months before, Ann had taken a keen interest in the radio man's religion. The philosophy of "mind over matter" appealed to the heiress, whose life had constantly been subjected to one determinist viewpoint or another. At the mayhem trial, she'd listened to a doctor say that her premature birth was to blame for her feeblemindedness. Then she'd listened as others objected that, no, it was her domestic environment that had doomed her. Then, after the trial, she'd been subjected to constant press predictions about her marriages. In fact, on the morning of Gertrude's funeral, she'd read one reporter's statement: "I wouldn't bet 160 to 1 that this thing lasts, the way it's been going." She was tired of being told where her life was headed.

Ann's insistence that she could become a mother also reflected the influence of classic myths about infertility. In the Western tradition, childless women are often told that they *can* conceive, if only they embrace a positive attitude or pray diligently. In Greek myth, the goddess Artemis blesses the mortals who make sacrifices at her altar. In the Old Testament, those who obey the Lord are promised fertility, among other blessings; and God "opens the womb" of faithful women, such as Abraham's wife Sarah. Generally, the only women who remain childless are those being punished for some grave sin. In the Bible, David's wife Michal is made barren for despising her husband. In early America, infertile women were often perceived to have been cursed for practicing witchcraft. The implication of these portrayals is clear: Whether she lacks faith or is atoning for other offenses, a woman who is infertile has only herself to blame.

This particular notion gained momentum in the 1940s, when medical experts increasingly believed that feminism was preventing women from becoming pregnant and that declining birth rates were a serious social concern. Without the technology even to know if a couple's infertility *was* attributable to the woman, many physicians began to blame infertility upon women's unconscious hatred for their spouses and their anger at having to do the child-rearing. After gaining rights at the polls and in workplaces, doctors claimed, women now wanted to wash their hands of motherhood. They preferred to pursue professional opportunities, rather than a decent-size family. Problematically, women's feelings of resentment about motherhood triggered spasms in the vaginal muscles, making conception impossible. Negative feelings about one's partner or one's own place in society could also disrupt the normal ebb and flow of hormones needed to reproduce, medical persons maintained. The solution to infertility, therefore, was for these women to quit their jobs or reduce their hours to focus on finding joy at home.

To promote domesticity, doctors published case studies of infertile women who left the workforce, or dropped to part-time employment, conceiving shortly thereafter. They also encouraged adoption as therapy. Adoption could trigger a "re-regulating of neuro and endocrine activity," one physician told peers of the

American Orthopsychiatric Association. It did so by compelling women to abandon their careers, thereby "breaking the vicious cycle" of women repudiating their roles and spewing bad eggs.

Because repressed fear and hostility were thought to undergird reproductive failure, psychoanalysis proved another popular treatment in the midcentury. In talk therapy, women could be trained to stop "emotionally boycotting" their fates, in the words of one psychoanalyst, and become more responsible citizens.

While she realized her infertility was not psychogenic, Ann nonetheless internalized the medical and scientific rhetoric surrounding childlessness, thinking pregnancy really was possible if she put her mind to it. Women's magazines abetted her thinking. *Ladies' Home Journal* and *Good Housekeeping* touted "miracle" pregnancies, profiling women who had been infertile for years before finally conceiving. These publications also wrote on new medical treatments, such as hormone therapy, X-ray treatment of the ovaries, and even tuboplasty to repair damaged fallopian tubes, which were alleged to be helping thousands.

Although seeming to conform to feminine ideals (pursuing motherhood against insurmountable odds), Ann's declaration of fertility was rather deviant. By claiming she would soon give birth, Ann refused the notion that she ought to be punished for her sexuality. She implicitly insisted upon her "fitness" for parenthood, despite having been declared "unfit" by psychologists, doctors, California courts, and even the American public. The heiress could have gone even further in adopting a child, but she didn't actually want one. She wanted to *be loved*, not show love. In husbands, she sought to compensate, not for the dolls she never had to dote upon, but for the father who had briefly adored her and the mother who never did. Her indifference to children aggravated members of the press, who preferred to think of childless women in constant yearning for a baby for whom to care, rather than as human beings with emotional needs of their own.

But even as she herself defied certain social conventions, Ann often belittled women by appealing to gendered stereotypes. Gertrude Nicholson was one such woman. Ann joined Frank in portraying Gertrude as jealous and unhinged, refusing to accept any responsibility for the breakup of the Nicholsons' marriage or for Gertrude's tragic death.

When pressed to explain the haste of his remarriage, Frank told reporters that he and Gertrude had grown hostile toward each other over the years. In fact, he said, his deceased wife had once come at him with a knife during an argument. She'd also thrown him out of the bed, breaking his leg. "I'm glad to be rid of a person who tried to kill me," Nicholson muttered, as Ann nodded in understanding. "Though she did throw the final curve at me, dying that way."

Ann agreed that there was nothing unusual about the timing of their marriage, given the circumstances. "When we all sat down together, we agreed that I would marry Frank as soon as she withdrew from the scene. Well, she withdrew." The heiress shrugged.

The newlyweds maintained that Gertrude had ended her life simply to embarrass them. For this, they bitterly resented her. "Gertrude is reaching out from the grave once more to make Frank's life miserable," said the new Mrs. Nicholson. "That's awfully spiteful, don't you think?"

The couple's attempts to gain the press's sympathy failed. A week later, at the official inquest into the suicide, Shirley Travis, Gertrude's child from a previous union, took the stand in the county courthouse to reveal incriminating facts about both Frank and Ann.

"Several weeks ago, Frank told my mother that he had met a girl and, as he put it, was 'madly in love with her,'" the young woman explained. "The girl was Ann Hewitt." The witness paused to allow onlookers to observe Ann shifting nervously in her seat in the front row. Satisfied, Shirley continued, "Last Monday, my stepfather brought Miss Hewitt out to the house, and they talked with my mother. Then, on Tuesday, he came back to the home to pick up some records for a radio program. He had the girl with him again, and they all talked once more."

Ann fiddled with the cuffs of her sleeve as she braced herself for the unfolding testimony.

"On Friday morning, I was staying with my aunt in Albany," Travis continued. "I telephoned my mother and suggested I come over so we could go shopping. She said she had an eleven a.m. date with Nick to talk about their trouble. So I went out by myself. Then that afternoon, a friend called. She said she'd phoned Mother and was alarmed by how drowsy she sounded. I rushed over to the house. When I got there, the police were already there, and my mother's stomach had been pumped."

Travis wiped a tear from her cheek. "She was conscious. I talked to her, and she seemed all right. She told me she had taken something to make her sleep. I had no idea it was fifty tablets."

The city coroner, who was directing the hearing, allowed her a moment before asking, "And then what happened?"

Travis took a deep breath. "Then my mother was taken out of house and put in the ambulance. I saw Nick and this girl sitting in a car a little way down the street, watching. Later at the hospital, Nick called, and I talked to him. At first, he denied being in front of the house with the woman, and then he said, 'Well I guess you got me, honey.'"

Those in attendance gasped and strained to see Nicholson, who was slumped in the first row next to Ann.

"My mother died at five thirty-five that night," said Travis, breaking into sobs. "I never got the chance to say goodbye to her." This witness then had to be escorted back to her seat. Audience members shook their heads and cast sympathetic glances when she passed.

Nicholson next took the stand. When asked about the last time he saw his wife, he answered, "I went to her house Friday morning, the day she died. I gave her $250 to buy some clothes."

"Were you watching from an automobile when she left in an ambulance?" the coroner asked.

Nicholson fidgeted in his seat. "Well, later that day, I visited a nearby liquor store. I saw an ambulance pull away from Gertrude's apartment, so I slowed down to see what was going on. That's why I phoned the hospital—I wanted to make sure she was all right. I was told she was. You can imagine how I felt when I learned a few hours later that she was dead."

"But you were planning to leave your wife," the coroner countered.

"That doesn't mean I wished her harm," said Nicholson.

"How long were you married?" the medical man asked.

"Three years."

"How long did domestic difficulties go on?"

"Over three years."

"When did the discord get so bad that you couldn't tolerate each other?"

Nicholson looked around for someone to object, but he had no lawyer present. It wasn't a criminal proceeding. "Isn't that tremendously personal?"

"Your wife is dead. We're just trying to understand why," said his questioner. "Did your wife ever take drugs?"

"Yes," Frank replied.

"Which ones?"

"Barbiturates, membutal, barbital, amytal—you name it. She loved them all." The audience collectively gasped, and Travis's face turned bright red.

Ann was also called to testify at the inquest, but the heiress refused to take the stand. "On what grounds?" asked the coroner. "This is an investigation into a suicide, not a criminal trial. There's no possibility of incriminating yourself." Ann merely shrugged from her seat. "Is it that you don't want to degrade yourself?" the coroner pressed. The heiress nodded.

Ann knew better than to think her testimony couldn't be used against her in the case of fraud and conspiracy. That afternoon, in the same courtroom, she and her husband had to go before a jury to explain how they managed to obtain signatures for their hurried marriage. Authorities suspected that Eugene Nicholson had helped them to obtain health certificates through a series of subterfuges and evasions. At this proceeding, Ann willingly took the stand. She stated that she had undergone a physical examination on the morning of her wedding in Dr. Pedar Bruguiere's home. (A different person had signed Frank's health certificate.) She claimed that her private physician, who maintained his medical license despite not having an official practice, had also performed the blood tests for her and Frank a few days earlier. The last point was false and would later result in perjury charges.

The couple was also compelled to explain why, when applying for a marriage license, they had listed an address in San Rafael at which neither was known. The Nicholsons didn't have a good answer to this question, but their silence wasn't adequate to void the marriage or launch a full investigation. In the end, Ann and Frank escaped the conspiracy charges and the court returned a verdict of "suicide unknown" in the matter of Gertrude's death. The toxicologist had found no trace of poison, and there was no physical evidence to suggest that the woman had been forced to consume an entire bottle of aspirin. Perhaps the lovers had coaxed the poor woman to take her life, but there was no way to substantiate this. A few months later, both Ann and Frank stood trial and were convicted of perjury for lying about the blood tests. But they managed to avoid jail and pay only a $1,500 fine.

Contrary to Ann's claims of poverty, the newlyweds had $1 million at their disposal, according to one New York reporter's calculation. "This should be enough for groceries even with a family," the *Daily News* writer quipped.

The Nicholsons moved to Nevada and lived quietly until 1950, when Ann shocked the public with the announcement that she was running for the US Senate. She and Frank had recently opened a nightclub and were seeking permits for a radio station in the city when she decided to enter public service. After going to the county clerk's office to file the paperwork for her candidacy and pay the required fee, Ann released a statement: "It's about time the women of Nevada were represented in Washington, D.C. I am going to the nation's capital to fight communism and help fix things up for the kids." She added that she intended to raise the standard of gold and silver.

Frank swiftly declared his support for Ann. "Nevada is about the last outpost of freedom, and Ann's been kicked around a lot as a little kid," he told a local newspaper. "She wants to do something to uphold the children and women because, after all, if there weren't any women there wouldn't be any future generations."

Some said Ann was trying to buy herself a seat. But Frank countered that Ann's wealth guaranteed her integrity. Unlike other candidates, she wouldn't be influenced by financial contributions. "She's got her own money to run her campaign and won't be tempted to take bribes once in office," he said. "In fact, she plans to divide her salary between the infantile paralysis fund and education."

But neither the press nor public ever got the chance to hear Ann's ideas for reforming the country. The next announcement she made merely stated her intentions to file for divorce. She didn't offer a reason, but those close to her knew that she and her husband frequently fought. "We just aren't compatible," Ann had told a friend.

"It's just a friendly parting of ways," Nicholson assured reporters. "We're the best of pals. We even had dinner together last night. And if she is defeated, I guess we'll be married again." According to Frank, it was Ann's political career that required her to cut ties with him. The nightclub and casino business simply weren't suited for the husband of a senator, he said.

A few weeks later, Ann quit the Senate race, citing health problems. "The divorce has placed a mental strain upon me, and I can't make the rigorous campaign that I would like," she said in a press statement. "I heartily endorse the Republican slate this year." Her vetted peers had no comment. None of them wanted to be associated with such a notorious woman.

Ann had never been that serious about going to Washington; she simply hadn't given up on trying to redeem her reputation from the damage of the trial. Though she didn't care much what people had to say about her selection of mates or other aspects of her life, she desperately wanted the world to know that she was not a moron. She once told a friend, "I always find myself on the defensive. I enter into every relationship with the idea that I will be thought feebleminded until I prove myself normal."

Later that fall, Ann took her fifth husband, a cowboy named Donald Charles Walter. This wedding barely made the news, as Ann's marital adventures were finally beginning to bore readers.

Less than one year later, she obtained a divorce and returned to Nicholson.

Little more was heard from the heiress. By the time of her death in February 1956, the public didn't even realize that she and Frank had moved to a ranch in Monterrey, Mexico, where the tentacles of the American press hadn't reached. In this citrus-covered valley, Ann finally released herself from the stigma of the sterilized heiress. Here she could walk through the piazzas of the shopping district and sit quietly in the Cathedral of Our Lady without a single person dropping a jaw, grabbing a companion's arm, and pointing in her direction. And she could have conversations with people who didn't pity or belittle her.

The former radio performer reported that on the day of her death, Ann had complained of a headache and retired to her room. He found her blue and cold several hours later. Three doctors signed the death certificate, attributing the cause of death to cancer. One of them had recently performed an operation removing a tumor from Ann's digestive organs.

"I never received notice of the death or a request for the remains to be repatriated," the American ambassador in Monterrey told the press, upon hearing the news. The reason for this, according to Nicholson, was simple: Ann had no wish to return to her home country. Frank buried Ann between an oak and cypress tree in the cemetery of Villa Santiago, two thousand miles from her parents' tombs in Brooklyn.

The heiress left her entire estate, which had dwindled to half a million dollars, to her husband. She awarded her half brother only $1, a traditional gesture for disinheriting someone from a will. Frank moved to Texas to invest Ann's money in the oil industry. There he briefly reunited with his first wife, daughter, and two new grandchildren before dying of cancer himself the following year.

Nicholson broke a final promise to be buried alongside Ann in her mausoleum in Monterrey. In the end, the heiress, who'd once claimed that she feared being alone more than anything else in the world, had been abandoned one last time.

In her final moments, when entire lives are said to unroll like a reel of film, Ann might have recalled happy times, such as toddling on her father's polished shoes as he practiced the fox-trot in their Paris apartment; walking hand in hand with the scientist down the pastry-scented streets; or even climbing Brougher Mountain to give her father's papers a decent burial, when she finally decided that no one on earth could ever replace him. The heiress had once reminisced to a friend, "It was after midnight. The coyotes were crying, the moon was high, and the desert still. I made a huge bonfire of the patents and blueprints. When I struck the match and the flames leapt high, there went all that was earthly of my father. There was no more."

After her death, Ann's name also flickered out. The press had other fashionable, unruly women, such as Elizabeth Taylor and Marilyn Monroe, to trail; and the world soon forgot that the sterilized heiress had ever existed.

17

OPERATION LAWSUIT

In 1972, *Good Housekeeping* profiled the troubles of a woman named Florence Caffarelli, whom the magazine described as "the last person you would expect to find in the eye of a storm." The twenty-six-year-old Peekskill, New York, housewife lived a quiet life with her truck-driving husband and her three children, ages three, seven, and eight. Florence enjoyed reading magazines and occasionally going out with her girlfriends, with whom she could be candidly honest about something she didn't initially have the courage to tell her doctor: She did not desire to have any more children.

Caffarelli was part of Operation Lawsuit, a class-action suit launched in 1971 to mobilize women who had been denied sterilization surgeries in private hospitals. Across the nation, doctors at private hospitals often followed arbitrary standards, such as the "120 Rule," to grant or refuse a patient's request for tubal ligation. This rule required that a woman's age multiplied by the number of her live children total at least 120 in order for her to obtain an irreversible operation. If women didn't meet this standard, the hospital board needed to approve the surgery. But without a good reason, many boards denied women their requests.

Caffarelli was one such woman. She became the face of the

lawsuit to advocate for middle-class white women's reproductive rights, during a time when many women, such as those affiliated with the famous Boston Women's Health Collective, were marching in the streets to demand access to tubal ligations, the Pill, abortion, and other contraceptive technologies.

The Peekskill housewife had first learned about tubal ligation, a new, noninvasive procedure that involved cutting and tying the fallopian tubes (rather than removing them), from the glossy pages of her magazines. When all of her children were sound asleep and her husband had turned off his reading lamp, Caffarelli would pull out her monthlies and look longingly at the pretty blondes and brunettes shown ice-skating or learning a new hobby after having undergone the procedure. These women explained that the world was their oyster now that their children attended school and they no longer had young ones to mind at home. They claimed tubal ligation had enriched their relationships with both their children and husbands. "I actually look forward to seeing my sons get off the school bus—because I'm not exhausted from changing nappies all day," said one. "After years of dreading sex, I finally enjoy it," said another. "I don't have to worry about it leading to another pregnancy."

A television appearance by H. Curtis Woods, the president of the Association for Voluntary Sterilization, also provided some insight on sterilization for Caffarelli. Founded in 1937 under another name to promote forcible sterilization of "defectives" in New Jersey, the now-nationwide association assisted middle-class women to obtain desired sterilizations. (The organization's leaders realized that the broader cause of reproductive freedom served the goal of making sterilization available to the communities those leaders perceived to need it—poor and minority women.) When the association's president appeared on her television set, Caffarelli had shushed her children and turned up the volume to hear Woods speak of the safety, efficacy, and popularity of tubal ligation. No more pills, which caused weight gain and uncomfortable side effects? No more condoms, which strained marriages? Or diaphragms or jellies, which were unreliable and a nuisance to use? Sterilization sounded too good to be true.

Before telling her husband that she was interested in the procedure, Caffarelli broached the issue among a few friends. "I happen to think that what I do with my own body is my own affair," she told her peers. "It's not up to a doctor to say what I can or can't do. Or what my family should look like."

Most of them agreed. "I can't imagine having to bring bottles and diapers back into my life," said one. "I do look fondly on those days... but I don't want to go back to them."

That night, Florence told her husband how she felt, and he agreed that they had absolutely completed their childbearing. Florence's spouse had seen how difficult it was for her to carry and labor with their children—especially Michael, the youngest. Florence had conceived this child while using an IUD, which caused her to cramp and bleed. She had been using this contraceptive method because she could not take the Pill, which caused an existing breast tumor to grow. The Caffarellis decided that Florence should have her tubes ligated.

Caffarelli had the option of an abortion, if she became unexpectedly pregnant. In New York, abortion was legalized, even though the landmark *Roe v. Wade* decision, which decriminalized abortion in all states, had not yet been handed down. But as she told *Good Housekeeping*, Florence preferred not to have to make the choice to obtain one. "I think every woman should be able to have an abortion if she wants one," she assured the magazine's readers. "But I don't think *I* could decide to have one."

Florence went to her doctor to tell him about her discontent with the IUD. "The side effects are awful, and there's no guarantee it will protect me. Michael is evidence of that," she explained. "And I'm not afraid of doing something permanent. I am perfectly content with my family size."

Florence's physician supported her decision, observing that another pregnancy could worsen her health. He'd hate to see her tumor grow from a flood of pregnancy hormones, he said. But the Peekskill Community Hospital refused Caffarelli's sterilization request. While administrators appreciated the contraindications to her pregnancy, they didn't think these qualified her for surgery. "We will not permit any such operation unless and until…a court directs it," they wrote.

This enraged Caffarelli. "How dare they? How dare they tell me and my doctor that I can't have this operation unless I'm in danger of imminent death?" she asked her physician. "I could cry to them about medical reasons—I might really die with another pregnancy—but why should I have to do that?"

Caffarelli decided to contact the authorities behind Operation Lawsuit, which she'd seen advertised in print and television. The class-action lawsuit was widely marketed to women across the nation, thanks to support from the Association for Voluntary Sterilization, the organization Zero Population Growth (another eugenic nonprofit, which appropriated environmentalist concerns to control the population of poor and minority communities), and the American Civil Liberties Union.

Lawyers agreed to take Florence's case, then charged Peekskill Community Hospital administrators with discriminating against her on socioeconomic grounds. These attorneys observed that, as the spouse of a truck driver, Caffarelli lived on a fixed income. In contrast to her peers with greater means, she could not afford to search private institutions until she found one willing to sterilize her.

It was true that upper-middle-class and wealthy women had greater access to sterilization, thanks to their ability to "doctor shop." This inequity became a core concern of Operation Lawsuit, which represented many lower-middle-class women like Caffarelli. Unfortunately for the lawsuit's organizers, most plaintiffs were only concerned with redressing discrimination against themselves, not their entire social class. As soon they gained access to sterilization procedures, they dropped their lawsuits.

Caffarelli received her operation on December 17, 1971, after agreeing to withdraw her request for monetary damages and policy changes. In contrast with her co-plaintiffs, Florence actually did recognize the need to secure wider reform and not simply achieve her individual goal. She had spent the previous year writing to New York legislators and speaking with the press about the importance of reproductive freedom. But her attorney worried that if she continued to publicly demand changes to hospital policy, she might lose the opportunity to receive surgery herself. Caffarelli accepted the counsel and abandoned her fight. She wasn't *really* cut out for activism, she decided after having her tubes tied. As her husband later told reporters, she was never "one of those radicals," and she only supported women's liberation "to a certain extent." In the end, Florence returned to her quiet life. She was now a liberated woman with hidden passions and hobbies to uncover.

Operation Lawsuit achieved some broader political success, including noteworthy legal wins against hospitals and medical centers. This was in no small part because of *Roe v. Wade*, which enshrined women's right to contraception, in addition to abortion, when decided in 1973. One of the most critical victories came in Massachusetts, where the First Circuit Court of Appeals ruled that a medical institution had to provide services to Robbie Mae Hathaway, a low-income woman with eight children and physical ailments that increased the risk of pregnancy complications. Hathaway had no choice but to seek her desired tubal ligation at her local hospital. (Her insurer did not cover sterilization, and the local medical center, Worcester City Hospital, was obligated to provide health care to medically indigent patients.) Many doctors would have liked nothing more than to snip a poor woman like Hathaway, even if she had never been on welfare. But Worcester City Hospital had a comprehensive ban against elective sterilizations. In denying her the procedure while granting other patients elective surgeries of comparable risk, the hospital had arbitrarily discriminated against Hathaway, her attorneys argued. The high court agreed, citing *Roe*.

Other Operation Lawsuit cases cited the Hathaway case, forcing hospital policy changes and overturning age/parity restrictions, such as the 120 Rule. The flurry of Operation Lawsuit cases across the nation prompted many hospitals to preemptively revise their policies to avoid litigation. It also prompted medical organizations and even some legislative bodies to amend sterilization guidelines in favor of women seeking the procedure.

But these amendments failed to address the problem of involuntary sterilization, which had intensified amid the baby boom. While middle-class white women faced pressure to birth children, poor and minority women were forcibly prevented from doing so for the same underlying reason: Medical authorities wanted whites to increase in population and African American, Mexican American, and indigenous peoples to decrease. In the 1970s, these women also waged war against the doctors doing harm, with even more monumental results.

18

MADRIGAL V. QUILLIGAN

Twenty-six-year-old Antonia Hernández was working at her desk at the Los Angeles Center for Law and Justice on East Olympic Boulevard when a curly-haired doctor came in with boxes of files and a startling claim: Thousands of women at County General Hospital had been sterilized without their informed consent. Bernard Rosenfeld claimed to know this because he'd been quietly documenting the abuse for months. After his shifts in the obstetrics unit, he'd go to his office and type notes from private conversations and record information from patients' charts. He'd transcribed dozens of conversations with medical residents who believed that Mexican Americans were having too many babies and that it was their job to intervene. Some cited overpopulation concerns, while others worried about welfare costs. Often, if informed that a patient targeted for sterilization was not on welfare, a resident responded, "Well, her children will be." One resident had remarked about Mexican Americans, "All they do is screw, drink, and drive around the city."

After extensively documenting his findings, Rosenfeld had written a full report, which described physicians performing surgeries without any consent or after "selling [the procedure] in a manner not unlike many other deceptive marketing practices." For instance, Rosenfeld explained, residents would exaggerate the need for surgical training, making patients feel as though they had to comply or else stall medical science. They also misrepresented the procedure as reversible, when it was not. By using the term *tubal ligation*, they implied that they were merely going to tie the fallopian tubes, when, in fact, they planned to cut them. And they cautioned that if patients didn't undergo the procedure, their health was endangered. In one case, a doctor had held a syringe in front of a mother in the throes of contraction, taunting, "Do you want the pain to stop? Do you want to go through this again? Then sign the papers!" Another physician had also withheld pain medication until his patient signed, telling her, "If you hadn't had sex, then you wouldn't be in so much pain."

Rosenfeld reported that he had already gone to the head of the obstetrics department with his findings. Edward Quilligan had denied that there was any such abuse occurring in his department and, Rosenfeld maintained, refused to even broach the issue with medical residents. After this, Rosenfeld had spent hours composing letters to journalists, civil rights groups, and government authorities, hoping to publicize the scandal and provoke reform. But none were moved by his story. Now he stood before Hernández seeking to gain the center's participation in a lawsuit to stop the practice.

Hernández's thoughts immediately went to her own mother, who had given birth at the medical center in question. Like the patients Rosenfeld described, she had been a working-class native Spanish speaker. Feeling a personal connection to the patients, the young attorney agreed to consider Rosenfeld's request. She knew that if she took on the case, the battle would no doubt resemble that of David and Goliath. She was fresh out of UCLA law school, working for a social justice organization with limited funding. Her twenty-nine-year-old colleague, Charles Nabarrete, was legally blind, making it difficult for him to quickly process documents and navigate the city. The hospital, on the other hand, would have the political and financial resources of the county at its disposal. But she couldn't say no.

After further conversations with Rosenfeld, Hernández began to search for plaintiffs. Having no information other than patients' names, she drove up and down the streets of Los Angeles looking for the women referenced in his records. Many women closed their doors in her face, claiming they wanted to forget about what happened. Others let her in, but spoke in hushed whispers so their family members in adjoining rooms couldn't hear. Hernández learned that many forcibly sterilized women were too afraid to tell their loved ones what had happened. According to their Catholic faith, sterilization, like abortion, was a mortal sin; and those who committed mortal sins risked eternal damnation. Women also kept quiet about their surgeries for fear of becoming undesirable in their partners' eyes. One forcibly sterilized woman told the young attorney that her husband had accused her of undergoing the procedure in order to be unfaithful. "Women do this to be with other men," he'd said. When she told him that wasn't true, he'd struck her.

In some cases, women had no idea that they had even undergone an operation. It pained Hernández to ask these women, "Do you know you were sterilized?" Others knew that they had been operated upon, but believed that their tubes had been tied, not cut. Therefore, they thought the procedure could be undone when they were ready for more children. When the young attorney told them otherwise, many were in disbelief. Others broke down in tears.

When Hernández approached hospital staff with her and Rosenfeld's findings, she found that most were reluctant to speak against a pillar of the medical community. Quilligan, known as "The Q," was a well-respected, Yale-trained physician who had helped the hospital to gain federal grants, including a $2 billion one from the US Department of Health, Education, and Welfare, which paid for an extensive renovation. This same grant, Hernández learned from a willing witness, had financed the minority women's sterilizations. Dr. Karen Benker told Hernández that, while a medical student at County General, she had heard Quilligan remark, "Poor minority women in L.A. county are having too many babies. They're a strain on society. It's good that they be sterilized." Quilligan, she said, then bragged about receiving a grant that he intended to use to "show how low [he could] cut the birth rate of Negro and Mexican populations in Los Angeles county." (Quilligan denied making these statements.)

The Los Angeles doctor wasn't the only physician to receive such a grant, Hernández's research revealed. In 1971, the Office of Economic Opportunity authorized federal funds earmarked for family planning services to be used for sterilization as part of President Lyndon Johnson's War on Poverty. Health clinics and hospitals across the nation used the new money to sterilize between 100,000 and 150,000 low-income women annually.

This push to sterilize poor women was partially spurred by the Civil Rights Act of 1964. When African Americans gained access to federal programs, many people feared the nation was going to be overrun with descendants of slaves. (They presumed black women would reproduce just to obtain welfare benefits designed for white mothers.) To prevent this, physicians in the South often operated upon African American women who presented in hospitals for abdominal surgery. The practice of involuntary sterilization was so common, even before the passage of the momentous civil rights bill, that it gave rise to the term *Mississippi Appendectomy*. Southern black women who developed abdominal conditions had to choose between pursuing less-proven home remedies and surrendering themselves to white doctors with who-knows-what agendas. But these women had no recourse, as their surgeries were seldom documented. Nor did indigenous women on reservations, where an estimated 25 percent were involuntarily sterilized through the federally funded Indian Health Service in the 1970s. For centuries, indigenous women had labored with midwives and healers; but beginning in the 1900s, when people began to be criminalized for using ceremonial practices in medical settings, they were forced to go to white-run hospitals. Here, as in the South, records were often falsified to indicate consent.

The push to sterilize poor, minority women also corresponded with a global effort to control dark-skinned populations. In the 1960s and '70s, sociological experts cautioned that overpopulation was going to create international chaos. Guy Irving Burch, director of the Population Reference Bureau and the American Eugenics Society, urged that "uncontrolled human reproduction not only favors the survival and the multiplication of the least gifted members of society; it menaces and in the long run will destroy human liberties and any chance for a world at peace." Burch believed—and many American doctors agreed—that poor people were responsible for depleting natural resources and degrading the environment, as a result of their unchecked fertility. In his 1968 bestseller *The Population Bomb*, Paul R. Ehrlich similarly warned of mass starvation and chaos as a result of too many (poor) people. To redress the "problem" of third-world fertility, many medical professionals went to India, Puerto Rico, and other underdeveloped regions to establish birth control clinics with funding from the federal government. They did so with funding from the Rockefeller Foundation, among other philanthropic organizations.

But these doctors didn't identify as eugenicists. In fact, many recoiled at the term, perceiving great difference between their work and that of Nazi Germany. After the war, eugenics had become synonymous with the Holocaust, obscuring the fact that the Third Reich had gotten its blueprints from Americans like Popenoe. This allowed doctors to insist that they were not targeting entire races or classes of people, but simply addressing the growing problem of poverty. Never mind that Hitler and the eugenicists before him were centrally concerned about dependency on the state, targeting sick and disabled persons perceived to drain public resources.

In California, the push to operate upon poor minorities with no known heritable defects coincided with World War II, as two noteworthy cases suggest. In 1941, just five years after the San Francisco trial for Ann Cooper Hewitt's sterilization, California authorities sent Andrea García, one of nine children, to the Pacific Colony for school truancy. Fearing that she was prone to have a large brood like her mother, officials at the institution forced the Mexican American under the knife. That same decade, colony authorities forcibly sterilized Fortuna Valencia because of her heritage and family size. Valencia had six children with her first husband before he died, then five with her second. Sometime after her final child, the welfare department put her on probation, claiming she was not to have any more children and that she must regularly appear before authorities. When Valencia resisted supervision, her children were declared wards of the court, and she was sent to the asylum. There she was given an intelligence test as a formality, but surprised officials by excelling on the test. Having no exam score to brandish against her, colony officials declared her feebleminded for another reason: her "social orientation."

Feebleminded might have continued to serve as a catchall term for anyone authorities did not want to reproduce but for two amendments to California's sterilization statute in 1952 and 1953. Prompted by an unsuccessful constitutional challenge to the statute, lawmakers deleted references to "idiocy," "fools," syphilis, and sexual perversion as conditions for sterilization. This made it difficult for asylum directors to sterilize women at will. Fortunately for them, physicians in private and public hospitals were more than willing to assume the role of controlling the population, as Hernández learned in 1974.

It didn't surprise the civil rights attorney when Quilligan denied having ever expressed concerns about poor, minority women's reproduction. After learning of the action she and Nabarrete were organizing with Rosenfeld's help, he insisted, "We're practicing good medicine." He merely admitted that the women in question should not have been approached to give consent for sterilization while in labor, saying "the timing was unfortunate."

Hernández knew that, if she and Nabarrete were to prevail, she needed to garner public support for the sterilized women. So she appealed to leaders of the Chicano rights movements in the city. Many officials didn't feel compelled to help her case, as they regarded sterilization abuse as secondary to other concerns, like workers' rights. But Chicana feminist organizations such as the Comisión Femenil Mexicana Nacional, the Chicana Welfare Rights Organization, the Chicana Rights Project of the Mexican American Legal Defense and Education Fund, and the Chicana Nurses Association agreed to lend a hand.

When Rosenfeld published his report, leading to a front-page story in the *Los Angeles Times*, the Comisión helped to organize public forums where women in the city could share their experiences. These Mexican American feminist activists also helped to form the Committee to End Forced Sterilization, which later organized demonstrations outside of County General. With helicopters circling above them and SWAT teams positioned on the hospital roof, activists held signs reading, OUR SISTERHOOD INCLUDES ALL WOMEN...JOIN US TO FIGHT FORCED STERILIZA-TION and STOP MEDICAL EXPERIMENTATION WITH POOR WOMEN. Members of the Los Angeles Women's Union, the Committee to Free Los Tres, and the Solidarity Band marched, too.

It wasn't long before these activists gained the attention of national organizations, such as the National Coalition Against Sterilization Abuse, which came to Los Angeles to fundraise for Rosenfeld. After the whistleblower had published his report, the Los Angeles hospital had charged him with moral turpitude, claiming he had violated patient confidentiality in publicizing his findings. Many high-profile feminists, including Jane Fonda, attended the fundraising event.

Hernández continued to work with Rosenfeld to identify poten-tial plaintiffs. Together the two identified 140 Mexican American women who claimed to have been coercively sterilized at the hospital during the last few years. Hernández and Nabarrete then selected from this group ten women to file a class-action suit: Guadalupe Acosta, Estella Benavides, Maria Figueroa, Rebecca Figueroa, Maria Hurtado, Consuelo Hermosillo, Georgina Her-nández, Dolores Madrigal, Helena Orozco, and Jovita Rivera.

The selected women each had a strong case for lack of informed consent, and not a single one was on welfare. Dolores Madrigal, the first plaintiff listed, had signed a consent form after being falsely told that her husband had signed it. Helena Orozco had signed after being told that physicians could treat her hernia only if she agreed to the surgery (and that, if untreated, her hernia could rupture, causing death). Rebecca Figueroa had signed under the impression that the procedure could be undone. Guadalupe Acosta had never signed a consent form at all. Nor had Georgina Hernández, whose physician was very blunt about his motivations: "Mexican people are very poor, and you should not have any more children because you can't support them."

In most cases, there had been no translators available, so doctors and nurses had communicated with patients, who had varying levels of English proficiency, with basic questions in English or Spanish. For instance, they'd asked, "*¿más niños?*" (more babies), thinking a shaking of the head implied consent for sterilization. If women resisted their efforts, doctors and nurses hadn't been afraid to threaten "*deportación*" (deportation). In fact, one resident had told a plaintiff, "We know you're here illegally. If you don't consent to this surgery, we'll call the feds right now and tell them you're here."

Hospital staff had also restricted communication between laboring women and their husbands, involving husbands only if patients resisted. In such cases, the doctor would tell the husband his wife's life would be on the line if she became pregnant again. Not knowing any better, husbands had pleaded with their wives to be sterilized.

There were a few sympathetic staff members at County General. Consuelo Hermosillo recalled that it was a nurse who had alerted her about the abuse during her prenatal visits. "I thought the surgery was necessary. They told me there was a limit of only three cesarean sections by law," she explained. But the nurse had said, "Don't be crazy. I've had five cesareans, and no one ever told me I needed to do anything about it." Hermosillo added that the white-capped woman had come to her bedside when no one was around and whispered, "Don't pay attention to any of the doctors here. All they want is to cut Mexican women's tubes." Had she not been under the influence of analgesics and anxious to deliver, she would never have signed the consent form.

Hernández and Nabarrete had little hope of recovering any damages for the plaintiffs; they opted for the class action simply to gain greater publicity in their efforts to compel the hospital to comply with new federal sterilization guidelines, including a mandatory seventy-two-hour waiting period between consent and surgery, established in response to mounting concerns around the country about the targeting of poor women of color. In addition to the hospital, the plaintiffs named as defendants the US Department of Health, Education, and Welfare, which oversaw the Office of Economic Opportunity; the California State Department of Health; the individual doctors who had performed the sterilizations; and the heads of the obstetrics department (Dr. Quilligan and his immediate subordinate, Roger Freeman).

Soon after the case was filed in 1975, a US District Court judge granted a preliminary injunction against the California Department of Health. Judge E. Avery Crary mandated that the department rewrite Spanish-language sterilization consent forms to a sixth-grade level, at which more than half of Mexican American patients at County General Hospital read. (The current forms, which did not describe the procedure or the lasting effect, were written at a twelfth-grade reading level.)

In 1977, the state agreed to hold three bilingual public hearings to further explore the issue of consent. Both individuals and organization leaders testified, urging officials to adopt federal guidelines, including a mandatory seventy-two-hour waiting period between consent and surgery. Latina activists encountered some resistance, not from the hearing's planners, but from the California representatives of the National Organization for Women and the National Association for the Repeal of Abortion Laws. The white representatives present didn't believe that the state should impose a mandatory waiting period. They believed a woman should have sterilization on demand, if she wanted it. Latina activists insisted that the provision was necessary to protect against medical abuse. Neither was willing to budge. The dispute signaled to Hernández and others that white feminists were only willing to support the cause if it didn't infringe upon their own political interests.

After the hearings, the Department of Health adopted the proposed guidelines, including the mandatory three-day waiting period. This victory emboldened Hernández and Nabarrete. "We've won everything we asked for," Nabarrete publicly declared.

But in April 1978, before the financial damages for plaintiffs could be decided, Crary died. The Los Angeles court assigned the case to conservative judge Jesse Curtis, a seventy-year-old Nixon appointee who resided on a yacht in the ritzy Newport Beach area. Despite the judge's leanings, Hernández and Nabarrete agreed to try the case by bench, rather than jury. They knew the sophisticated legal arguments required an expert in the law.

In late May 1979, the proceedings began, and the now-thirty-year-old Hernández appeared to argue the case of her career. She and Nabarrete alleged that the plaintiffs' civil and constitutional rights to bear children had been violated. They boldly drew upon the brand-new *Roe v. Wade* decision, which affirmed a woman's reproductive choice, to make this case. They saw no reason why *Roe* couldn't be used to create a more comprehensive framework of reproductive justice—one that protected the rights of poor, minority women and not just middle-class white women.

But the defense attorneys swiftly moved to dislodge the case from its civil rights roots. William Maskey and Nancy Menzies petitioned the court to drop Quilligan and Freeman from the case, arguing that the two physicians had no direct involvement in the ten sterilizations in question. Judge Curtis agreed and further found there was no class action—just ten battery cases connected by a common theme. Though reframed as ten plaintiffs opposing ten defendants, *Madrigal v. Quilligan* continued to be tried as a single case. For the next two weeks, Hernández and Nabarrete laid out their argument.

They called the ten plaintiffs to testify, along with Dr. Benker, a New York consent expert, a psychologist who had examined all of the women, and an anthropologist analyzing the women's trauma from a cultural perspective. Judge Curtis attempted to prevent the last from taking the stand, drawing upon stereotypes to do so. "Look, the court knows—everybody knows—the Mexican people have strong feelings about a big family," he said. "I don't anticipate that he's going to tell us anything we don't already know." When Hernández and Nabarrete refused to strike Dr. Carlos Vélez-Ibáñez, claiming his insights were critical, he said, "Fine. But you're wasting your money."

Vélez-Ibáñez told the court that six of the plaintiffs had hidden their surgeries from their siblings (and three from their mothers), feeling such profound shame about their condition. He further related that several of the plaintiffs were now experiencing marital problems due to their infertility and that one plaintiff's common-law husband had abandoned her and her children after learning of her operation. Motherhood was central to the plaintiffs' Chicana culture. In fact, for the plaintiffs, to be *una mujer* (a woman) was to be a mother, Vélez-Ibáñez testified. When sterilized, the women had been severed from their former selves: "For each woman, her sense of continuity with the past had been fractured, her sense of self-worth had been shattered, self-blame had been internalized, and a new social identity of impotence had been generated...The final effect was acute depression."

Curtis interrupted the expert to ask if he could quantify the plaintiffs' infertility in "dollars and cents," implying the cultural deficits meant little to the court.

The judge similarly appeared unconvinced by Dr. Benker, who took the stand on June 7. This witness spoke about the systemic sterilization abuse and discrimination against Mexican American women, which she claimed to have witnessed "on an almost daily basis" as a medical student at the hospital. Benker told the court that physicians believed Mexican women were making babies all the time. Thinking two children were sufficient to satisfy a woman's maternal instincts, they advocated for sterilization. Benker testified that she and a few other students had heard Quilligan comment on his plans to utilize the federal grant to lower the African American and Mexican American birth rates in Los Angeles. According to her, several students had reacted to the remark with surprise, while a physician nodded in agreement, citing "poverty and over-population." She also told of a time that she and a few residents had been making rounds when one boasted of having sterilized a nineteen-year-old African American the night before. When a peer questioned the propriety of sterilizing a patient who was so young and who had only one child, the resident had smugly responded, "Oh, I'll sterilize any woman."

But Judge Curtis refused to believe that there was a plot to target low-income minority women in Los Angeles. He noted that there was never a hospital rule instructing employees to push sterilization on any group of women and that Quilligan was never present when women were coerced to consent to surgery. The judge further refused to acknowledge any concerns with the doctors' denigrating remarks about Mexican Americans: "I do not think it is surprising that you might find a doctor who believes that people who are inclined to have big families shouldn't, and particularly for good medical reasons, undertakes to persuade a person not to have a large family." Such individuals were perfectly within their rights: "There is a big segment of the people in this country, and not only in this country but in the world, who believe that one of the prime causes of our social and economic problems are big families where the parents are not able to either socially or economically support them. The people who have that belief . . . are just as entitled to their beliefs as people who feel as the plaintiffs do here."

For Curtis, the primary question was whether or not the attending doctors had overridden the wishes of patients—and if so, what their medical justifications for doing so were.

Hernández couldn't help but rise to her feet at this moment in the trial. "I do not believe that any of the doctors have indicated that there was a medical indication for the sterilization operation," she said.

Curtis conceded this point, but countered, "Neither has there been any evidence at this point that the hospital or anyone has used any social reason for bringing sterilization about."

Hearing Curtis persistently deny any wrongdoing, as well as demean Mexican Americans, Hernández wasn't shocked when, after all the testimony had been delivered, the judge ruled in favor of the defendants. Still, she struggled to stomach his opinion, delivered in late June: "There is no doubt that these women have suffered severe emotional and physical stress because of these operations. One can sympathize with them for their inability to communicate clearly, but one can hardly blame the doctors for relying on these indicia of consent which appeared to be unequivocal on their face and which are in constant use in the Medical Center." In other words, the tragedies were simply due to a breakdown in communication—

one that might have been avoided if the plaintiffs were able to speak the language of the country. The judge went on to argue that if the plaintiffs weren't so culturally inclined toward such enormous families, they might not have found themselves in such an unfortunate position.

Unable to face the court, Hernández raced outside. Nabarrete was right behind her. "Don't cry," he urged. So she put on a brave face for the gathered reporters. Nabarrete told these crowds that, if upheld by a higher court, Judge Curtis's decision would result in thousands more Mexican American women being sterilized against their will. It was hard to overstate the detriment of the case to civil rights, he said.

Hernández and Nabarrete appealed the ruling the following year. But the higher court denied their appeal. Though probably celebrating the conclusion to the case, County General physicians reflected with indignation, "We busted our asses to provide care for people and got sued for it."

Hernández was heartbroken. So were the plaintiffs, some of whom had risked their marriages and familial relationships to testify. Hermosillo had not told her spouse about her participation. She'd secretly ridden the bus to the courthouse, hoping her words would help to protect other women from suffering the same fate. Others had brought their children along and left them in the car, not wanting to reveal to friends or family members that they were participating in a sterilization trial.

Hernández took comfort in knowing that the case was transforming sterilization practices for the better. The various coalitions and community action groups formed to support the victims were too powerful for hospital or state authorities to ignore. By bringing scrutiny to County General's abusive practices, Mexican American feminist activists had succeeded in changing hospital policy.

Though welfare benefits weren't threatened in any of the plaintiffs' cases (none received them), activists had also raised awareness about the rights of recipients. They knew that sterilization abuse often occurred when individuals did fear a loss of benefits. A recent US District Court case on the East Coast had called attention to this fact. *Relf v. Weinberger* involved two poor, intellectually disabled African American girls in the South, whose mother signed a consent form for their sterilization thinking their benefits would be revoked if she didn't. (The mother was also falsely told that her daughters were receiving birth control shots, rather than being permanently sterilized.) Horrified by the violation of the girls' rights, the district court judge had ruled that federal funds for family planning services could not be used for the involuntary sterilization of poor or mentally incompetent persons. Estimating that over one hundred thousand low-income women underwent sterilization with tax dollars each year, Judge Gerhard Gesell had written, "The dividing line between family planning and eugenics is murky."

Latina activists in California further debunked the myth that welfare benefits could be revoked based on a patient's immigration status. (Until 1996, when President Bill Clinton signed the Personal Responsibility and Work Opportunity Reconciliation Act, undocumented immigrants were eligible for certain public programs besides emergency Medicaid and nutrition assistance.) And they had encouraged welfare beneficiaries to recognize their dignity and refuse the notion that poor people were parasitic. Yolanda Navas of the Comisión Femenil insisted in her public speeches and writing that those who cooked, cleaned, or cared for others were no different than those who reported to the office or factory Monday through Friday; all were part of the workforce. This perspective offered an important counterpoint to mainstream feminism, which focused on liberating women from "demeaning" household work.

Such an emphasis on human dignity also contrasted sharply with the tactics used in Ann's case over forty years before. Focused on establishing the unlawfulness of Ann's surgery, the witnesses for the prosecution had never questioned the ethics of sterilization. They'd simply tried to prove Ann undeserving of the surgery by virtue of her education and intellectual abilities, and Maryon's failings. This approach obstructed the fact that classism, ableism, and misogyny had allowed Ann's mother and physicians to commit their crimes in the first place.

In Northern California, other activist groups took up the cause initiated by the Los Angeles women. The Chicana Rights Project of the Mexican American Legal Defense and Educational Fund came together with other Bay Area organizations to petition the California Department of Health for more stringent regulations of sterilizations (rather than leaving it up to hospital boards to decide whether or not to adopt federal regulations imposed on publicly funded sterilizations). Members of these groups and others increased public awareness about the crisis by creating print materials about abuse in hospital settings and contributing stories on the topic to magazines such as *Agenda*, the publication of the National Council of La Raza. The Coalition for Medical Rights also initiated a letter-writing campaign, in which women from across the state wrote to lawmakers about their experiences with sterilization abuse.

But Latina activists' crowning achievement came in 1979, the same year that Hernández was tapped to serve as counsel for the US Senate Judiciary Committee. Inspired by Hernández, Nabarrete, and the ten plaintiffs in his district, State Assemblyman Art Torres took action to repeal California's sterilization laws. The repeal officially ended seven decades of state-sanctioned eugenic violence, which had impacted over twenty thousand men and women in state-run institutions—one-third of all the sterilization victims in the country and more than double the number in any other state. Torres envisioned this appeal would also halt the practice of sterilization abuse in hospitals, where procedures were falsely recorded as voluntary.

Other states had already begun to repeal their own sterilization laws. Indiana, which passed the first sterilization law in the nation, had repealed its statutes in 1974. So had Virginia, whose laws had secured the Supreme Court's blessing of eugenics with Carrie Buck's case. And thanks to the advocacy of women of color, including a chief tribal judge who testified on sterilization abuse at the United Nations Convention on Indigenous Rights in 1977, new federal regulations offered further protections than those established in 1976. For instance, for publicly funded sterilizations, the federal government extended the mandatory waiting period from three to thirty days, except in cases of emergency abdominal surgery and premature delivery.

But even with these important legislative measures, involuntary sterilization has remained a serious problem in the United States and around the world. And as Hernández knew from the very beginning, no revision to the law could ever take away the trauma of the women whose bodies were mutilated.

A few years after the case, Maria Figueroa climbed the fence of a bridge overpass near her home by City Terrace. She couldn't bear to live anymore. Her husband had abandoned her, and she felt like a ghost of a woman. If it weren't for an old man who left his car to plead with her, she might have mustered the courage to jump. Guadalupe Acosta died tragically after her partner left her and her children. Conseulo Hermosillo continued to dream of conceiving another child, despite her condition. She told Hernández about this fantasy: "I always dream I have my baby. I dream I get to Mexico with the baby. People want to see him, but I won't show them because I have a surprise. A miracle...he's something that's mine that nobody else can see. That's what I dream."

19

ANOTHER REVEAL

On July 7, 2013, Center for Investigative Reporting journalist Corey Johnson published a shocking story that resulted in an extensive investigation of the prison system in California, followed by new legislation. Johnson posited that between 2006 and 2010, 148 women inmates had been sterilized without consent or under dubious conditions, such as coerced consent or not understanding the procedure's permanence. He further suggested, based on state documents and interviews, that another hundred inmates might have been involuntarily sterilized since the late 1990s, and that many more had been unsuccessfully pressured to undergo surgery. Many of the women, housed at either the California Institution for Women in Corona or Valley State Prison for Women in Chowchilla, had already given birth to multiple children and served multiple prison sentences.

Thirty-four-year-old Christina Cordero was one of these women. Cordero told Johnson that a doctor began pressuring her to undergo a tubal ligation as she prepared to give birth to her sixth child while in prison. "The closer I got to my due date, the more he talked about it," said Cordero, who was serving time for auto theft. "He made me feel like a bad mother if I didn't do it." She eventually relented.

Other women were pressured to consent to sterilization while in labor and under the influence of pain medication. Kimberly Jeffrey, who actually managed to refuse sterilization, told Johnson she was sedated and strapped to a surgical table when a physician approached her, saying, "So we're going to be doing this tubal ligation, right?" (Jeffrey had previously refused the procedure when it was mentioned at a prenatal care visit.) Even when the doctor continued to pressure her, she remained firm. She'd heard rumors of medical staff trying to take women's uteruses.

Daun Martin, a medical supervisor at Valley State Prison, insisted that the surgeries were performed to empower inmates. By preventing women from becoming pregnant, this official said, doctors gave those women a chance to get a job and rehabilitate themselves. Dr. James Heinrich, one of the physicians contracted to perform the operations, claimed that he was providing an important service to low-income women, who were at risk for pregnancy complications due to a history of cesarean sections. He explained that scar tissue develops with each cesarean and that, if scar tissue inside the uterus tears during pregnancy or labor, there is a risk of blood loss or even death. It's not common practice to offer tubal ligations to women who have had cesarean sections, an expert told Johnson. In cases where the risk of complications is high, women are generally offered intrauterine devices, implants, or another reversible method of birth control.

When pressed, Heinrich betrayed that he was motivated to prevent the birth of babies likely to qualify for public assistance. Asked about the $147,460 he received for his services, Heinrich said, "Over a ten-year period, that isn't a huge amount of money, compared to what you save in welfare paying for these unwanted children—as they procreated more." Heinrich further suggested that the women accusing him and his colleagues of involuntary sterilization were fabricating events "to stay on the state's dole somehow." He told the reporter, "They all wanted it done. If they come a year or two later saying, 'Somebody forced me to have this done,' that's a lie. That's somebody looking for the state to give them a handout."

Johnson's investigation prompted a state audit, which affirmed the journalist's findings of abuse over an eight-year period. According to the state auditor's report, released in 2014, 144 women in the prison system (4 less than Johnson identified) underwent a bilateral tubal ligation, though only 39 did so under conditions of absent or dubious consent. In twenty-seven of these thirty-nine cases, the operating physician had failed to sign a form certifying the inmate's competence and understanding of the surgery's permanent effect. In eighteen, the required waiting period was not satisfied. In six cases, both requirements were violated. Targeted inmates shared a profile: They typically tested below a high school level of reading proficiency, had been pregnant five or more times, and were between twenty-six and forty years of age.

Even if a history of cesareans was a valid concern, the operating physicians had violated the law. In response to the audit, California governor Jerry Brown signed a bill banning sterilization as a form of birth control for women inmates of county jails, state prisons, and other detention centers. The bill made an exception for life-threatening situations, but mandated extensive counseling from independent physicians to prevent medical abuse. The new law also afforded protection to employees of correction facilities reporting violations of the law.

But eugenic practices extend well beyond California prisons. In other parts of the country, the criminal justice system has promoted court-ordered sterilizations as a condition of sentences. In 2009, a West Virginia judge required a twenty-one-year-old mother to undergo tubal ligation as a term of her probation for a marijuana possession. In 2015, news broke that prosecutors in Nashville, Tennessee, were stipulating birth control in plea deals with certain defendants. More recently, a judge in that state issued a standing order promising women a thirty-day sentence reduction in exchange for a birth control implant. (He also offered men a sentence reduction in exchange for a vasectomy.) The judge explained his order by saying, "I hope to encourage [the inmates] to take personal responsibility and give them a chance, when they do get out, not to be burdened with children." Echoing the authorities of Ann's day, who insisted sterilization was protective, rather than punitive, he added, "This gives them a chance to get on their feet and make something of themselves."

Prison inmates and criminal defendants are not the only individuals at risk of coercive practices. Disabled, transgender, intersex, and substance-dependent individuals are also subjected to sterilization abuse—which is only one mechanism for regulating reproduction, as eugenicists well knew. Immigration restrictions and welfare reforms provide other means of population control. When authorities refuse entry to "pregnant pilgrims" or when policy makers propose to deny citizenship to the soil-born children of non-citizens (pejoratively termed "anchor babies"), they seek to prevent the birth of certain kinds of people within their borders. Likewise, cuts to prenatal care under Medicaid and caps on welfare benefits based on family size constitute deliberate measures to prevent poor women from reproducing. This becomes very clear when the lawmakers promoting such policies suggest the need to stop women from having babies "just to get another few hundred dollars a month."

The Cooper Hewitt case helped to lay the groundwork for these social policies. By rearticulating the concept of parental fitness, the case repackaged eugenic principles for the modern era. And by declaring the potential dangers of the domestic environment, the case affirmed the need for both medical and nonmedical experts to intervene in reproductive practices based on their own arbitrary moral judgments. It allowed for concerns about population control, immigration, and welfare costs to supplant concerns about defective genes.

Long after the heiress and her mother faded from the spotlight, and even after the so-called sexual revolution of the '60s and '70s, Americans have generally continued to believe what the 1936 case decided: that while pleasure may be a universal right, procreation most certainly is not.

20

REMEMBERING ANN

New Yorkers strolling through Cooper Square, the East Village neighborhood where Cooper Union sits, or past the impressive English Georgian-style building on 91st Street, which houses the Cooper Hewitt Smithsonian Design Museum, might know a bit about the iconic American family behind the two institutions. But chances are, they haven't heard the sordid tale of one of its descendants and her mother. The sole biography of the Cooper Hewitt family only briefly mentions Ann and Maryon; and there is virtually no record of either woman within the Cooper Hewitt family collections.

Mortified by the scandalous women and their feud, Peter's siblings removed papers and records relating to Ann and Maryon from the items eventually donated to one of three institutions bearing the family's legacy: Cooper Union for the Advancement of Science and Art; the union's museum (now the design museum, housed in the former home of Andrew Carnegie); and Ringwood Manor, a National Historic Landmark administered by the Division of Parks and Forestry within the New Jersey Department of Environmental Protection. In trying to remove what they perceived to be a stain on the saga of a great family, the Hewitt siblings helped to erase

eugenics from the public memory while upholding the movement's ideals. The family members may not have bankrolled or
publicly supported sterilization campaigns, as many of their peers
did, but they shared eugenicists' disdain for women thought to be
disruptive.

Peter's siblings were correct in thinking that Ann's sterilization case undermined everything the family dynasty symbolized,
though not because of anything Ann did. Legendary men like
Peter, his father, and his grandfather represented the supposedly
unlimited opportunity available to Americans with ambition, as
well as the seemingly forward march of scientific thought. These
men further suggested that hard work inevitably leads to prosperity
and that ingenuity invariably advances human civilization. Ann's
story revealed that, in fact, many lives are constrained by the
perceived defects of one's birth or social circumstances—and that
science often reinforces fatalist narratives about people in the name
of social progress.

From a young age, Ann was fully aware of her paternal aunts'
and uncles' hatred for her. But she had no idea that there
was one Cooper Hewitt who hadn't shared their disdain: Lucy.
Unbeknownst to even her parents, Peter's first wife had bowed out
of her marriage for Ann's sake. Lucy knew that Peter was never
going to love her and that there was no use maintaining appear-
ances if it meant keeping him from the child she'd never been able
to give him. Whereas Peter's siblings questioned his paternity, then
declared Ann illegitimate upon his death, Lucy saw Ann as a child
only she could make valid (by allowing Peter to claim her). She
died in 1934 at her bluff-top estate in New Windsor, New York,
never knowing what became of Ann. She'd devoted the last decade
of her life to raising prizewinning livestock.

Ann never enjoyed such a successful second act, as she was

branded by the sterilization case until her final years in Mexico. Still, while a victim of familial wounds, medical abuse, and a relentless press, she managed to defy certain narratives about her. Contrary to her mother and doctors' claims that she was an invalid, too sick to lead an ordinary existence, she found much pleasure in life, pursuing painting and other passions. She once remarked that her eye for beauty was "one of the most precious gifts of her life"—one that no one could ever take away from her. And contrary to her mother's and later the press's claims that her defects rendered her unlovable, Ann believed she could be treasured. She knew that her mother's hatred for her probably stemmed from the fact that she'd been so dear in her father's eyes.

Ann also challenged the prevailing sentiment that women should be nurturing, submissive, and self-controlled. Even after being excoriated by the national press for her perceived moral failures, the fur-wearing heiress refused to allow conservative mores to interfere with her pursuit of love. Her string of working-class husbands suggests that she cared little what people thought of women who paid the mortgage from their own checkbooks, just as her refusal to adopt suggests that she didn't much care how the public regarded women without children who didn't spend every single moment dreaming of one.

With her many marriages, Ann drew numerous comparisons to her mother over the years. But those likening her to Maryon failed to appreciate that, in marriage, the two women pursued vastly different aims—in each case, what had been lacking in childhood. For Maryon, it was material comforts; for Ann, deep and abiding love. The heiress had fleetingly experienced such love while her father was alive, and she spent all of her adulthood chasing it.

Her desire for love was so intense that she often appealed to the very patriarchal ideals through which members of the press diminished her. In 1936, casting herself as innocent and worthy of love required her to cast her mother as a monster. Though her claims of abuse were founded, she stirred social anxieties by portraying Maryon as someone who either neglected her daughter or demanded total obedience though guilt, shame, and other means of psychological manipulation. The heiress understood that such a definitive characterization of Maryon would incite Americans, many of whom feared for the future of the family.

In maligning Maryon, and later Gertrude, Ann failed to appreciate the common wounds that she and these other women bore. In her own pain, she didn't see theirs. And longing to dodge the public's vicious scrutiny, she subjected them to the same. It never occurred to her to do what the *Madrigal* plaintiffs did decades later—uplift other women to resist those doing collective harm.

But Ann did show great generosity to all women when she decided to forgive her mother for her heinous crime. This might have been the boldest act of her life. After years of estrangement, Ann appeared at Maryon's graveside in Brooklyn and refused to indulge the public's desire to witness the dramatic humiliation of a woman perceived to embody the most unforgivable flaw, that of being unfit for motherhood. Having been tried for the same crime, Ann may have intuited that there was something frightening about the public's eagerness to condemn Maryon as a monster, even if her mother had indeed acted monstrously and even if she had been the one to first portray Maryon as such.

Observers attributed Ann's behavior to the emotional deficiencies of her childhood: "She never gained independence from the woman who controlled her. Not even a vile act could sever her from her abusive parent." But perhaps, in this moment, Ann simply saw Maryon for what she was: a human being. In showing compassion to the woman who had inflicted so many scars, the heiress undermined the intense misogyny surrounding women like her. She denied that it was others' job to rebuke those who failed to resemble the ideal mother. Most of all, in forgiving Maryon, Ann implicitly acknowledged the dignity and worth of socially outcast women, including herself.

AUTHOR'S NOTE

This is a work of creative nonfiction. The primary events, data, and attributed media quotes are factual, though certain quotes have been edited for readability. Some scenes, dialogue, and narrative details have been constructed for dramatic purposes. These elements, intended to bring Ann and other historical figures to life, are inspired by newspaper records, private correspondence, archival materials, court transcripts, and historical commentary, which can be found in the annotated bibliography. In an effort to give readers a sense of the worlds inhabited by these figures, I have used jargon and turns of phrase encountered in my research, especially found in the society pages that extensively reported on Ann and her parents.

I have greatly relied upon Wendy Kline's analysis of the Cooper Hewitt case and its relation to the broader eugenics movement in her book *Building a Better Race: Gender, Sexuality, and Eugenics from the Turn of the Century to the Baby Boom*. Alexandra Minna Stern's *Eugenic Nation: Faults and Frontiers of Better Breeding in Modern America*, Rebecca M. Kluchin's *Fit to Be Tied: Sterilization and Reproductive Rights in America, 1950–1980*, Dorothy Roberts's *Killing the Black Body: Race, Reproduction, and the Meaning of Liberty*, and Elena Gutiérrez's *Fertile Matters: The Politics of Mexican-Origin Women's Reproduction* have also informed the historical themes of this book. The themes recounted here do not present a comprehensive portrait of eugenics, but merely offer a few windows into a movement that continues to shape policies and lives.

ACKNOWLEDGMENTS

This book owes itself to so many generous and talented people, beginning with Maddie Caldwell, editor extraordinaire. The first moment I spoke with her, I knew she was the one to help me bring this story into the world. Time and again, she put her finger on problems I could only vaguely sense, pressed me to ask the hard questions, and gave me the courage to answer them. Ann and Maryon came to life on these pages thanks to her.

I could not have asked for a better team than the one at Grand Central Publishing. Like Maddie, Jacqui Young showed such enthusiasm for this story and graciously put up with my many first-time-author queries. She keenly intuited the book's more buried themes and found ways to bring them to the fore in promotional material. I'm incredibly grateful to cover designer Yang Kim, production editor Carolyn Kurek, copy editor Laura Jorstad, marketer Morgan Swift, and publicist Staci Burt for all they've done for this book.

Where would I be without my fairy godmother and literary agent, Marya Spence, who believed in this story when it was just sprouting and understood even then that it urgently needed to be told? She, along with Clare Mao, provided invaluable insights on early drafts, for which I am deeply indebted. Many thanks also goes to Natalie Edwards at Jankow & Nesbit for providing such vital support on everything from cover images to jacket copy.

I would not have been so blessed to have landed Marya were it not for Karah Preiss, who happened to read my July 2019 *Narratively* story on Ann and immediately put the two of us in touch. Of course, I must thank the editors at *Narratively* for accepting my strange pitch about a sterilized heiress, polishing the story until it sparkled, and then helping it to reach so many readers, including Karah. Much gratitude to Lynne Peskoe-Yang and Brendan Spiegel.

At various stages throughout the writing of this book, I had the opportunity to share my research in leading publications, whose editors sharpened my thinking about eugenics and its legacy. Special thanks to Lenika Cruz (*Atlantic*), Ben Huberman (*Longreads*), Carly Goodman (*Washington Post*), Jason Linkins (*New Republic*), and Alexandra Barylski (*Marginalia Review of Books*). Alexandra, along with her colleagues, has kindly allowed me to reproduce passages of my published essay here.

They say that PhDs never stop hearing the editorial voice of their advisers, and I'm fortunate to have Linda Kauffman's voice still guiding me. Linda, thank you for permitting me no shortcuts, nor too many uses of any single verb. Thanks also to Lee Konstantinou and Marcel Cornis-Pope for pushing me to be a better scholar, thinker, and writer.

This book would not exist were it not for Wendy Kline's historical research, which first introduced me to Ann and contextualized her case. As I have stated elsewhere, I have greatly relied on Wendy's insights in my own analysis of Ann's case. I came to her work only after nonchalantly taking up a hair-raising book of poems by Molly McCully Brown about women inmates at the Virginia State

Colony for Epileptics and Feebleminded. Haunted by the stories, I had to know more about the eugenics movement and swiftly dove down the rabbit hole. The following archivists assisted me and, in some cases, provided materials: Sue Shuttle of Ringwood Manor, Loma Karklins of the California Institute of Technology, and Linnea Anderson of University of Minnesota Libraries.

Finally, I'm blessed to have the love and support of my family. My parents and first readers have read—and saved—thousands of pages of my writing over the years. Where I cringe at old work, they only beam with pride. My in-laws have logged many hours caring for my kids to allow me quiet time for writing. My spouse and sounding board, Matt, has endured days and even months of my chewing over a single idea; and my little ones, Grace and Henry, bring daily joys, even if not calm. This book is dedicated to the three of them.

BIBLIOGRAPHY

CHAPTER ONE: THE STERILIZED HEIRESS

Annotated Bibliography

Some of the passages in this chapter originally appeared in an essay for *Narratively* (2019).

Details related to Ann's civil lawsuit can be found in chapter 4 of Kline (2001), Payne (2010), and the news stories cited below, some of which appear in the Association for Voluntary Sterilization Papers. For the most detailed coverage of Ann's claims of abuse at her mother's hands, see her stories, as told to Enid Hubbard, in the *San Francisco Examiner*. Readers interested in Peter Cooper Hewitt and his ancestors should consult Raymond (1901) and Guerin (2012).

A brief history of salpingectomy can be found in chapter 3 of Kline.

References

200 Offer to Aid Ann in Trial Here. (January 13, 1936). *San Francisco Examiner*, 6.
$500,000 Operation. (January 20, 1936). *Time*, 20.
Accuses Mother in Court. (January 24, 1936). *New York Times*, 2.
Association for Voluntary Sterilization Papers. Social Welfare History Archives at University of Minnesota. Box 14, Folder 20.
Battle of Alienists Indicated in Heiress' Sterilization Suit. (January 9, 1936). *Richmond Times-Dispatch*, 5.

Farley, Audrey. (July 8, 2019). The Curious Case of the Socialite Who Sterilized Her Daughter. *Narratively.* Available at: https://narratively.com/the-curious-case-of-the-socialite-who-sterilized-her-daughter.

Guerin, Polly. (2012). *The Cooper-Hewitt Dynasty of New York.* History Press, Charleston.

Hewitt, Ann Cooper. (January 10, 1936). Ann Hewitt's Own Story: As Told to Enid Hubbard. *San Francisco Examiner*, 6.

———. (January 11, 1936). Ann Hewitt's Story: As Told to Enid Hubbard. *San Francisco Examiner*, 6.

———. (January 12, 1936). Ann Hewitt Tells of Imprisonment: As Told to Enid Hubbard. *San Francisco Examiner*, 5.

———. (January 13, 1936). Accuses Mother of Inebriety: As Told to Enid Hubbard. *San Francisco Examiner*, 6.

———. (January 14, 1936). Ann Wins Fight for Freedom: As Told to Enid Hubbard. *San Francisco Examiner*, 12.

Hubbard, Enid. (January 10, 1936). Ann Haunted by Mirror. *San Francisco Examiner*, 10.

Kline, Wendy. (2001). *Building a Better Race: Gender, Sexuality, and Eugenics from the Turn of the Century to the Baby Boom.* University of California Press, Berkeley.

Letter from Nurse Offers Help to Girl. (January 11, 1936). *San Francisco Examiner*, 4.

Payne, G. S. (April 2010). The Curious Case of Ann Cooper Hewitt. *History Magazine*, 1–4.

Raymond, Rossiter. (1901). *Peter Cooper.* Riverside, Boston.

CHAPTER TWO: "OVER-SEXED"

Annotated Bibliography

Ann's "sex complex" is discussed by Kline (2001) in her fourth chapter. News accounts, cited on the next page, elaborate on Mrs. Cooper Hewitt's claims that Ann had an adolescent masturbation habit and overfondness for boys.

Discussion of Victorian sexual norms, as well as anxiety about early-twentieth-century women's resistance to such norms, can be found in chapters 1 and 3 of Kline, Preiss (2004), Preiss and Simmons (1989), and Odem (1995). For discussion of religious anxiety about changing sexual practices and the "liberated" woman, see DeBerg (2000). All of these scholars connect such sexual anxieties to concerns about the future of the white race; however, readers can find more in-depth analysis of race and sexuality in Roberts (1997). Roberts discusses how women of color were perceived to be immoral well before the twentieth century, despite the fact that many became pregnant out of wedlock only after being forcibly raped by white masters.

For in-depth analysis of the xenophobia fomenting in the early decades of the twentieth century, see Okrent (2019) and chapters 3, 4, and 5 of Black (2003).

Theodore Roosevelt's labeling of childless individuals as "race criminals" appears in a letter to Bessie Van Horst (1902). Importantly, Roosevelt was merely building upon Edward A. Ross's popular notion of "race suicide," discussed by Lovett (2007). For discussion of the Progressive response to the sexual habits of salesgirls and other workingwomen in the early twentieth century, see chapter 4 of Odem.

References

Affidavit Deceived Ann, Says Parent. (January 8, 1936). *San Francisco Examiner*, 2.

Black, Edwin. (2003). *War Against the Weak: Eugenics and America's Campaign to Create a Master Race*. Four Walls Eight Windows, New York.

Calls Ann Overly Romantic. (January 10, 1936). *New York Times*, 2.

DeBerg, Betty. (2000). *Ungodly Women: Gender and the First Wave of American Fundamentalism*. Mercer University Press, Macon.

Heiress Impresses in Testimony Accusing Mother and Doctors. (January 24, 1936). *Medform Mail Tribune*, 6.

Hewitt Doctors Defend Surgery as Authorized. (August 19, 1936). *Daily News*, 3.

Kline, Wendy. (2001). *Building a Better Race: Gender, Sexuality, and Eugenics from the Turn of the Century to the Baby Boom*. University of California Press, Berkeley.

Lovett, Laura L. (2007). The Political Economy of Sex: Edward A. Ross and Race Suicide. *Conceiving the Future: Pronatalism, Reproduction, and the Family in the United States, 1890–1938*. University of North Carolina Press, Chapel Hill: 77–108.

Odem, Mary E. (1995). *Delinquent Daughters: Protecting and Policing Adolescent Sexuality in the United States, 1885–1920*. University of North Carolina, Chapel Hill.

Okrent, Daniel. (2019). *The Guarded Gate: Bigotry, Eugenics, and the Law That Kept Two Generations of Jews, Italians, and Other European Immigrants out of America*. Scribner, New York.

Preiss, Kathy. (July 2004). Charity Girls and City Pleasures. *OAH Magazine of History* 18.4: 14–16.

Preiss, Kathy, and Christina Simmons (eds.). (1989). *Passion and Power: Sexuality in History*. Temple University Press, Philadelphia.

Roberts, Dorothy. (1997). *Killing the Black Body: Race, Reproduction, and the Meaning of Liberty*. Vintage, New York.

Roosevelt, Theodore. (October 18, 1902). Letter to Bessie Van Vorst. Available at: https://www.theodorerooseveltcenter.org/Research/Digital-Library/Record.aspx?libID=o18 3324.

Sensational Story Hinted on Schooling. (January 9, 1936). *San Francisco Examiner*, 3.

Tell of Hewitt Operation. (January 9, 1936). *New York Sun*.

CHAPTER THREE: REMAKING THE WORLD

Annotated Bibliography

A few passages have been reprinted from an essay I contributed to *Marginalia Review of Books* (2019).

A thorough discussion of the origins of the eugenics movement, as well as key figures Francis Galton, Charles Davenport, Harry Laughlin, and Margaret Sanger, can be found in Black (2003). Among other topics, Black discusses the formation of the Eugenics Record Office, the religiosity of certain eugenic crusaders, and the collaboration between eugenicists and Protestant church leaders in America. For more on religion and eugenics, see Rosen (2004). For a survey of religious leaders' mixed response to Ann's sterilization, see "Sterilization Hit, Upheld by Leaders" (1936).

Sanger's legacy and investment in eugenics is contested by historians, with some saying she merely aligned birth control with race betterment to benefit the former. The second chapter of Roberts (1997) intervenes in this debate, suggesting that Sanger did not share the view of most eugenicists that certain races were *genetically* inferior. Rather, she believed it was unchecked fertility that caused certain ethnic groups to experience poverty and disease. This somewhat softer view was still very problematic, and it led to many racist policies, argues Roberts.

On the importance of philanthropic support for eugenics, see chapters 4 and 6 of Black and chapter 4 of Okrent (2019). Black discusses such families as the Rockefellers, Carnegies, and Harrimans, while Okrent gives special attention to the Harriman family matriarch, Mary.

Carrie Buck's case is the central subject of Lombardo (2010) and Cohen (2016). Both describe Buck's early life, pregnancy by presumed rape, and the conspiracy between her attorney and the superintendent of the Virginia Colony, which resulted in the landmark Supreme Court decision upholding the legality of forcible sterilization.

Films as a form of eugenic propaganda are discussed by Pernick (1996). Both the Better Babies and Fitter Families contests are discussed in the Eugenics Image Archive. For a wider discussion of eugenics in popular culture, see Currell and Cogdell (2006).

The ascent and then seeming decline of eugenics is addressed in chapter 4 of Kline (2001). Here Kline also discusses California eugenicists Paul Popenoe and Ezra Gosney and the founding of the Human Betterment Foundation in Pasadena, which had a formative influence on Nazi Germany. Further information about the Human Betterment Foundation can be found in the E. S. Gosney and the Human Betterment Foundation collection at California Institute of Technology. For more on Adolf Hitler's adoption of ideas and tactics from the American eugenics movement within the context of eugenics, see chapter 15 of Black's volume. On the decline of hereditarian science and the rise of environmentalism in the context of eugenics, see chapter 1 of Kluchin (2011).

References

Black, Edwin. (2003). *War Against the Weak: Eugenics and America's Campaign to Create a Master Race*. Four Walls Eight Windows, New York.

Cohen, Adam. (2016). *Imbeciles: The Supreme Court, American Eugenics, and the Sterilization of Carrie Buck*. Penguin, New York.

Currell, Susan, and Christina Cogdell (eds.). (2006). *Popular Eugenics: National Efficiency and American Mass Culture in the 1930s*. Ohio University Press, Athens.

E. S. Gosney and the Human Betterment Foundation. California Institute of Technology.

Eugenics Image Archive. Dolan DNA Learning Center at Cold Spring Harbor Laboratory. Available at: http://www.eugenicsarchive.org/eugenics/list_topics.pl?theme=43.

Farley, Audrey. (October 18, 2019). The Revival of Raced-Based Medicine: Eugenics, Religion, and the Black Experience. *Marginalia Review of Books*. Available at: https://marginalia.lareviewofbooks.org/revival-of-raced-based-medicine-eugenics-religion-and-the-black-experience.

Kline, Wendy. (2001). *Building a Better Race: Gender, Sexuality, and Eugenics from the Turn of the Century to the Baby Boom*. University of California Press, Berkeley.

Kluchin, Rebecca M. (2011). *Fit to Be Tied: Sterilization and Reproductive Rights in America*. Rutgers University Press, New Brunswick, NJ.

Lombardo, Paul A. (2010). *Three Generations, No Imbeciles: Eugenics, the Supreme Court, and Buck v. Bell*. Johns Hopkins, Baltimore.

Okrent, Daniel. (2019). *The Guarded Gate: Bigotry, Eugenics, and the Law That Kept Two Generations of Jews, Italians, and Other European Immigrants out of America*. Scribner, New York.

Pernick, Martin. (1996). *The Black Stork: Eugenics and the Death of "Defective" Babies in American Medicine and Motion Pictures Since 1915*. Oxford University Press, Oxford.

Roberts, Dorothy. (1997). *Killing the Black Body: Race, Reproduction, and the Meaning of Liberty*. Vintage, New York.

Rosen, Christina. (2004). *Preaching Eugenics: Religious Leaders and the American Eugenics Movement*. Oxford University Press, Oxford.

Sterilization Hit, Upheld by Leaders. (January 8, 1936). *San Francisco Examiner*, 7.

CHAPTER FOUR: MAYHEM

Annotated Bibliography

For a summary of sterilization practices in California in the first three decades of the twentieth century, as well as insights on the application of the legal concept of "mayhem" to sterilization cases, see Miller and Dean (1930), Stern (2011), and chapter 4 of Kline (2001). For more information on the nature of salpingectomy, see chapter 3 of Kline.

A physician's early response to Ann Cooper Hewitt's case, with insights on the frequency of abortions performed in private practice and without the patient's consent, is provided by "A Dangerous Assumption" (1936).

On the medical profession's assumption of authority over deviant sexual behavior, with the referenced quote from the editor of *The Medical Record*, see Hansen (1992) and Oosterhuis (2012). See also chapter 2 of Kline on this subject. Here Kline discusses the role of the Sonoma State Home, where record numbers of individuals were sterilized after 1920 as officials' tactics shifted from segregation to surgery.

References

Calls Ann Overly Romantic. (January 10, 1936). *New York Times*, 2.

A Dangerous Assumption. (January 18, 1936). *New York Medical Week* 15.4.

Doctor Defends Sterilization. (January 15, 1936). *San Francisco Examiner*, 5.

Hansen, Bert. (1992). American Physicians' "Discovery" of Homosexuals, 1880–1900: A New Diagnosis in a Changing Society. *Framing Disease: Studies in Cultural History* (eds. Charles E. Rosenberg and Janet L. Golden), Rutgers University Press, New Brunswick, NJ: 104–133.

Heiress Impresses in Testimony Accusing Mother and Doctors. (January 24, 1936). *Medform Mail Tribune*, 6.

Heiress Will Not Sign Complaint Against Mother. (January 12, 1936). *St. Louis Dispatch*, 3.

Hewitt Doctors Defend Surgery as Authorized. (August 19, 1936). *Daily News*, 3.

Kline, Wendy. (2001). *Building a Better Race: Gender, Sexuality, and Eugenics from the Turn of the Century to the Baby Boom*. University of California Press, Berkeley.

Lack of State Law Told in Hewitt Case. (January 10, 1936). *San Francisco Examiner*, 6.

Miller, Justin, and Gordon Dean. (March 1930). Liability of Physicians for Sterilization Operations. *American Bar Association Journal*: 158–161.

New Evidence Hunted in Girl Sterilization. (January 10, 1936). *San Francisco Examiner*, 6.

Oosterhuis, Harry. (April 2012). Sexual Modernity in the Works of Richard von Krafft-Ebing and Albert Moll. *Medical History* 56.2: 133–155.

Police Decide on Charges in Sterilization. (January 10, 1936). *Middletown Times Herald*, 8.

Prosecutor to Act if Ann Signs. (January 11, 1936). *New York Times*, 16.

Stern, Alexandra Minna. (2011). From Legislation to Lived Experience: Eugenic Sterilization in California and Indiana, 1907–79. *A Century of Eugenics in America* (ed. Paul A. Lombardo), Indiana University Press, Bloomington.

Sweeping Probe. (January 8, 1939). *San Francisco Examiner*, 2.

Two Doctors Held in Ann Hewitt's Case. (February 20, 1936). *New York Times*, 3.

CHAPTER FIVE: THE NEWCOMER

Annotated Bibliography

An overview of Gilded Age New York is provided by Crain (2016). Crain discusses the legendary feud between the Astor and Vanderbilt families, emblematic of the tension between the city's "old rich" and "new rich." Here, too, readers will find history on the financial impact of the Civil War in New York, the rise of "robber barons," and the increasing popularity of hotel living. See Lears for more general history on the first few decades of the century, not only in New York, but across the nation.

Sarah Bernhardt's unconventional life and the culture of celebrity are explored by Marcus (2019). Importantly, Marcus notes tension between the press and the public with regard to controversial figures like Bernhardt, making the point that conservative journalists and society writers often failed to convince their readers to adopt their same judgments about women. Though Marcus's discussion of Bernhardt focuses on the nineteenth century, it is useful for understanding Maryon's reception in the early twentieth.

For a legal and cultural history of divorce in the twentieth century, see Difonzo (1997).

References

Awful Shadow That Menaces Baroness d'Erlanger's Daughter. (June 24, 1923). *San Francisco Chronicle*, 14.

Crain, Esther. (2016). *The Gilded Age in New York, 1870–1910*. Black Dog & Leventhal, New York.

Difonzo, J. Herbie. (1997). *Beneath the Fault Line: The Popular and Legal Culture of Divorce in Twentieth-Century America*. University of Virginia Press, Charlottesville.

Lears, Jackson. (2009). *Rebirth of a Nation: The Making of Modern America, 1877–1920*. Harper Perennial, New York.

Marcus, Sharon. (2019). *The Drama of Celebrity*. Princeton University Press, Princeton, NJ.

Marital Merry-Go-Round of Maryon Andrews—Continent to Continent. (January 6, 1926). *San Francisco Chronicle*.

Martin, Martha. (January 12, 1936). Daughter's Suit Jolts. *Daily News*, 52–53.

Mrs. Bruguiere and Former Daughter in Law Said to Have Eyes on $600,000 U. of C. Bequest. (December 28, 1911). *San Francisco Call*, 1.

Mrs. McCarter's All-Star Troupe of 5 Husbands. (November 25, 1934). *San Francisco Examiner*, 85.

New Twist in Bruguiere Tangle; Dr. Pedar Sued by Second Wife. (July 23, 1912). *San Francisco Examiner*, 3.

Peter Cooper Hewitt, Noted Inventor, Dead. (August 26, 1921). *Standard Union*, 6.

Physician Will Reveal All Matrimonial Secrets Necessary, Is Whisper. (July 25, 1912). *San Francisco Call*, 22.

Story of Baby Boy Is Read in Bruguiere Suit. (September 4, 1912). *San Francisco Call*, 22.

The Widow Discusses Her Sex. (July 5, 1906). *Town Topics: The Journal of Society.* 56.1: 16. New York Public Library.

Will the Gay Divorcee Mme. Bruguiere Now Gain Social Recognition? (January 12, 1919). *Philadelphia Inquirer*, 55.

CHAPTER SIX: THE CHRYSALIS

Annotated Bibliography

The changing nature of the press and the adoption of yellow journalism are discussed by Bessie (1942). "Ballyhoo" news—news with over-the-top publicity—is examined by Allen (1931), who offers the Hall-Mills double murder case as an example. More details about that case can be found in my article for *Contingent Magazine* (2020).

Discussion of cultural anxiety surrounding venereal disease can be found in Parascandola (2008), the third chapter of which describes the detainment of thirty thousand women during World War I. For analysis of the eugenicist logic of public health campaigns to eradicate sexually transmitted disease, see Lombardo (2017).

"Dollar princesses" are the subject of books by Ferry (2017) and De Courcy (2018). Both explore the allure of a title for wealthy nineteenth-century women. Their insights are useful for understanding Maryon Cooper Hewitt's motivations.

Josephson (1934) offers one of the first detailed histories of the "robber barons," who rose to power during or shortly after the American Civil War and engaged in business practices not meeting the public's moral standards, leading to calls for sweeping reform. Josephson also discusses the various laws violated by such men.

References

Allen, Frederick (1931). *Only Yesterday: An Informal History of the 1920s.* Harper & Row, New York.

Awful Shadow That Menaces Baroness d'Erlanger's Daughter. (June 24, 1923). *San Francisco Chronicle*, 14.

The Baroness d'Erlanger Is Named in Conspiracy; Charges Brought by Nurse Imprisoned in New York. (September 3, 1922). *Washington Times*, 27.

Bessie, Simon M. (1942). The Influence of the Tabloid. *The Press and Society: A Book of Readings* (ed. George L. Bird). Greenwood, Westport, CT: 183–186.

Child May Lose Peter Cooper Fund. (March 11, 1922). *New York Times*, 3.

Choice of Cash, Fourth Spouse Up to Pretty Widow. (October 1921). *Star Tribune*, 6.

Cost Her $488,393 to Marry a Husband She Could Not Live With. (July 17, 1927). *San Francisco Examiner*, 106.

De Courcy, Anne. (2018). *The Husband Hunters: American Heiresses Who Married into the British Aristocracy.* St. Martin's, New York.

Downs, Kenneth T. (May 1, 1936). Ann Cooper Hewitt's Suit Recalls Mother's Sensational Career. *Journal Times*, 24.

Dr. Bruguiere Legally Wed, Judge Decides. (April 15, 1913). *San Francisco Examiner*, 3.

Farley, Audrey. (March 8, 2020). Lovers Under an Apple Tree. *Contingent Magazine*. Available at: https://contingentmagazine.org/2020/03/08/lovers-under-an-apple-tree.

Ferry, Julie. (2017). *The Transatlantic Marriage Bureau.* Quarto, Islington, UK.

Hewitt, Ann Cooper. (January 10, 1936). Ann Hewitt's Own Story: As Told to Enid Hubbard. *San Francisco Examiner*, 6.

———. (January 11, 1936). Ann Hewitt's Story: As Told to Enid Hubbard. *San Francisco Examiner*, 6.

———. (January 12, 1936). Ann Hewitt Tells of Imprisonment: As Told to Enid Hubbard. *San Francisco Examiner*, 5.

———. (January 13, 1936). Accuses Mother of Inebriety: As Told to Enid Hubbard. *San Francisco Examiner*, 6.

———. (January 14, 1936). Ann Wins Fight for Freedom: As Told to Enid Hubbard. *San Francisco Examiner*, 12.

Josephson, Matthew. (1934). *The Robber Barons: The Great American Capitalists, 1861–1901.* Harcourt, Brace, New York.

Lombardo, Paul A. (Spring 2017). A Child's Right to Be Well Born: Venereal Disease and the Eugenic Marriage Laws, 1913–1935. *Perspectives in Biology and Medicine* 60.2: 211–232.

Marital Merry-Go-Round of Maryon Andrews—Continent to Continent. (January 6, 1926). *San Francisco Chronicle*.

Martin, Martha. (January 12, 1936). Daughter's Suit Jolts. *Daily News*, 52–53.

Mrs. McCarter's All-Star Troupe of 5 Husbands. (November 25, 1934). *San Francisco Examiner*, 85.

The Much Married Maryon. (June 4, 1939). *San Francisco Examiner*, 89.

Noted Inventor Gone. (August 31, 1921). *Salt Lake Tribune*, 6.

Parascandola, John. (2008). *Sex, Sin, and Science: A History of Syphilis in America.* Praeger, Santa Barbara.

Saunterings. (July 21, 1917). *Goodwin's Weekly.*

Too Beautiful for "The 400." (October 14, 1914). *San Francisco Examiner*, 26.

Why Brainy Men Often Marry Frivolous Wives. (November 16, 1919). *Richmond Times-Dispatch*, 67.

CHAPTER SEVEN: AN ACCIDENT

Annotated Bibliography

The racial undertones of Maryon's claim that Ann was attracted to men in uniform are discussed by Kline (2001). For discussion of the roots and implications of the "degeneration theory" that Maryon implicitly invoked, see Oosterhuis (2012) and Pick (1989).

On the Kallikak family and psychologist Henry Goddard, see chapter 2 of Roberts (1997) and chapter 5 of Black (2003). Both discuss Goddard's development of a classification system to diagnose and ultimately weed out feeblemindedness. For information on Lewis Terman's appropriation of Goddard's classification system (and the intelligence tests of French physician Théodore Simon and French psychologist Alfred Binet), see chapter 2 of Kline. Terman's Stanford-Binet was administered to Ann.

A rich reading of the flapper as a conservative symbol is offered by Simmons (1989). Simmons explains how psychologists, marriage manual writers, and sex educators in the early decades of the century softened the jazz-listening, bobbed-hair, and sexually liberated woman into an emblem of monogamous, heteronormative sexuality. This tactic allowed traditionalists to grant some gains to women, while reminding them to keep their eyes on marriage and babies.

References

Affidavit Deceived Ann, Says Parent. (January 8, 1936). *San Francisco Examiner*, 2.

Ann Cooper Hewitt's Mother Attempts to Commit Suicide. (February 29, 1936). *Owensboro Messenger*, 1.

Ann's Birth in Paris Told. (January 9, 1936). *San Francisco Examiner*, 3.

Black, Edwin. (2003). *War Against the Weak: Eugenics and America's Campaign to Create a Master Race*. Four Walls Eight Windows, New York.

Calls Ann Overly Romantic. (January 10, 1936). *New York Times*, 2.

Goddard, Henry. (1921). *The Kallikak Family: A Study in the Heredity of Feeble-Mindedness*. Macmillan, New York.

Kline, Wendy. (2001). *Building a Better Race: Gender, Sexuality, and Eugenics from the Turn of the Century to the Baby Boom*. University of California Press, Berkeley.

Lawyer Backs Mother's Acts. (January 9, 1936). *San Francisco Examiner*, 3.

Mrs. Hewitt Has Relapse. (March 16, 1936). *New York Times*, 4.

Mrs. Hewitt Still Very Ill. (March 4, 1936). *New York Times*, 10.

Oosterhuis, Harry. (April 2012). Sexual Modernity in the Works of Richard von Krafft-Ebing and Albert Moll. *Medical History* 56.2: 133–155.

Pick, Daniel. (1989). *Faces of Degeneration: A European Disorder, 1848–1918*. Cambridge University Press, Cambridge.

Roberts, Dorothy. (1997). *Killing the Black Body: Race, Reproduction, and the Meaning of Liberty.* Vintage, New York.

Simmons, Christina. (1989). Modern Sexuality and the Myth of Victorian Repression. *Passion and Power: Sexuality in History* (eds. Kathy Preiss and Christina Simmons), Temple University Press, Philadelphia: 157–177.

Stepbrother Denies Cruelty. (January 13, 1936). *New York Times*, 17.

Tell of Hewitt Operation. (January 9, 1936). *New York Sun.*

CHAPTER EIGHT: A NEW ANN

References

200 Offer to Aid Ann in Trial Here. (January 13, 1936). *San Francisco Examiner*, 6.

Ann's Mother in N.J. Hospital. (February 29, 1936). *San Francisco Examiner*, 1.

Ann Unmoved at News of Mother's Attempt. (February 29, 1936). *San Francisco Examiner*, 7.

Girl Normal Says Physician in East. (January 8, 1936). *San Francisco Examiner*, 2.

Hewitt, Ann Cooper. (January 10, 1936). Ann Hewitt's Own Story: As Told to Enid Hubbard. *San Francisco Examiner*, 6.

———. (January 11, 1936). Ann Hewitt's Story: As Told to Enid Hubbard. *San Francisco Examiner*, 6.

———. (January 12, 1936). Ann Hewitt Tells of Imprisonment: As Told to Enid Hubbard. *San Francisco Examiner*, 5.

———. (January 13, 1936). Accuses Mother of Inebriety: As Told to Enid Hubbard. *San Francisco Examiner*, 6.

———. (January 14, 1936). Ann Wins Fight for Freedom: As Told to Enid Hubbard. *San Francisco Examiner*, 12.

Letter from Nurse Offers Help to Girl. (January 11, 1936). *San Francisco Examiner*, 4.

Mentality of Young Heiress Is Questioned. (January 9, 1936). *Cumberland Evening Times*, 1.

New Report Favors Ann. (January 9, 1936). *San Francisco Examiner*, 3.

CHAPTER NINE: FUGITIVE PRISONER

Annotated Bibliography

Ezra Gosney's full remarks on the Hewitt case, published in the *Pasadena Star News*, can be found in the Association for Voluntary Sterilization Papers.

References

$3,500 Bail Set for Mrs. Hewitt. (July 1, 1936). *Central Jersey Home News*, 1.

Ann Cooper Hewitt's Mother Attempts to Commit Suicide. (February 29, 1936). *Owensboro Messenger*, 1.

Ann Hewitt's Mother Held for Mayhem. (February 29, 1936). *Daily News*, 3.

Gosney, Ezra S. (February 5, 1936). Sterilization Explained. *Pasadena Star News*. Found in Association for Voluntary Sterilization Papers, Social Welfare History Archives, University of Minnesota Libraries. Box 14, Folder 20.

Martin, Martha. (January 12, 1936). Daughter's Suit Jolts. *Daily News*, 52–53.

Miss Hewitt Called "Nut," Says Witness. (February 19, 1936). *Town Talk*, 2.

Mrs. Hewitt to Remain. (April 30, 1936). *Nebraska State Journal*, 2.

Report "Mental Age" of Jurist as 12 Years. (February 18, 1936). *Wilkes-Barre Times Leader*, 14.

CHAPTER TEN: PLOTTING

Annotated Bibliography

Letters between Paul Popenoe and I. M. Golden appear in the E. S. Gosney and the Human Betterment Foundation Papers at the California Institute of Technology. A copy of Ezra Gosney's remarks published in the *Pasadena Star News* appears in the Association for Voluntary Sterilization Papers. In the remarks, Gosney claims that there is no record of individuals having formally complained about being forcibly sterilized. In fact, many individuals in California had filed civil and criminal complaints or pursued other means to resist sterilization or seek damages after the fact. Some of these cases are discussed by Lira and Stern (2014), who argue that Mexican Americans were particularly fueled to resist sterilization practices because of their Catholic faith.

For a detailed discussion of how Ann's case symbolized the eugenics movement's transition from hereditarian to environmental frameworks, see Kline (2001). Kline argues that, facing criticism from scientific leaders, eugenicists realized the need for a tactical shift—and this shift was under way before Ann's case came into the spotlight, as evidenced by Huntington (1935). But as the eugenicists connected to Ann's case surely intuited, a favorable ruling in the high-profile court drama could greatly helped to cement the new avenue. See also chapter 1 of Kluchin (2011) on eugenic leaders' awareness of the need to rebrand the movement, prior to World War II.

References

E. S. Gosney and the Human Betterment Foundation. California Institute of Technology.

Gosney, Ezra S. (February 5, 1936). Sterilization Explained. *Pasadena Star News*. Found in Association for Voluntary Sterilization Papers, Social Welfare History Archives, University of Minnesota Libraries. Box 14, Folder 20.

Huntington, Ellsworth. (1935). *Tomorrow's Children: The Goal of Eugenics*. Wiley, New York.

Kline, Wendy. (2001). *Building a Better Race: Gender, Sexuality, and Eugenics from the Turn of the Century to the Baby Boom*. University of California Press, Berkeley.

Kluchin, Rebecca M. (2011). *Fit to Be Tied: Sterilization and Reproductive Rights in America*. Rutgers University Press, New Brunswick, NJ.

Lira, Natalie, and Alexandra Minna Stern. (Fall 2014). Mexican Americans and Eugenic Sterilization: Resisting Reproductive Justice in California, 1920–1950. *Aztlán: A Journal of Chicano Studies* 39.2: 9–22.

CHAPTER ELEVEN: THE WIZARD

Annotated Bibliography

Peter's life and childhood are captured by his brother's books on the family (Hewitt 1943, 1946). Edward Hewitt tells of the Hewitt boys' many adolescent pranks, inventions, and privileges at the family's Lexington Avenue and Ringwood homes. Guerin (2012) offers another perspective on Peter and his siblings, including his three sisters, two of whom devoted their lives to the family's philanthropic projects.

For discussion of the increasing cultural authority of science in the Gilded Age and Progressive Era, see Ehrenreich and English (1978) or the more recent work of Keel (2018). Keel discusses how nineteenth-century scientists' need to overcome the "trappings" of Christianity resulted in terribly racist and shoddy science.

Neurasthenia—essentially a nineteenth-century diagnosis of "burnout"—is the subject of Schuster (2011). Schuster explains that medical and scientific experts mostly agreed that modern ways of working and living were to blame for the nervous problems increasingly experienced by men and women.

Lucy Cooper Hewitt's notoriety on stage can be referenced in Murphy (2014). Here Murphy also discusses the significance of *tableaux vivants* for upper-class women in the late nineteenth century, who may have felt constrained by social conventions.

The "self-made man" myth was first explored in-depth by Wyllie (1954), who traced the term to statesman Henry Clay. As Wyllie discusses, the notion that anyone can rise from rags to riches has long had a strong hold on Americans, who tend to associate personal success with business success.

References

Another Police Outrage. (May 15, 1890). *New York Times*, 1.

Ehrenreich, Barbara, and Deirdre English. (1978). Science and the Ascent of the Experts. *For Her Own Good: Two Centuries of the Experts' Advice to Women*. Anchor, New York: 76–108.

Father Changed His Opinion. (July 20, 1904). *Fairmont West Virginian*, 6.

Greatest Light Yet Produced. (March 1, 1903). *Wichita Daily Eagle*, 17.

Guerin, Polly. (2012). *The Cooper-Hewitt Dynasty of New York*. History Press, Charleston.

Hewitt, Edward R. (1943). *Those Were the Days: Tales of a Long Life*. Duell, Sloan and Pearce, New York.

———. (1946). *Ringwood Manor, the Home of the Hewitts*. Trenton Printing Company, Trenton.

Hewitts Give Plays in Private Theater. (February 26, 1908). *New York Times*, 7.

Is a Great Invention. (February 2, 1902). *Detroit Free Press*, 36.

Keel, Terrance. (2018). *Divine Variations: How Christian Thought Became Racial Science*. Stanford University Press, Palo Alto, CA.

A Light Better than Daylight. (January 26, 1913). *San Francisco Call*, 6.

Mayor Hewitt's Son. (May 16, 1980). *Hartford Courant*, 2.

Mercury Vapor Lamp May Work Wireless Marvels. (December 6, 1914). *Oregon Daily Journal*, 63.

Murphy, Shannon. (April 29, 2014). She Wore Steels of Spur. *Cooper Hewitt Blog*. Available at: https://www.cooperhewitt.org/2014/04/29/she-wore-spurs-of-steel.

Raymond, Rossiter. (2013). *Peter Cooper*. Riverside, Boston.

Schuster, David. G. (2011). *Neurasthenic Nation: America's Search for Health, Happiness, and Comfort, 1869–1920*. Rutgers University Press, New Brunswick, NJ.

Weddings in the City. (April 28, 1887). *New York Tribune*, 5.

The Wonderful Hewitt Lamp. (June 18, 1903). *Salina Herald*, 1.

Wyllie, Irvin G. (1954). *The Self-Made Man in America: The Myth of Rags to Riches*. Rutgers University Press, New Brunswick, NJ.

Yesterday's Weddings. (April 28, 1887). *New York Times*, 5.

CHAPTER TWELVE: LOVE OR THE LAMP

Annotated Bibliography

Thomas Malthus's watershed theory on the nature of poverty and its influence on Englishmen such as Herbert Spencer is discussed in chapter 2 of Black (2003). According to Black, the wealthy classes had long perceived themselves to be inherently superior, but few considered withholding charity to let the poor die off, as Malthus had proposed. This changed in the early twentieth century, when eugenicists managed to convince Northeast millionaires that they needed to "cure evils at their source," in the words of John D. Rockefeller. By this, the oil magnate meant preventing the reproduction of people perceived bound to live in squalor because of their genetic defects.

For more on the Rockefeller, Harriman, Kellogg, and Carnegie families' financial and public support for eugenic programs, see chapters 4 and 6 of Black and chapter 4 of Okrent (2019).

President Warren Harding's nationalist campaign and his support for eugenics upon assuming office are discussed by Berman (2015). Not discussed, but of note: Harding's vice president elect Calvin Coolidge penned an editorial (1921) shortly before being sworn in, in which he advocated for stringent immigration restrictions. In a piece titled "Whose Country Is This?" Coolidge wrote, "Biological laws tell us that certain divergent people will not mix or blend. The Nordics propagate themselves successfully."

Information on the Second International Eugenics Congress, held in New York in September 1921, can be found in chapter 2 of Okrent.

References

Berman, Russell. (August 14, 2015). Warren G. Harding's Terrible Tenure. *The Atlantic*. Available at: https://www.theatlantic.com/politics/archive/2015/08/warren-g-harding-nan-britton-affair/401288.

Black, Edwin. (2003). *War Against the Weak: Eugenics and America's Campaign to Create a Master Race*. Four Walls Eight Windows, New York.

Carnegie, Andrew. (1889). The Gospel of Wealth. Reprinted in *The Gilded Age and Progressive Era: A Documentary Reader* (eds. William A. and Susannah J. Link), Blackwell, Hoboken.

Coolidge, Calvin. (February 1921). Whose Country Is This? *Good Housekeeping*, 14.

Cooper Hewitt Denies Wife Wants to Part. (July 31, 1921). *Daily News*, 46.

Craydon, Barbara. (September 19, 1920). Love or the Lamp? *El Paso Times*, 39.

Okrent, Daniel. (2019). *The Guarded Gate: Bigotry, Eugenics, and the Law That Kept Two Generations of Jews, Italians, and Other European Immigrants out of America*. Scribner, New York.

P. C. Hewitt Estate in Trust to Widow; Funeral Is Held. (September 15, 1921). *New York Herald*, 9.

Peter Cooper Hewitt Quits Democratic Party. (October 4, 1920). *New York Tribune*, 2.

Peter Cooper Hewitt Sees Great Possibilities in Aerial Warfare. (November 7, 1915). *Detroit Free Press*, 92.

Will the Gay Divorcee Mme. Bruguiere Now Gain Social Recognition? (January 12, 1919). *Philadelphia Inquirer*, 55.

CHAPTER THIRTEEN: THE CRIMINAL TRIAL

Annotated Bibliography

Paul Popenoe's and I. M. Golden's letters to each other following Judge Raglan Tuttle's dismissal of the criminal mayhem case against the two doctors can be found in the Ezra S. Gosney and Human Betterment Foundation Papers. In Golden's letter accepting Popenoe's congratulations, the attorney attaches a copy of Judge Tuttle's written decision.

A thorough analysis of the implications of the criminal case appears in chapter 4 of Kline (2001). Here Kline notes the lack of protests and riots following Judge Tuttle's decision, which she reads as a sign of widespread public support of eugenics and its burgeoning emphasis on the domestic environment as a means to determine maternal unfitness. Kline mentions Fred Hogue's column in the *Los Angeles Times Sunday Magazine* (1936), which printed a letter from a reader in support of eugenics. (Hogue claimed to have received many such letters.)

Kline also discusses how the Cooper Hewitt case intervened in legal debates about the application of "mayhem" to sterilization cases. She argues that, by denying that criminal mayhem had been committed against Ann, the court implicitly sided with those claiming that the purpose of sexuality was pleasure, not reproduction. Such a notion marked a departure from Victorian thought—and would be reflected in sterilization practices for years to come.

Paul Popenoe's writings on Mexican Americans, whom the eugenicist perceived to be "hyperbreeding" inferiors, are discussed in Stern (2005). For discussion of efforts to reduce the black birth rate in the South during the same time period, see chapter 2 of Roberts (1997).

References

Ann Hewitt Duped into Sterilization, She Tells Court. (August 15, 1936). *New York Daily News*, 5.
Court Throws Out Ann Cooper Hewitt Case. (August 20, 1936). *New York Times*, 12.
Doctor Defends Sterilization. (January 15, 1936). *San Francisco Examiner*, 5.
Dramatic Story of Ann Told on Stand. (August 15, 1936). *San Francisco Examiner*, 5.
Ends Cooper Hewitt Case. (September 1, 1936). *New York Times*, 44.
Ezra S. Gosney and Human Betterment Foundation Papers. California Institute of Technology. Box 11, Folder 9.
Girl Hits Back at Mother. (January 10, 1936). *New York Times*, 2.
Hewitt, Ann Cooper. (January 10, 1936). Ann Hewitt's Own Story: As Told to Enid Hubbard. *San Francisco Examiner*, 6.

———. (January 11, 1936). Ann Hewitt's Story: As Told to Enid Hubbard. *San Francisco Examiner*, 6.

———. (January 12, 1936). Ann Hewitt Tells of Imprisonment: As Told to Enid Hubbard. *San Francisco Examiner*, 5.

———. (January 13, 1936). Accuses Mother of Inebriety: As Told to Enid Hubbard. *San Francisco Examiner*, 6.

———. (January 14, 1936). Ann Wins Fight for Freedom: As Told to Enid Hubbard. *San Francisco Examiner*, 12.

Hewitt Doctors Defend Surgery as Authorized. (August 19, 1936). *Daily News*, 3.

Hogue, Fred. (October 25, 1936). Social Eugenics. *Los Angeles Times Sunday Magazine*, 31.

Hubbard, Enid. (January 10, 1936). Ann Haunted by Mirror. *San Francisco Examiner*, 10.

Hyman, A. D. (August 15, 1936). Heiress Pawn, Says Counsel for Doctors. *San Francisco Examiner*, 1.

Kline, Wendy. (2001). *Building a Better Race: Gender, Sexuality, and Eugenics from the Turn of the Century to the Baby Boom.* University of California Press, Berkeley.

Legal Sterilization. (August 20, 1936). *San Francisco Examiner*, 2.

Plot Charged in Mayhem Case. (August 15, 1936). *Courier-Journal.*

Roberts, Dorothy. (1997). *Killing the Black Body: Race, Reproduction, and the Meaning of Liberty.* Vintage, New York.

Stern, Alexandra Minna. (July 2005). Sterilized in the Name of Public Health. *American Journal of Public Health* 95.7: 1128–1138.

CHAPTER FOURTEEN: BURYING THE STERILIZED HEIRESS

Annotated Bibliography

A summary of mid-twentieth-century popular thought on women's emotions and fertility can be found in Epstein (2003). For a taste of both the anti-scientific and patronizing attitudes directed at childless women of the era, see "Emotional Compensations for Childless Wives Offered" (1950). A more trans-historical overview of stereotypes of childless women is offered by Kimball (2019). Kimball discusses, for instance, how infertile women have been portrayed as destructive monsters dating back to Greek mythology.

An analysis of the "blunderer"—the aloof male who doesn't know how to emotionally or sexually satisfy his mate—is offered by Simmons (1989). Simmons reads the figure as a sign that cultural authorities had let go of Victorian notions of man's natural depravity in order to preserve male dominance in a world where women increasingly denied male needs. Roberts (1997) clarifies that white men who raped slaves were seldom considered to be depraved—and that men of color are still perceived as violent brutes, despite the waning of Victorian value systems.

References

Ann Bradstreet Reported Ill. (July 7, 1939). *New York Times*, 18.

Ann Cooper Hewitt's 10,000 Marriage Proposals. (September 20, 1936). *Philadelphia Inquirer*, 122.

Ann Cooper Hewitt's Love for Working Men. (September 14, 1941). *Tennesseean*, 55.

Ann Cooper Hewitt Wed for 3rd Time. (August 11, 1941). *Herald-News*, 11.

Ann Hewitt Files Suit for $50,000. (August 14, 1937). *San Francisco Examiner*, 11.

Ann Hewitt Says "I'm Through." (January 16, 1938). *San Francisco Examiner*, 3.

Ann Hewitt's Mother Dies Penniless. (May 1, 1939). *San Francisco Examiner*, 1.

Court Holds Hewitt Case. (December 24, 1936). *New York Times*, 13.

Doctor in Hewitt Case Succumbs. (January 25, 1937). *Nevada Journal*, 3.

Emotional Compensations for Childless Wives Offered. (December 12, 1950). *Lansing State Journal*, 21.

Epstein, Randi Hutter. (2003). Emotions, Fertility, and the 1940s Woman. *Journal of Public Health Policy* 24.2: 195–211.

First Happy Chapter Opens for Heiress. (October 9, 1937). *San Francisco Examiner*, 5.

Fowler, Gene. (1936). The Sterilized Heiress. Reprinted in H. Allen Smith's *The Life and Legend of Gene Fowler* (1977). Macmillan, New York.

Heiress Ann Hewitt's New Compensation Husband. (April 23, 1939). *Tennessean*.

Heiress Begins Life Anew; "Happy for First Time." (October 11, 1937). *Evening Sun*, 3.

Hewitt Heiress Dies Here at 55. (May 1, 1939). *New York Times*, 42.

Hewitt Trial Dropped. (December 16, 1936). *New York Times*, 2.

Kimball, Alexandra. (2019). *The Seed: Infertility Is a Feminist Issue.* Coach House, Toronto.

Maryon Hewitt, Once Worth Millions, Dies Alone and Unattended. (May 1, 1939). *Californian*, 1.

Mrs. Cooper Hewitt Loses Extradition Fight. (December 8, 1936). *New York Times*, 27.

Mrs. Hewitt, in Court, Waives a Hearing. (October 2, 1936). *New York Times*, 18.

Ready for Mrs. Hewitt's Trial. (December 9, 1936). *New York Times*, 17.

Roberts, Dorothy. (1997). *Killing the Black Body: Race, Reproduction, and the Meaning of Liberty.* Vintage, New York.

Simmons, Christina. (1989). Modern Sexuality and the Myth of Victorian Repression. *Passion and Power: Sexuality in History* (eds. Kathy Preiss and Christina Simmons), Temple University Press, Philadelphia: 157–177.

Ucker, William. (November 7, 1937). Can Ann Be Happy Without a Baby? *New Orleans Item.*

CHAPTER FIFTEEN: MR. MARRIAGE

Annotated Bibliography

Some of the content in this chapter appeared in a 2019 *Longreads* essay.

Popenoe's turn to "positive eugenics" is well documented in chapter 5 of Kline (2001), Ladd-Taylor (2001), and Lepore (2010), all of whom discuss his prolific counseling career, his popular advice column "Can This Marriage Be Saved?" in *Ladies' Home Journal*, and his influence on "traditional family values" crusaders in the late twentieth century. James Dobson's ties to Popenoe are discussed in David Popenoe (1991). For a parallel discussion of Popenoe's colleague (and co-author) Roswell Johnson's embrace of positive eugenics, see Slavishak (2009). Slavishak argues that Johnson abandoned sterilization mandates for "a more therapeutic stance that cast individual decisions in the context of managed family life." Eugenics' movement from the public to the private sector in more recent decades is discussed by Roberts (2005) and Black (2003).

Details about Popenoe's private life, including rumors of scandal, can be found in David Popenoe (1991), as well as Lepore. According to Popenoe, claims that "the man who saved marriages had a troubled one himself" haunted the marriage counselor for much of his career, despite there being no true scandal. David Popenoe's support of strict sex-gender norms is discussed by Smith (2017). His attitudes on marriage and parenthood are outlined in greater detail in his own book (2005).

References

Black, Edwin. (2003). *War Against the Weak: Eugenics and America's Campaign to Create a Master Race.* Four Walls Eight Windows, New York.

Farley, Audrey. (June 2019). We Still Don't Know How to Navigate the Cultural Legacy of Eugenics. *Longreads.* Available at: https://longreads.com/2019/06/19/we-still-dont-know-how-to-navigate-the-cultural-legacy-of-eugenics.

Kline, Wendy. (2001). *Building a Better Race: Gender, Sexuality, and Eugenics from the Turn of the Century to the Baby Boom.* University of California Press, Berkeley.

Ladd-Taylor, Molly. (2001). Eugenics, Sterilization, and Modern Marriage in the USA: The Strange Career of Paul Popenoe. *Gender & History* 13: 299.

Lepore, Jill. (March 22, 2010). Fixed. *The New Yorker.* Available at: https://www.newyorker.com/magazine/2010/03/29/fixed.

Popenoe, David. (1991). Remembering My Father: An Intellectual Portrait of "The Man Who Saved Marriages." A publication of the Institute for American Values. Available at: http://americanvalues.org/catalog/pdfs/wp-10.pdf.

———. (2005). *War Over the Family.* Transaction, Piscataway.

Popenoe, Paul. (1953). *Can This Marriage Be Saved?* Macmillan, New York.

Roberts, Dorothy E. (2005). Privatization and Punishment in the New Era of Reprogenetics. *Faculty Scholarship at Penn Law* 579. Available at: https://scholarship.law.upenn.edu/faculty_scholarship/579.

Slavishak, Edward. (January 2009). From Nation to Family: Two Careers in the Recasting of Eugenics. *Journal of Family History* 34.1: 89–115.

Smith, Laura. (September 15, 2017). In the 1920s, This Man Brought Marriage Counseling to America to Save the White Race. *Timeline.* Available at: https://timeline.com/popenoe-eugenics-marriage-counseling-faa8aacb0f3d.

CHAPTER SIXTEEN: THE INQUEST

Annotated Bibliography

For a history of blood tests as a means to regulate marriage on eugenic grounds, see Lombardo (2017). Lombardo notes that more than forty states, including California, required blood tests for much of the twentieth century. While state officials claimed to have an interest in preventing stillbirth and affliction from disease, blood tests were also meant to combat interracial coupling, as Johnson (2018) explores. Experts associated certain diseases, such as Tay-Sachs and sickle cell anemia, with certain groups (Jewish and African American persons, respectively).

For discussion of the pressure upon infertile women to pray or embrace more positive attitudes, dating back to the days of the Old and New Testaments, see Kimball (2019). See also Epstein (2003) on the blaming of women for their infertility. Surveying 1940s expert advice and popular writing, Epstein notes that infertile women's struggles were exploited to warn of the dangers of abandoning domestic life for a professional career. Epstein further observes how fertility therapies, such as talk therapy, were geared toward pushing women to accept their fates in the home.

References

Ann Cooper Hewitt Attends Funeral of New Husband's Second Wife at Sacramento. (September 24, 1947). *Nevada State Journal*, 10.
Ann Cooper Hewitt Divorcing Roy. (May 11, 1950). *Daily Independent Journal*, 5.
Ann Cooper Hewitt's Love for Working Men. (September 14, 1941). *Tennesseean*, 55.
Ann Cooper Hewitt Will File. (March 17, 1950). *Reno Gazette Journal*, 11.
Ann Weds Again. (September 8, 1950). *Nevada State Journal*, 3.
Epstein, Randi Hutter. (2003). Emotions, Fertility, and the 1940s Woman. *Journal of Public Health Policy* 24.2: 195–211.
Heiress Ann Cooper Hewitt Dies in Mexico Ranch House. (February 11, 1956). *Journal Herald*, 37.
Heiress's Marriage Linked to Suicide of Groom's Wife in S.F. (September 23, 1947). *San Francisco Examiner*, 1.
Johnson, Kirk A. (2018) *Medical Stigmata: Race, Medicine, and the Pursuit of Theological Liberation*. Palgrave Macmillan, London.
Kimball, Alexandra. (2019). *The Seed: Infertility Is a Feminist Issue*. Coach House, Toronto.
Lombardo, Paul A. (Spring 2017). A Child's Right to Be Well Born: Venereal Disease and the Eugenic Marriage Laws, 1913–1935. *Perspectives in Biology and Medicine* 60.2: 211–232.
She's Going to Have a Boy. (October 5, 1947). *Daily News*, 116.

CHAPTER SEVENTEEN: OPERATION LAWSUIT

Annotated Bibliography

Operation Lawsuit is the subject of chapter 4 of Kluchin (2011), which chronicles the efforts of "fit" (white) women to secure reproductive rights in the 1970s. Here Kluchin describes the cases of both Florence Caffarelli and Robbie Mae Hathaway. She notes that Hathaway's case was only decided after being dismissed multiple times. While it bolstered other cases around the nation, it also ushered in new challenges for Operation Lawsuit and the broader reproductive rights movement in the form of spousal consent and conscience clauses. Husbands filed suits to prevent their wives from obtaining surgeries without their permission; and doctors filed suits to seek protections for refusing to perform surgeries on moral grounds.

Kluchin claims that Operation Lawsuit benefited from the racial privilege of plaintiffs, but struggled because of such plaintiffs' unwillingness to fight for collective change.

References

Cadden, Vivian. (May 1972). A Very Private Decision. *Good Housekeeping*, 148.
Kluchin, Rebecca M. (2011). *Fit to Be Tied: Sterilization and Reproductive Rights in America*. Rutgers University Press, New Brunswick, NJ.

CHAPTER EIGHTEEN: *MADRIGAL V. QUILLIGAN*

Annotated Bibliography

The *Madrigal v. Quilligan* case is the subject of chapter 3 of Gutiérrez (2009) and Stern (2005). Both discuss the impact of Johnson's War on Poverty upon sterilization rates in the early 1970s, as well as the increasing alarm surrounding overpopulation in the post–World War II years. See Manian (2018) for more detailed profiles of the ten plaintiffs.

The court transcripts of *Madrigal v. Quilligan* (1978) are housed in the Carlos G. Vélez-Ibáñez Sterilization Research Collection. They can be accessed online. Many of the plaintiffs, along with defendant Edward Quilligan, attorneys Charles Nabarrete and Antonia Hernández, and physician Bernard Rosenfeld, appear in the film *No Más Bebés*, which aired on PBS in 2016.

For a discussion of the Relf sisters and sterilization abuse in the South, see Dorr (2011). For discussion of the cases of Fortuna Valencia and Andrea García, see Lira and Stern (2014). The latter more broadly discusses Mexican American resistance to forcible sterilization in California from 1920 to 1950, providing historical context for the actions of the *Madrigal* plaintiffs. See Theobald (2019) on involuntary sterilization on native reservations in the United States.

Roberts (1997) discusses how the Civil Rights Act intensified prejudice against black women, who became known as "welfare queens" soon after qualifying for the federal programs designed for and long enjoyed by white mothers. See chapter 5 for discussion of the redoubled push to control reproduction in African American communities in the decades following the landmark bill. On the immediate impact of the Personal Responsibility and Work Opportunity Reconciliation Act on immigrants, see Gutiérrez and Espenshade et al. (1997).

References

Dorr, Gregory Michael. (2011). Protection or Control? Women's Health, Sterilization Abuse, and *Relf v. Weinberger. A Century of Eugenics in America* (ed. Paul A. Lombardo), Indiana University Press, Bloomington.

Espenshade, Thomas J., Jessica L. Baraka, and Gregory A. Huber. (December 1997). Implications of the 1996 Welfare and Immigration Reform Acts for US Immigration. *Population and Development Review* 23.4: 769–801.

Evidence Mounts That Thousands Victimized by Unregulated, "Voluntary" Sterilization Programs. (December 8, 1974). *Poughkeepsie Journal*, 10A.

Gutiérrez, Elena R. (2009). *Fertile Matters: The Politics of Mexican-Origin Women's Reproduction.* University of Texas Press, Austin.

Lira, Natalie, and Minna Stern. (Fall 2014). Mexican Americans and Eugenic Sterilization: Resisting Reproductive Justice in California, 1920–1950. *Aztlán: A Journal of Chicano Studies* 39.2: 9–22.

Madrigal v. Quilligan Court Transcripts. (1978). Carlos G. Vélez-Ibáñez Sterilization Research Collection, 20, Chicano Studies Library, University of California at Los Angeles.

Manian, Maya. (2018). The Story of *Madrigal v. Quilligan*: Coerced Sterilization of Mexican-American Women. Preliminary draft of essay submitted to *Reproductive Rights and Justice Stories.* Available at: https://papers.ssrn.com/sol3/papers.cfm?abstract_id=3134892.

No Más Bebés. (2016). Directed by Renee Tajima-Peña. Produced by Virginia Espino. Moon Canyon, Los Angeles.

The Politics of Sterilization. (1971). Chicago Women's Liberation Union. Available at: https://www.cwluherstory.org/health/the-politics-of-sterilization.

Roberts, Dorothy. (1997). *Killing the Black Body: Race, Reproduction, and the Meaning of Liberty.* Vintage, New York.

Stern, Alexandra Minna. (2005). *Eugenic Nation: Faults and Frontiers of Better Breeding in America.* University of California Press, Santa Barbara.

———. (July 2005). Sterilized in the Name of Public Health. *American Journal of Public Health* 95.7: 1128–1138.

Stop Forced Sterilization Now. (Undated). Committee to Stop Forced Sterilization. Available at: http://freedomarchives.org/Documents/Finder/DOC46_scans /46.StopForcedSterilizationNow.pdf.

Theobald, Brianna. (2019). *Reproduction on the Reservation: Pregnancy, Childbirth, and Colonialism in the Long Twentieth Century.* University of North Carolina Press, Chapel Hill.

CHAPTER NINETEEN: ANOTHER REVEAL

Annotated Bibliography

The recent abuses within the California prison system were first uncovered by Corey G. Johnson (July 7, 2013). The journalist's findings prompted a state audit, the results of which were published in June 2014. The audit confirmed abuse, though on a smaller scale than Johnson claimed.

More detail on sterilization abuse of disabled, transgender, intersex, and substance-dependent individuals can be found in World Health Organization (2014). For discussion of immigration restrictions and welfare caps as means of controlling the fertility of certain kinds of people, see Gutiérrez (2011) and Roberts (1997).

References

California State Auditor. (June 2014). Sterilization of Female Inmates. Available at: https://www.auditor.ca.gov/pdfs/reports/2013-120.pdf.

Gutiérrez, Elena R. (2009). *Fertile Matters: The Politics of Mexican-Origin Women's Reproduction.* University of Texas Press, Austin.

Hunter, Lee. (August 23, 2017). The U.S. Is Still Forcibly Sterilizing Prisoners. *Talk Poverty.* Available at: https://talkpoverty.org/2017/08/23/u-s-still-forcibly-sterilizing-prisoners.

Johnson, Corey G. (July 7, 2013). Female Inmates Sterilized in California Prisons Without Approval. *Reveal.* Available at: https://www.revealnews.org/article/female -inmates-sterilized-in-california-prisons-without-approval.

———. (July 11, 2013). Lawmakers Call for Investigation into Sterilization of Female Inmates. *Reveal.* Available at: https://www.revealnews.org/article/lawmakers-call -for-investigation-into-sterilization-of-female-inmates.

———. (August 14, 2013). Calif. Lawmakers Seek Legislation to Prevent Prison Sterilization Abuse. *Reveal.* Available at: https://www.revealnews.org/article/calif -lawmakers-seek-legislation-to-prevent-prison-sterilization-abuse.

———. (September 26, 2014). California Bans Coerced Sterilization of Female Inmates. *Reveal.* Available at: https://www.revealnews.org/article-legacy/california -bans-coerced-sterilization-of-female-inmates.

Rosenblatt, Kalhan. (July 21, 2017). Judge Offers Inmates Reduced Sentences in Exchange for Vasectomy. *NBC News*. Available at: https://www.nbcnews.com/news/us-news /judge-offers-inmates-reduced-sentences-exchange-vasectomy-n785256.

Roberts, Dorothy. (1997). *Killing the Black Body: Race, Reproduction, and the Meaning of Liberty*. Vintage, New York.

Tennessee Prosecutor Fired Over Plea Bargains Involving Female Sterilization. (April 1, 2015). *The Guardian*. Available at: https://www.theguardian.com/us-news/2015/apr /01/tennessee-prosecutor-fired-female-sterilization-plea-bargains.

World Health Organization. (2014). Eliminating Forced, Coercive and Otherwise Involuntary Sterilization. An interagency statement by OHCHR, UN Women, UNAIDS, UNDP, UNFPA, UNICEF, and WHO. Available at: https://www.unaids.org/sites /default/files/media_asset/201405_sterilization_en.pdf.

CHAPTER TWENTY: REMEMBERING ANN

References

Ann Cooper Hewitt's 10,000 Marriage Proposals. (September 20, 1936). *Philadelphia Inquirer*, 122.

Guerin, Polly. (2012). *The Cooper-Hewitt Dynasty of New York*. History Press, Charleston.

Hewitt, Ann Cooper. (January 14, 1936). Ann Wins Fight for Freedom: As Told to Enid Hubbard. *San Francisco Examiner*, 12.

Lucy Work Hewitt Dies of Pneumonia. (March 22, 1934). *New York Times*, 22.

"Woodburn Hall's Eccentric Owner Kept Strange Company." (April 28, 2015). *Poughkeepsie Journal*. Available at: https://www.poughkeepsiejournal.com/story/news/local/2015/04 /28/dateline-history-woodburn-hall/26523817.

READING GROUP GUIDE

THE UNFIT
HEIRESS

DISCUSSION QUESTIONS

1. At the time of publishing, this case was eighty-five years old. Why do you think the author chose to write about it now?

2. Each side of the court case, as well as society at large, tried to use Ann and Maryon's personal lives to discredit them. How are a woman's sexuality and personal affairs similarly weaponized to this day?

3. There is little question that Maryon is a villain of this story, but how was she also a victim of a society that believed women should adhere to strict norms? Are there ways society's treatment of her influenced her treatment of Ann?

4. How did attitudes toward immigrants and African Americans shape Ann's early life and subsequent court case? Do you see any ways that fears about "good stock" continue to guide policy in the United States?

5. Legislating her reproductive rights is the most prominent way doctors and judges sought to control Ann in this narrative. What are other, subtler instances of the state or society exerting control over Ann? Do you feel any of those pressures in your day-to-day life?

6. There is no question that Ann's socioeconomic status benefited her, from the attention her case got to the legal guidance she was able to procure, but are there ways it hurt her as well?

7. What are the pitfalls of giving any profession, in this case that of medicine, the right to make moral judgments? How do we rely on doctors or medical scientists to shape human behavior?

8. Peter isn't necessarily relevant to the central action, aside from providing a contrast in parenting styles with Maryon and being responsible for the fortune the two women are fighting over, yet the author dedicates a chapter to his upbringing. What is gained by juxtaposing his and Ann's adolescence and opportunities?

9. How did the press try to shape Maryon's and Ann's stories, and to what ends? Do you think *The Unfit Heiress* posthumously gives both women a fairer portrayal by viewing them through modern standards or not?

10. After the first court case has concluded, Ann regrets pursuing it because of the damage it did to her mother, and ultimately refuses to testify in California, despite the deep pain Maryon

has caused her. Do you think she made the right choice? Would you have acted similarly?

11. The prosecutor trying the two doctors for criminal mayhem did not challenge the legality or ethics of sterilization—only the lawfulness of sterilizing Ann. Accordingly, he and various witnesses drew upon very classist, sexist, and ableist arguments. How did these same arguments shape sterilization practices for decades to come? How did they come to bear on the court proceedings in Los Angeles in the late 1970s?

12. Like Ann, the Operation Lawsuit plaintiffs pursued legal recourse for themselves at the expense of more collective change. Do you believe their cases underscore the importance of supporting other women? Why or why not?

YOUR
BOOK
CLUB
RESOURCE

VISIT
GCPClubCar.com

to sign up for the **GCP Club Car** newsletter, featuring exclusive promotions, info on other **Club Car** titles, and more.

GRAND
CENTRAL

FOREVER

12

TWELVE

LEGACY
LIT

balance

ABOUT THE AUTHOR

AUDREY CLARE FARLEY is a scholar of twentieth-century American culture. She holds a PhD in English literature from the University of Maryland, College Park. Her essay on Ann Cooper Hewitt, published in *Narratively*, was the publication's second-most-read story of the year. Her writing on other topics has appeared in the *Atlantic*, the *Washington Post*, the *New Republic*, and many other outlets. She lives in Hanover, Pennsylvania. Her next book, *Girls and Their Monsters: The Genain Quadruplets and the Making of Madness in America*, explores the lives of four sisters diagnosed with schizophrenia, following a troubled childhood. She lives in Hanover, Pennsylvania.